COUNTERATTACK:
The West's Battle Against the Terrorists

COUNTERATTACK:
The West's Battle Against the Terrorists

by Christopher Dobson
and Ronald Payne

Facts On File, Inc.
460 Park Avenue South, New York, N.Y. 10016

COUNTERATTACK:
The West's Battle Against the Terrorists

Library of Congress Cataloging in Publication Data

Dobson, Christopher.
    Counterattack: the West's battle against the terrorists.

    Includes index.
    1. Terrorism—Prevention. I. Payne, Ronald. II. Title.
HV6431.D6   363.3'2   82-1589
ISBN 0-87196-526-7   AACR2

Printed in the United States of America
10 9 8 7 6 5 4 3 2 1

Contents

Introduction: The Mounting Tide of International Terrorism

Terrorism is part of the human condition. There are always men and women who are prepared to use violence to achieve their political ambitions, to murder when their arguments fail, to persuade by means of the bomb. Terrorism ebbs and flows like the tide, one moment crashing frighteningly on the foreshores of our lives, then retreating to lie quiescent, gathering strength for its next assault. It is inevitable that the assault will take place in one form or another, with greater or lesser impact, every few years. But at no time has the assault been fiercer, more ruthless, more sustained or caused more permanent social, legal and political changes than during the last decade.

Many circumstances combined to bring this about. The speed of travel and instant communications that can bring the reality of a terrorist incident into everybody's home are important factors. The very fact that some 400 potential hostages are packed into the metal shell of a jet airliner hundreds of times a day and sent hurtling through the skies provides terrorists not only with a target whose cosmopolitan innocence imbues it with a "there but for the Grace of God" emotionalism, but one that is packaged with a supermarket flair, ideal for selling through millions of television sets.

The development of plastic explosives and compact automatic weapons gave the terrorists the weapons to exploit their targets. They were often better armed than the police forces that had to deal with them. In Munich, for example, the Palestinians used Kalashnikov automatic rifles—the weapon of revolution—while the police were armed with single shot rifles.

And then there was the general ambience of the seventies which favored terrorist operations. Mao Tse-tung spoke of guerillas living among the peasant population like fish in the sea. In Europe middle-class university students, indoctrinated by those false prophets, Sartre and Marcuse, created an intellectual climate in which urban terrorism could flourish. The same bourgeois products of Europe's post-war prosperity turned to violence when the ambitions festered by the student riots of 1968 were seen to have no substance. It was as much anger at their own impotence as their desire to make a revolution persuaded them to take up the gun. What increased the fury of these peculiar revolutionaries was that they failed to gain any support from the workers, the very people for whom they were supposed to be making the revolution. The workers had far more sense than to be led astray by the chic philosophers who preached the beauty of violence without regard to the misery it causes.

These developments coincided with the launching in England and Northern Ireland of one of the periodic tidal waves of Irish violence. The hitmen of the IRA are by no means the same political animals as the international terrorists. Predominantly working class and nationalist, their philosophy is far removed from the lecture room and the comfortable life. They are the exceptions to the normal terrorist profile in Western Europe, and as a leading expert on the movement, Dr. Richard Clutterbuck, has said of both the IRA and the extremist Protestant groups, "They are the only terrorist organizations in the world which even in their leadership have practically no intellectuals."

Nevertheless, the resurgence of terrorism in Ireland made the IRA gunmen into a de facto ally of the European and Arab extremists. At the same time America's young men were reacting violently to being drafted to fight and sometimes to die in Vietnam, and a propaganda campaign against U.S. involvement in that desperately mishandled war provided acts of terrorism against America and its supporters with a cloak of righteousness. Then there was the most important factor of all: the Palestinians and their war against Israel. The Arab armies of Egypt, Syria and Jordan had been defeated in the Six Day War in 1967, and until 1973 they were in no condition to go to war against Israel's efficient and highly motivated forces. Various Arab groups took it upon themselves to carry on the war by other means and the only way they could wage war was by terrorism. Amply, but often capriciously, provided with weapons, money, training grounds and diplomatic cover by the Arab states that adopted and occasionally founded the groups, they attempted to fight guerilla war in the Gaza Strip and on the West Bank. But it was a short-lived campaign; the guerillas were defeated for the time being. And so they took their war to Europe, where they discovered left-wing intellectual support for their cause, based on the premise that since Israel depended for its survival on the United States any blow struck at Israel was a blow against the American "war machine." Some of the Arab groups, especially the Popular Front for the Liberation of Palestine, also professed a Marxist-Leninist philosophy that blended well with the socially destructive views of the European revolutionaries. Of course, it was not all philosophy and theory. In return for help in carrying out operations and providing "safe houses," the Palestinians were generous with weapons and "scholarships" to their Middle Eastern training camps.

When all these various threads came together, the pattern gave the impression of a subtle and powerful world plot. But this was not true. It simply happened that the circumstances and conditions in various parts of the world gave rise to an upsurge of terrorism among people who, because of modern communications, could co-ordinate their actions when it suited them and because they had all read the same books—Marcuse, Sartre and the technicians of terror: Che Guevara, Frantz Fanon and Carlos Marighilla—appeared to act according to some great master plan. Certainly the Soviet Union was interested in keeping the pot boiling because of its belief that anything which caused trouble for the West provided prospects for the spread of communism. The Russians offered weapons, training and political support for the Arab groups, arguing that they were oppressed people fighting a "war of liberation."

They funded subversive magazines, such as *Konkret* in West Germany, for which Ulrike Meinhof was a star writer. They used Lumumba University in Moscow as a selection course for Third World students chosen for training as leaders of "liberation armies." The Venezuelan assassin Carlos spent some time at Lumumba before ostensibly being expelled, but there is good reason to believe that he kept his connections with the KGB.

The most comprehensive account to date of the way in which the Soviets train terrorists came from Adnan Jaber, commander of the PLO squad that killed six Israelis in an ambush at Hebron in May 1980.

Jaber, who was later captured by the Israelis, gave an interview, with Israeli permission, to David Shipley of *The New York Times* just before he was due to be tried. He said he had received six months of intensive training at Sokhodnaya, a village some 20 miles from Moscow. The course, conducted by Soviet civilian and military instructors, encompassed propaganda, political, tactical and weapon training. Its specific purpose was to prepare young men to take command of units 30 strong. He found it invaluable but somewhat outdated, for he felt that more modern techniques of guerilla war imparted to other Arab groups who had gone to Vietnam were more valuable.

It is known that Palestinians have also gone for training at Sanprobal, near Simferapol on the Black Sea. There a six-month course was offered to them as well as to Libyans, South-Yemenis, Iraqis and Algerians. Instruction included advanced explosives work, bomb making, and training in biological and chemical warfare.

Another Soviet ploy was to make use of such men as Henri

Curiel, himself eventually assassinated by right-wing terrorists in Paris, to maintain liaison with European terror groups. The Soviets also employed Cuba to play a surrogate function in their attempts to turn the wave of terrorism to their own advantage, to train terrorists and to drum up support for "freedom fighters" throughout the Third World.

Secretary of State Alexander Haig, who narrowly escaped death from an IRA-style culvert bomb in 1979 when he was Commander of Allied Forces in Europe, has no doubts about the Russian role. He told a congressional committee: "It is the Soviet Union which bears responsibility today for the proliferation and hemorrhaging of international terrorism as we have come to know it. I think it is time this issue be addressed publicly and stated forthrightly, no matter how much anguish it may give us."

He told the committee that literally thousands of Third World embryo terrorists were receiving training in the Soviet Union, Eastern Europe and Libya and that if the United States did not move to contain the spread of terrorism, "we will find it within our borders tomorrow."

Haig's statement was welcomed by the anti-terrorist community because it gave notice that President Reagan's new administration had made the combatting of international terrorism one of its key objectives. The Central Intelligence Agency was ordered to prepare a special report on the Kremlin's involvement.

When the Foreign Assessment Center of the CIA issued its annual report in the summer of 1981 it concluded that the Russians were deeply engaged in support of revolutionary violence and that "such violence frequently entails acts of international terrorism."

Claire Sterling in *The Terror Network* mapped out the links between the multifarious inernational groups and traced them all back to Moscow during "Fright Decade 1." Despite some tendentious interpretations of events, this wide ranging book caught the imagination of the new Reagan Administration and Sterling became one of the first to give evidence at Senate Committee hearings on security and terrorism. *The Terror Network* takes the deep conspiracy view of the rise of terrorism, for which the plotters in the Soviet Union, Cuba and Libya are held responsible.

There can be no doubt about the involvement of the KGB and GRU, as we ourselves first publicized in *The Carlos Complex,* but that does not mean that these organizations planned or caused terrorism in the first place. It is almost as fruitless for writers in the West to blame the KGB for all ills as it is for the propagandists of the left to see the hand of the CIA in all international mischief. The role of the Soviet organs of state was to exploit to the advantage of the USSR a new form of violence plaguing the Western world.

A great deal of evidence has been accumulated from captured terrorists, such as Adnan Jaber, who have been trained at Soviet schools. The Russians themselves argue that their courses are planned to help men and women engaged in justified wars of liberation against colonialist oppression and deny the label "schools of terrorism." Occasionally they confuse matters by attacking what they call terrorism. According to a Soviet spokesman Haig's denunciations are "a gross and malicious deception."

The Soviets further obfuscate the issue by accusing governments supported by the Western powers of resorting to "state terrorism," by which they mean the efforts of these governments are to fight back against armed insurrection mounted by revolutionary groups with links to Moscow. And who could be more guilty of state terrorism, even against its own citizens, than the Soviet Union?

Conor Cruise O'Brien, the Irish statesman and journalist, has neatly disposed of this Soviet argument by pointing out that when a terrorist organization claims to be a liberation movement engaged in guerilla warfare it is simply trying to invest itself with a form of legitimacy that it conspicuoulsy lacks. He argues that: "The force used by a democratic state against the terrorist is legitimate, while the violence of the terrorist is not."

Certainly terrorism needs to be defined, for definition is the basis of all the statistics upon which data must be assessed. The United Kingdom Prevention of Terrorism Act 1976 sets out a pragmatic and robust description: "Terrorism means the use of violence for political ends, and includes any use of violence for the purpose of putting the public or any section of the community in fear."

That is the guideline we intend to use in this book, and under it the Soviet Union is guilty of training, arming and financing groups that practice terrorism. An obvious example is the Palestine Liberation Organization, which though now considered respectable itself, controlled Black September and supported the Popular Front for the Liberation of Palestine. They chose to call themselves liberation movements, but they carried out acts of terror, such as the massacres at Lod Airport and in Munich, and they murdered the U.S. Ambassador, Clee Noel, at Khartoum.

There seemed to be no doubt in the mind of Defense Secretary Caspar Weinberger when he declared: "There is good clear evidence that the Soviets have been participating in the training of groups, that for want of a better term, can be called terrorist groups."

Dr. Samuel Francis, an American expert in terrorist affairs, summed up the case against the Soviets in a Heritage Trust pamphlet: "The assistance takes the form of weaponry training, propaganda and disinformation, and operational support—i.e., aid in travelling, the establishment of false identities, provision of medical and legal help." Quite correctly, he added the important warning upon which we too insist: "This is not to say that the Soviets control or plan international terrorism, but it is clear that the perpetrators of terror could not operate as efficiently as they do without Soviet assistance."

A side benefit for the Soviets is that the Iron Curtain countries have remained free of international terrorism. The Palestinians, anxious not to offend their suppliers, have refrained from carrying out a single operation on Communist soil.

A balnce sheet of international incidents published by the CIA showed that from 1968 to 1979 terrorists carried out 3,336 attacks, with a peak in 1976 of 413. Of these only 12 occurred in the Soviet Union and Eastern Europe.

In 1981 the National Foreign Assessment Center of the CIA produced revised figures for the same period which claimed that there had in fact been, 6,714 incidents of international terrorism, including 760 in 1980. New categories added to the list recorded 1,008 threats, 58 hoaxes and 121 cases of conspiracy. The report noted a sharp increase in right-wing terrorism in Europe highlighted by the bomb attacks at the 1980 Munich Oktoberfest and at the railway station in Bologna, Italy. But it also confirmed that the Soviets were deeply involved in support of revolutionary violence which also entailed acts of international terrorism. For the first time the report mentioned Russians among the victimized nationalities.

The most publicized attack in the Soviet Union was the still unexplained explosion in a Moscow underground station. From Communist China no hint of terrorist activities emerged until the autumn of 1980 when the government admitted that terrorists were responsible for an explosion in Peking.

The terrorist figures for the decade reveal, incidentally, that Americans too are much safer at home than abroad, for of the 1,275 North Americans who were victims of terror attacks in the period 1968–78 only 84 were attacked inside North America. During that time most of the 990 Western European victims of terrorism were assaulted in their own countries.

CIA analysts commenting on these figures drew the conclusion that "terrorists continue to prefer operations in the industrialized democracies of Western Europe and North America. More than half of all incidents were recorded in these regions." When the international terrorists demonstrate by their acts that they have more enemies in the West worthy of attack than they have in the Communist countries, it is only reasonable to suppose that perhaps one reason for this is that behind the Iron Curtain they also have more friends.

The reason is not hard to discover. Most of the international terror groups favor an extreme left philosophy: they want to destroy the capitalist and bourgeois regimes. And this is true even of the very far left, which claims to hate Soviet state capitalism as much as it hates the West, for there is little sign of such people bringing enlightenment to Moscow by bomb and bullet.

Moreover, only the capitalist countries provide the liberal atmosphere and the rule of law that paradoxically enables the terrorists to survive and operate. Yet the terrorists and their supporters scream "foul" when their legal rights are infringed by the authorities. In the USSR opposition to Soviet rule is ruthlessly suppressed. It would take a very brave or extremely foolhardy man to attempt to set up a terrorist organization there. In the West things are different. Major political decisions are still arrived at by free argument. Dissent is part of the fabric of democracy.

In no country was this more fervently venerated, until the advent of the Baader-Meinhof gang, than in West Germany. At one time any hint of the formation of an elite police or army group to counter terrorism would have raised a great howl of protest both inside and outside West Germany. It was a political impossibility. And so the Germans were woefully unprepared when the wave of terrorism struck.

They were not alone. The British, concentrating on the Provisional IRA and having mopped up the Angry Brigade anarchists by conventional police methods, tended to be complacent in the belief that the net set to catch the Irish terrorists would also pick up any international terrorists who appeared on the scene. The French had a revulsion against secret armies following the long Algerian war, and with a large Arab population living in France in "Bidonvilles," which were almost impossible to police, they became positively embarrassed by the amount of information on the activities of Arab terrorists being force-fed to them by the Israelis. The Italians, shortly to become the victims of the Red Brigades and its associated groups, at first thought that the threat to law and order came only from Arabs and Israelis fighting their exported war of kill and counter-kill. They therefore concentrated on the strangers in their midst rather than upon their own disaffected youth. The Dutch believed that the South Moluccan immigrants might riot in the streets but did not know that a group had been trained in a Palestinian camp and were preparing to hijack a train. Neither did they know that Dutch people were forming a terrorist support group called Red Help, and were in sympathy with Baader-Meinhof.

The Americans, busy with political scandals at home and closely scrutinizing the affairs of the CIA and the FBI in the light of Watergate scandals, and still suffering from the after effects of the Vietnam war, were also unprepared at first for the new threat. Yet, although the law paid little heed at first, homebred groups such as the Weathermen and the Symbionese Liberation Army were plotting to emulate similar movements in Europe, and the universities became hotbeds of revolutionary fervor in the sixties.

The lack of understanding and preparation was worse in those special units of the armed forces which are also needed to deal with overseas incidents. Suffering from the trauma of defeat in Vietnam, the U.S. Army had retired to lick its wounds and rethink its role in the modern world.

Only the Israelis seemed prepared to slug it out with terrorism and sometimes their methods showed such desperate enthusiasm that they appeared to the outside world to be indistiguishable from those of the terrorists. The Israelis themselves realized this when one of their hit teams assassinated the wrong man at Lillehammer in Norway in 1973, mistaking an innocent Algerian waiter for the architect of the Munich massacre, Ali Hassan

Salameh. It took the Israelis another five and a half years to get Salameh, blowing him up with a car bomb in Beirut. They also killed four of his bodyguards and six innocent passersby, including a British secretary, 34-year-old Susan Wareham.

It was Salameh's Munich spectacular that marked the turning point. The Olympics, being held in Germany for the first time since the notorious Hitler Olympics in Berlin in 1936, were supposed to display to the world that the new, liberal Germany had been accepted back into the family of nations.

What it did display, in horrifyingly clear television pictures, was that the era of the international terrorist had arrived. A gang of Black September terrorists, with logistic support from German and French sympathizers, seized control of the Israeli athletes' dormitory in the Olympic village, killing two of the team and taking nine hostages. The terrorists demanded the release of 200 Palestinians imprisoned in Israel, but the Israelis, in keeping with their practice of never giving in to terrorism, refused and sent their own experts to Munich to help plan the rescue of the hostages. Meanwhile the authorities agreed to give the terrorists an aircraft to take them and the hostages to Egypt—at that time the arch enemy of Israel.

The Germans set up an ambush at Furstenfeldbruck Airport, and when the terrorists emerged from the the helicopters that had carried them to the airport, five sharpshooters opened fire. They were not sharp enough. Five of the terrorists died and three surrendered, but before they did so they killed all nine hostages and a police sergeant.

The Palestinians claimed a great victory. The sole purpose of the operation, they argued, was to draw attention to their right to a homeland in Palestine. Their cause, they feared, was going by default. The Arab states were powerless to defeat the Israelis and the world regarded them as merely a nuisance.

"Why should the rest of the world sit back in comfort and watch the Olympics while we, the dispossessed, live in squalor?" was the rationalization. The Palestinians succeeded brilliantly, for the modern world can stand almost any shock except having its sport interrupted. The Munich massacre did precisely what it was intended to do: it made the world take notice of the Palestinians.

But while the operation had succeeded beyond the planner's expectations—and here it must be emphasized that Yasser Arafat bears as much responsibility as anybody for the massacre because Black September was merely a cover name for teams drawn from the ranks of Arafat's Fatah organization under the command of his deputy, Salah Khalef—it also set in motion a series of measures that were eventually to prove deadly to terrorism.

The outrage at Munich finally roused European governments into realization of the dangers they were facing from the mounting tide of international terrorism. But there was still a long way to go before effective measures could be put into operation, for the truth is that Europe had been taken by surprise when the hijackers, kidnappers and assassins first began to strike within its comfortable confines. Their acts were not expected in countries with established democracies where the rule of law and constitutional practice made it possible to change governments and policies by the simple process of voting. In Europe there was no need for terrorism; that was the kind of unpleasantness to be expected in Latin American tyrannies.

The various groups of terrorists easily coalesced to attack across frontiers. There were not many of them, perhaps a thousand really active persons ready with gun and bomb. Their informal, clandestine organizations, uninhibited by any kind of public opinion within their ranks, helped them plan transfrontier operations.

It is in the nature of Western societies to listen to arguments. Their first response to terror had been to ask whether perhaps the terrorists had reasonable demands, and if so, should they not be heard and attempts be made to study their aims and deal with their grievances. In this case it was a pointless exercise and only delayed the adoption of firmer methods to stop the bloodshed first and ask questions afterward. That is why it took years for Western Europe to achieve the degree of cooperation that terror groups had achieved in months.

Since 1938, when Prime Minister Neville Chamberlain made a deal with Hitler, Munich had been the symbol of appeasement; it now became the watchword for what might be called "rearmament against terror." The governments at last looked at the forces they possessed to cope with a Munich-style incident and they found them wanting. Great Britain was lucky; it had a ready-made army unit, the 22nd Special Air Service Regiment, which could fill the role and that regiment had already studied the problems posed by international terrorism. Therefore, when then

Prime Minister Edward Heath assigned them to the role, they were not only willing but ready for the job.

West Germany also took the step it had put off for so long. So appalled was the government by the failure of the ambush at Furstenfeldbruck that it felt it had to cut through the bureaucracy which hampered action by individual police forces of the *länders* and create a new force as a Federal unit, controlled by the central government.

There was one at hand, the Federal Border Guard, and a special commando unit was formed within the Guard to take over anti-terrorist duties. Called *Grenzschutzgruppen 9* (GSG9), it earned its spurs at Mogadishu in 1977. The Dutch gave the anti-terrorist role to their Marines. The Italians called in the paramilitary *Carabinieri*. The Spaniards, already heavily involved in combating the Basque nationalist ETA group, which had many links with international groups, and the growth of both left wing and neofascists groups, also kept a watching eye on the Arab militants who passed through on the way to Northern Europe and on the Israelis, who were in turn watching the Arabs. The old-fashioned *Guardia Civile* were given all these tasks to perform and, not surprisingly, did not do particularly well. Special Operations Group, a new force modeled on the SAS, now spearheads anti-terror operations. The French had their own methods, confident that their numerous police organizations could deal with terrorism in metropolitan France, while the Parachute Division would handle any trouble in the remnants of the French Empire and those former members of the empire that still relied on the French army for protection. The Americans set up a committee called the Inter-Departmental Group on Terrorism, headed by Armin Meyer, a former Ambassador to Lebanon. It consisted of the Secretary of State, the U.S. Ambassador to the United Nations and the heads of the Central Intelligence Agency and the Federal Bureau of Investigation. Its task was to "coordinate information, consider tactics and set up task forces in cases of emergency." But it had no funds and no troops. Of all the nations faced by the danger of international terrorism, only Israel took direct action. The day after Munich, Prime Minister Golda Meir unleashed hit teams, which would roam the world seeking out the men responsible for the massacre. For them it was an "eye for an for an eye, a tooth for a tooth."

These were just the first steps taken by individual nations

feeling their way into the political, military and social minefields of the counter assault on terrorism. What was sadly lacking was any proper international cooperation. The Israelis were only too anxious to persuade other countries to take part in the fight against Arab terrorists and thereby share some of the opprobrium that surrounded their own lethal activities. They flooded Western European governments and police forces with information about terrorists, their movements and planned actions, but in many cases there was little that those countries could do under existing laws and, as the French complained, the mass of information gathered by Israeli agents, who had infiltrated the Arab groups, and disseminated by Mossad was just too much for them to manage.

The first tentative moves toward an international counterattack on terrorism were delayed and weakened by nationalistic and political antagonism and the differences in the legal codes of the countries involved. The French were notoriously unhelpful. They committed a series of acts that resulted in further outrages. They arrested Frazeh Khelfa, the Black September killer who was responsible for the attempted assassination of the Jordanian Ambassador in London. But, despite British attempts to have him extradited to stand trial, the French released him. They also arrested the German terrorist Wilfried Böse but, despite knowing his connection with Carlos, they simply put him across the German border. Böse later led the hijackers who were killed by Israeli commandos at Entebbe. Fear of upsetting the flow of oil and other trade from the Mideast also affected French calculations and it was for these economic-diplomatic reasons that they released the notorious Abu Daoud, one of Black September's commanders, after they had arrested him in Paris in 1977. Daoud, who had once devised a plot to kill King Hussein of Jordan, had arrived in Paris under an assumed name for the funeral of the Palestine Liberation Organization's representative, who had been murdered by a dissident PLO group. The French had taken photographs of the funeral party and had circulated them to friendly police forces asking for information. The British identified Daoud and the French police promptly arrested him, much to the embarrassment of the government because he had been introduced to senior government officials and entertained at the Quai d'Orsay.

Once the Israelis learned of his arrest, they named him as one of the planners of Munich and demanded his extradition. The West Germans also prepared papers for his extradition. But the French, under no illusions about the reaction of the Arab world if they handed Abu Daoud over to the Israelis or the Germans, performed a brilliant piece of legal sleight of hand and set him free. For the French, national considerations are paramount. In June 1981, for example, they refused to extradite the Basque nationalist Tomas Linaza to Spain despite well-documented evidence that he was involved in a bombing that killed six *Guardia Civile* officers. The reason for the refusal was that the French decided not to risk antagonizing Basques who live on their side of the frontier.

Because of the problems incurred in setting up official international cooperation—the United Nations was as usual divided, with many of its member states actively supporting the terrorists—it was left to individual police officers and soldiers to use the "old boy" network to establish channels for passing intelligence and, occasionally, for taking part in joint actions. Some of this unauthorized cooperation was originally carried out under the cover of Interpol. But that organization's charter says that it may only undertake criminal work and must not engage in "political" activities and therefore it acted under severe constraints. Officials at its headquarters in suburban Paris are still chary about discussing its role in the struggle against terrorism, and while there is no doubt that it had played a part, acting as a collating and distribution center for information, even that task has now been taken over by the German anti-terrorist computer data base at Wiesbaden. NATO, which has studied the terrorists, their arms and logistics for its own purposes, has proved to be of greater value than Interpol, passing on its intelligence assessments to the security organizations of its member nations.

What is astonishing is that while governments were waking up to threats posed by international terrorism, the academic world remained largely skeptical and often dismissive. There are exceptions: in England Dr. Richard Clutterbuck, at the Department of International Politics and Political Violence, University of Exeter, and Professor Paul Wilkinson of the Department of International Relations, Aberdeen University, occupy an honorable position among those who realized the dangers of terrorism and the need to gather and spread information about terrorists, their philosophies and their techniques. The same must be said of

Professor Stephen Sloan in the Political Science Department at the University of Oklahoma, who has carried out effective research by conducting simulated terrorist incidents using his students and local security forces. Brian M. Jenkins at the Rand Corporation was doing invaluable work compiling chronology of terrorism in reports for the Department of State and Defense Advanced Research Projects Agency. He has written wisely and wittily on many terrorist subjects.

It is difficult to pinpoint the incident that made terrorism appear to be a worthy and respectable subject for academics. Probably it was the exposure of Carlos and the international ramifications of his network which convinced them that the upsurge of bombing and assassination and the taking of hostages for political gain was no ephemeral affair, no aberration that would pass quickly. However, once they began to understand what was going on, university teachers in political science departments jumped on the bandwagon. It gave the authors of this book some pleasure to be asked for information by men who had earlier taken a lofty attitude toward such work but who had suddenly realized that there were reputations to be made and professorial chairs to be won in this newest of "trendy subjects."

Businessmen were much quicker off the mark. When South American terrorist groups started to kidnap rich men and company executives and hold them ransom for large sums of money, the prospects of making money out of fighting terrorism became apparent. It was risky but the profits matched the risk. Over the past 10 years the security business has proved to be one of the world's fastest growing industries. Lloyds of London offers not only insurance against being kidnapped but companies that will provide negotiators skilled in cutting the size of the ransom as well as "bringing 'em back alive."

There are companies that sell armor-plated cars, teach chauffeurs escape and evasion driving, and others which provide all these services. Most of them have staff who were once members of security services and maintain close ties with those services.

Public attention has been concentrated on the handful of successful and spectacular actions carried out by special forces. This is natural for Entebbe, Mogadishu and the Iranian Embassy siege in London were events of high drama. They were famous victories which delighted public opinion grown restive under constant attack and had made Americans and Europeans feel, as they do when faced with a resurgence of street crime and mugging, that nothing could be done to strike back at the aggressors.

But it would be wrong to neglect the equally important though less spectacular measures that have been taken in the same cause—the containment of terror. Slowly and carefully, as is the way in democracies, governments have altered and adapted their policies. They have made significant changes in police and security organization, in training and tactics. Legal steps have been taken to handle the new threat and judicial and penal systems have been devised to respond to the challenge of terrorists who are ably supported by revolutionary lawyers.

When all these components of the fight against terrorism are put together they make a formidable force. What we intend in this book, having detailed the growth of the terrorist groups in our previous book *(The Terrorists, Facts On File)*, is to tell the story of the anti-terrorist forces and how they went into action. We shall also describe the controversies surrounding these special forces and the way in which laws were altered to enable them to operate. In some cases nations were asked to surrender rights it had taken them long years to win in order to fight the terrorists. We shall also show how the private security services have grown to become almost a second arm of the law; and we will point to the way ahead and the dangers along the path.

1.

Terrorism and the World Community

Within a few weeks in the spring of 1981 President Reagan was shot in the chest as he left the Hilton Hotel in Washington by a deranged young man; Pope John Paul II, blessing the crowds in St Peter's Square, Rome, was hit in the stomach with a bullet fired by a Turk from the Grey Wolf terrorist group; and Provisional Irish Republican Army detonated a bomb at Sullom Voe oil terminal in the Shetlands while it was being inaugurated by Queen Elizabeth.

Then, as the Queen was riding at the head of a Sovereign's Escort of the Household Cavalry, her ceremonial bodyguard, to the Trooping of the Color in London, a 17-year-old boy fired shots at close range from a replica Colt revolver. Had the bullets been real she would have been assassinated.

In the autumn President Muhammed Ali Rajai of Iran and his Prime Minister were killed by a terrorist bomb in Teheran. Weeks later terrorists in the uniform of the Egyptian army murdered President Anwar Sadat with bursts of Kalashnikov fire while he was reviewing a ceremonial parade in Cairo.

Once again terrorists and lone gunmen had turned to assassination as a tactic to draw public attention. The 1981 CIA report on international terrorism confirmed the trend: "The number of terrorist incidents apparently aimed at causing casualties—most notably assassination attempts—increased dramatically in 1980."

Growing international cooperation, changes in the law, improved security and police methods and the actions of the special anti-terror forces made operations more difficult for the aggressors in many fields. But they were still active, and thwarted in their attempts at hijacking and hostage taking, they reverted to the oldest tactic—assassination. In many ways this is the most difficult form of terrorism to guard against.

When it becomes more hazardous to sieze aircraft, terrorists hijack buses or trains; when there is more risk involved in murdering diplomats or businessmen, they again resort to attacking statesmen, religious leaders and Royalty, who, because of their position, cannot be totally protected. In the nature of things the President, the Pope, the Queen cannot live in bullet-proof ivory towers, for they must be seen to appear in public.

But attempts to murder them often have a contrary effect to that desired by the would-be assassins. The attempt of the life of the Pope horrified Roman Catholics throughout the world—and not just Roman Catholics. Even before President Reagan was shot he had already made promises to combat terrorism. When he himself became victim of an assailant's bullets, there were clear signs that the U.S. would close ranks and take firmer action against this scourge. Acts of terror can be useful in mobilizing public opinion in favor of resolute action.

In the dawn of modern terrorism it was a political murder that first drew international attention to the problem of how to counter such violence. In October 1934 King Alexander of Yugoslavia, and Louis Barthou, the French Foreign Minister, were assassinated in Marseilles.

The Council of the League of Nations, the model for the later

United Nations, discussed this serious event and made a resolution: "The rules of international law concerning the repression of terrorist activity are not at present sufficiently precise to guarantee efficiently international co-operating in this matter."

That statement remains true nearly half a century later. For, because of the deep differences of opinion and political ideology, international bodies are not capable of developing a unified policy for action against terrorism.

After World War II and the creation of the United Nations the subject was taken up again. Even then it was not directly tackled. But in the high-flown terms of the Universal Declaration of Human Rights were to be found references guaranteeing the "right of life and security of the person." It laid down that nobody should be subject to torture or to cruel, inhuman or degrading treatment or punishment. In another covenant it was recommended that, "no one shall be arbitrarily deprived of his life."

Such worthy clauses have not been notable for their application in the jungle of international relations. They were simply marginal notes in international statements which might be interpreted later in different ways, according to the political point of view of the interpreter.

Other United Nations declarations set down all manner of general statements which could provide ammunition for those countries and organizations seeking to justify the violence of their methods in demanding change. For example, the international body provided the admirable statement that every state had a duty to refrain from forcible actions which deprived peoples of their right to self-determination.

A Declaration of Principles of International Law (international bodies given half a chance will always add as many capital letters as possible to their declarations) gave with one hand, and took away with the other. For it stated, "In their actions against and resistance to, such forcible action *in pursuit of their right to self-determination,* such peoples are entitled to receive support . . . "

It does not take the argumentative skill of an international lawyer to adapt that as clear support for any bunch of guerillas or terrorists who care to read the script. It is easy enough to use the declaration as justification for any kind of murderous activity undertaken in the name of securing the sacred right of self-determination. And of course self-determination is an acceptable, even noble idea, were it not for the ugly fact that the kind of aggressive campaign which sometimes secures it— theoretically—in the Third World often brings to power a gang of political thugs who will ensure that the unfortunate people under their control will never again have the opportunity to exercise it.

Whenever the United Nations steeled itself to get to grips with the concept of terrorism, it always ended up in a kind of trap. For it is trying against all the odds to be all things to all nations. Its first attempt to "do something" came in the wake of the Olympic massacre at Munich when Kurt Waldheim, its Secretary-General, called upon the UN to deal with the menace of international terrorism. Little more needs to be said about the efficacy of its response than to quote the lengthy title of the study which clearly reveals the seeds of its own confusion.

> Measures to prevent international terrorism which endangers or takes innocent human lives or jeopardizes fundamental freedoms, and study of the underlying cause of those forms of terrorism and acts of terrorism which lie in misery, frustration, grievance and despair, and which causes some people to sacrifice human lives including their own, in an attempt to effect radical changes.

It is not surprising that UN went on talking about this for five years. The very wording, beneath the committee compromise cliches, shows a kind of sympathy with terrorism. United Nations thinking is still dominated by the great assaults on colonialism and imperialism, which provided its assemblies with such rich food in the sixties and seventies. That was the time when the alliance of Third World states with support from the Soviet Union—and occasionally from a United States still conscious of its own revolutionary origins and dislike of European imperial history—condemned first Great Britain and then France.

Indeed the first and perhaps only great successes of terrorism in its strategic aims of removing governments and seizing power were registered at that time. Terrorist attacks combined with political and economic circumstances forced the British withdrawal first from Palestine, then from Cyprus and from Aden. The same tactics were important in the successful campaign to force France out of Algeria, although there was also a full scale guerilla war being fought there.

So far as the British were concerned economic difficulties at home and public dislike for foreign involvements rendered them more than willing to withdraw. Their main hesitation came because the three colonial problems, Palestine, Cyprus and Aden, were countries with radically divided populations where it was virtually impossible to hand over power without precipitating civil war.

Significantly the terrorism, which all Western countries are now attempting to master, developed from those countries. Tactics used then—assassination, hostage taking and bombing—were copied later. But the difficulties created by the withdrawal of colonial power also left warring and discontented factions: Arabs against Jews, Greeks against Turks, and Marxist Arabs against capitalist Arabs. Their schisms nurtured the new terrorism.

In fact the debates at the United Nations were simply extensions of the terror war with words replacing bomb and gun. This was the only step forward which they achieved. Those countries which supported terrorism harangued the West about "freedom struggles" and the iniquities of "colonialist and racialist terror." Indeed when the matter came up for discussion by an Ad Hoc Committee on International Terrorism in 1973 the Third World had little to contribute other than attacks on "state terrorism," a form of the art which exists in fact largely in Third World states where more peaceful ways of conducting affairs have not yet developed.

We know that there are numerous states, members of United Nations, which are brutal and oppressive. In their territories the state apparatus of security is so strong that there is no means of changing the system. Those are the countries, either Communist or Fascist in leaning, where indeed it might seem reasonable for young men and women to use force, and fight to overthrow unbearable systems where public opinion and true debate are not permitted by dictators and committees of dictators. But those are the very countries that in general are immune from terrorist attacks.

The basis of power is that the states control the means to prevent people even assembling to form guerilla bands. In such states weapons are not available to idealists who have other ideas about government. Such governments therefore do not wish to talk about terrorism. Yet, they urge people they call resistance fighters to overthrow democratic governments in the West. Terrorism can only be effective in liberal areas of the world, and those are the very places where the tyrants wish to impose their will. We in our part of the world do not need terrorism. For, by legally demonstrating, by appealing to public opinion and ultimately by peacefully voting it is possible to change policies and methods, without the ugly necessity of going out into the streets to murder in such a cause.

The only achievements at the UN were legal measures dealing with certain specific forms of terrorism. The General Assembly did adopt a convention on the prevention and punishment of crimes against "internationally protected persons, including diplomatic agents." This was ratified by enough member states for it to come into effect.

The hijacking of aircraft by terrorists drew attention to the problem caused by the new wave of violence. The Cubans from Castro's island were fore-runners of this form of frightfulness and the Palestinians took it up, inducing by example almost every rebel with or without a cause, but equipped with a revolver, to try his hand. Few states were willing to condone such continued attacks which affected everyone, without regard to race, creed, color or class. As early as 1963 the Tokyo Convention set down legal principles for dealing with offenses aboard aircraft and established rules to ensure the return of hijacked aircraft and their passengers. But it did not come into force until 1969, by which time individual countries were already taking their own and more effective measures to tighten aircraft security.

In 1970 the Hague Convention on hijacking was signed, and it came into force the following year. It required contracting states, either to permit extradition of hijackers to their country of origin, or to prosecute them under the legal code of the state where they were arrested. The Convention also recommended acceptance of the principle that it is a crime for any person to board an aircraft and to seize it in flight, or to gain control over it by force of arms or threats. In most countries that is considered a crime anyway whatever the nationality of the hijacker might be and in whatever state the aircraft is registered.

The Hague Convention was followed by another formulated in Montreal in 1971. This time an international quorum extended the scope of international law to include attacks upon airports and grounded aircraft. It also established the principle that severe penalties should be awarded for such offenses. But still there were no effective international sanctions to ensure enforcement, and there were no agreed provisions to punish states that gave help and sanctuary to hijackers. Eventually the United Nations brought itself to pass a resolution in the General Assembly condemning hijacking. But again it was the individual nations most incensed by the new form of air piracy that took the effective measures by strengthening airport security, and by threatening to shut down airline services to countries which assisted the hijackers.

At the height of the hijack era of 1969-73 it was well known that such countries as Cuba, South Yemen, Iraq, Libya and Algeria actively helped groups engaged in seizing aircraft. This did not stop those countries from joining in talks at the international meetings on how to stop such violence. In the case of the Arab countries this was sheer hypocrisy, for the hard line Arab states provided not only sanctuary but also helped to finance international terrorists, provided them with arms and explosives, and ran training courses to teach them how to carry out their missions.

Because the hijacking of aircraft had become a nuisance to both countries concerned, the United States and Cuba concluded a hijack pact in 1973. This unlikely arrangement between mutually hostile states came about largely because a good many of those who seized aircraft and forced them to fly to Cuba were criminals and psychopaths of no great political interest. What the consenting parties agreed to do was to return aircraft, their crews, passengers and the hijackers. To save his revolutionary pride Castro added a caveat to the effect that Cuba could refuse to hand over guaranteed, fully paid up hijackers affiliated to a national liberation movement. Nonetheless the pact played a significant part in putting a stop to the air piracy that had afflicted that region in the early seventies.

An even more important international move to discourage aircraft grabbing was made at the Bonn Summit meeting in July 1978. The heads of government of Canada, France, Italy, Japan, the United Kingdom, the United States and West Germany agreed to sanctions against states which aided and abetted the hijacking of aircraft. Experts met later to discuss ways and means of implementing this agreement. There is no doubt that it has contributed to making the world airlines safer for passengers.

Western governments had discovered a way of getting at those countries which backed the hijackers. Even Arab hard-line members of the terrorist supporters' clubs were reluctant to continue their aid, if the price of it was having their airline communications with the outside world disconnected. The Bonn agreements came late, after strong defensive measures adopted by the Western countries had already curbed the hijackers. Nevertheless they formed a useful function in displaying unity against the terrorists and their backers.

The real question at issue is whether some terrorist acts, regardless of the legitimacy or otherwise of the cause, are more justifiable than others. For example, many people of opposing political views might agree that it would have been reasonable to assassinate Hitler or Stalin. But, would it have been thinkable to seize a train, or an aircraft carrying German or Russian children, and kill them one by one until the dictator resigned? It might well be argued that faced with comparable cases, in less extreme form, the only role for international law is to try to categorize acts of terrorism even though in its present state it is unlikely to be able to do anything very much to prevent them.

In this context a United Nations study on the subject had some sensible thoughts.

> Even when the use of force is legally and morally justified there are some means, as in every form of human conflict, which must not be used; the legitimacy of cause does not legitimize the use of certain forms of violence, especially against the innocent. This has long been recognized even in the customary laws of war.

If this line of thought were followed the most satisfactory course of action for international bodies would be to try to produce a kind of Geneva Convention which regulates conventional warfare, to set down ground rules for acceptable terrorisms. We fear, however, that it would be a long and unrewarding task.

The supporters of terrorism have already tried to use the Geneva Convention in a totally different sense. They argue that terrorists who are arrested should be treated as prisoners of war and not as criminals, for terrorist organizations like to keep their men in play even after they have been captured. It is another tactical stage to rouse public opinion with reasonable sounding claims that they should have the special status of political prisoners.

Useful work has in general been done by like-minded regional groups of states. After the wave of diplomatic kidnappings in the late sixties and early seventies in Latin America, the Organization of American States formulated a Convention to "Prevent and Punish Acts of Terrorism taking the form of crimes against persons and related extortion that are of international significance." The aim of the wording was to designate the kidnapping of such persons as a common crime, thereby making it possible for the criminals to be extradited and punished. But because Latin American states have traditionally held that the principle of political asylum is inviolate, legal opposition to the new measures has slowed down its ratification and implementation.

It is Western Europe that most progress has been made in international coordination. The Western liberal democracies, although they were slow and reluctant to respond to the attack upon their institutions, did eventually take a number of practical steps. Coordination at first was largely of an informal nature on the "old boy net" of police and soldiers from the countries concerned. But after the Munich massacre in 1972 Ministers of the Interior of the European Economic Community, backed by their police forces and intelligence services, set up machinery for discussion and multilateral cooperation, largely through the instigation and coaxing of the British government. A series of ministerial meetings since then have drawn into the Common Market's security system outside countries such as Austria, Japan and Switzerland—for even the Swiss cannot remain neutral in the terror wars.

In fact multilateral cooperation between national police and intelligence forces has progressed more rapidly than joint ventures in the political and judicial aspects of the defense against terrorism. The International Criminal Police Organization— Interpol—with its headquarters just outside Paris, already existed before the terrorist challenge became apparent. Although it was useful up to a point, the constitution under which it had been set up insisted that it should confine its activities to dealing with crime, and not all the governments who enrolled their policemen into the international organization were convinced that terrorism was a crime. Nevertheless, Interpol has had its uses as a line of communication between different forces. For example, the Athens police were able to identify the West German terrorist, Rolf Pohle, from Interpol pictures, and to detain him.

But clearly other organs of police liaison were needed. There is now a permanent structure of police cooperation especially among EEC member states. In a thoughtful series of articles under the title, "Europe Against Terrorism," written by James Sarazan, some details of this organization were published in *Le Monde*. The French newspaper revealed that the network was named TREVI (terrorism, radicalism, and violence international), after the subjects with which it is principally concerned. Since 1977 TREVI has regularly brought together police chiefs from EEC countries. It is a formalization of the police "old boy" network. For day-to-day consultation and liaison each of the national forces has a coordination bureau. *Le Monde* stated that the French police bureau was secretly located near the Champs Elysées, though its name and address did not figure in any official list. In Britain it works from New Scotland Yard under the title of European Liaison Section of the Special Branch.

Controllers of the secret intelligence services involved in the war on terror have regular meetings in Switzerland, and their top secret discussions are described as gatherings of the Club of Berne. The only EEC country not represented at present is the Republic of Ireland. Non-EEC members are Israel and Switzerland.

In addition to the organizations already mentioned, the North Atlantic Treaty Organization has itself set up a useful system for exchange of information on terrorists, their organization, techniques, and the weapons at their disposal. Joint training visits and exchanges of security people among NATO countries as well as among those of EEC are now a regular feature. All this is in addition to bilateral arrangements between the security forces of individual nations. The NATO anti-terrorist network is particularly useful because it provides possibilities for the Americans to coordinate with European allies in this field. The Canadians, too, with their own experience of anti-terrorist operations conducted by the Royal Canadian Mounted Police make a useful contribution. With growing awareness of the need for concerted allied action to counter Soviet moves to exploit terrorism for its own purposes the role of NATO in the struggle is likely to grow.

Such are the practical defensive measures taken in Europe. Even though Western Europe has had more terrorist experience over the last two decades than any other part of the world, action was less speedy when it came to arranging judicial cooperation. The most noteworthy event in this field was an initiative by the Council of Europe in formulating a Convention on the Suppression of Terrorism. It was signed by seventeen out of the nineteen member states in January 1977. The two countries which did not sign were the Republic of Ireland, whose own long-standing difficulties in the field of terrorism have produced a permanent condition of ambivalence, and Malta, whose President, Dom Mintoff, was at the time flirting with Colonel Qaddafi of Libya, the paymaster of international terrorism who uses assassins to kill Libyan political opponents in exile.

The aim of the Convention was to persuade European states to treat all terrorist acts as criminal ones. Listed among such acts were assassination, kidnapping, hostage-taking, bomb attacks including use of grenades and rockets, and hijacking. In dealing with such attacks the states were urged to exclude those arrested from political offense clauses which in the past had been used to justify refusal to permit extradition. In some cases there were technical and constitutional difficulties in agreeing to such a practice. So states facing such difficulties were obliged by the Convention to bring suspects to trial before courts in their own jurisdiction. Although the Convention was quickly signed a number of countries showed less enthusiasm when it came to ratifying it. After a year only 5 member states had completed this process, Austria, Denmark, Sweden, the United Kingdom and West Germany. Those most reluctant to ratify were Belgium and France. Both countries excused themselves by declaring that their constitutions committed them to the principle of political asylum.

In addition to this difficulty the Convention contained an escape clause allowing extradition to be refused when an offense was deemed by the state concerned to be political or politically motivated. We are back to the initial dilemma for, essential though it may be to ensure safeguards of liberty in liberal societies, we also need judicial reforms that can prevent violent men taking advantage of the very freedoms which they insult and try to destroy. When violence "for political ends . . . putting the public in fear . . . " is intentionally extended to countries or citizens of those countries not directly involved in the dispute, that is international terrorism. We all know what such definitions mean, for they are sensible ones. But are they precise enough to persuade nation states to give up contitutional rights they have carefully formulated? Western states are rightly cautious when confronted by requests to abandon the right of political asylum. They are equally reluctant to prosecute non-nationals for crimes committed outside their own territory on the say so of a neighboring state.

Practical measures are necessary to meet the challenge of the men of violence. But we must not be too censorious with the lack of success of government attempts to change the laws. There is a built-in safety device in the slowness of the deliberations. For while operational necessity calls for the tactical cooperation of the security forces, care must be taken to ensure that laws do not get enshrined which bring about the punishment of the innocent for the sin of the guilty. For example, it would be tragic if under a West European law it became possible for the Soviet Union to demand the extradition of a Polish trade union leader who had fled westwards to avoid persecution, on the grounds that he was a terrorist with no rights to political asylum. In France the European Convention on the Suppression of Terrorism aroused a good deal of controversy, for it was seen as a threat to the idea of France as a traditional country of asylum for the persecuted.

There are dangers in overstressing the concept of international terror. For when that is recognized, and when Western governments set up special forces and police liaison groups to cope with it, terrorist suspects under arrest can argue that they are people in a special category. At this point it becomes more difficult for liberal governments to sustain the legally convenient argument that terrorists are simply criminals. For do criminal activities justify the elaborate state mechanism being set up to counter their activities on an international scale? It is because of reservations of this kind that the process of making fair and reasonable law strong enough to ward off an unusual and strong threat becomes so slow and difficult.

In North America both the United States and Canada faced similar problems in the same political area. How can civilized and open societies of the Atlantic Alliance respond effectively to the challenge of unscrupulous, totalitarian and Marxist forces of terror without harming the structure of their political societies?

Canada was the first victim in North America of a strong and dangerous native terrorist campaign. In the late sixties French Canadian separatists in Quebec launched a violent series of attacks. They culminated in October 1970 with the kidnapping of James Cross, the British Trade Commissioner for Quebec. Prime Minister Pierre Trudeau decided on a firm line of action, and refused to give in to their demand for a ransom of $500,000, and the release of members of the organization already in prison. The *Front du Libération du Quebec* (FLQ) then seized Pierre Laporte, Minister of Labor in the Quebec Provincial government, and eventually he was murdered. Mr. Cross was more fortunate. Though he was held by the terrorists for three months, they finally agreed to release him after Trudeau agreed to a deal whereby three of the kidnappers and four of their relations were flown to Cuba in a Canadian military aircraft. Although to this extent the Ottawa government did make a partial surrender the affair is of great importance in the history of counter assaults on terrorism. For immediately after the kidnapping Prime Minister Trudeau determined to rid Canada of the FLQ and their friends by fighting with all the means at his disposal.

He took the extreme step in 1970 of invoking the War Measures Act which enabled him to call in the army. For six months he was able to saturate the Montreal area with troops, a procedure which pinned down terrorist groups and allowed the police and the Royal Canadian Mounted Police, which handles security in Canada, to concentrate all their manpower in tracking down the cells which had organized the kidnappings and murders. Armed with sweeping powers to search and arrest suspects for questioning the security forces rounded up 340 suspects. Even so it took nine weeks to track down those responsible for the murder of Laporte. Prime Minister Trudeau, of course, came in for strong criticism from liberals. Sternly he rebuked them, "There are a lot of bleeding hearts around . . . All I can say is let them bleed."

Years later when Canada had again become peaceful, David Barrett, head of the opposition New Democratic Party, who is by no means a supporter of terrorism, told an international conference on the subject: "The scar on Canada's record of civil liberties which occurred ten years ago is a classic illustration of how the state, in an attempt to combat terrorism, overstepped its boundaries and actually threatened its own citizens. Democratic governments cannot legitimately establish consent by the use of force."

Nevertheless Pierre Trudeau's repression of the FLQ and its allies ridded Canada of terrorism for a whole decade. It is only fair to point out that the repression was accompanied by political measures, such as compulsory French courses for English speakers in order to erode the nationality barrier, and heavy investment in the French-speaking minority areas, which helped to rob the terrorists of moderate support. And, of course, civil liberties were restored once the crisis was over. In the summer of 1981 charges were made against 16 members of the RCMP and one former member, for offenses such as arson, breaking and entering and theft while they were taking part in the emergency campaign. Among them was a former assistant commissioner, the second highest rank in the force, and 11 officers were charged in connection with a break in at the offices of a Montreal computer company which kept a record of the names of members of the *Parti Québecois,* the main separatist group.

Excesss may have been committed during the crisis. Yet Canada has emerged as a nation no less free and democratic than it was before it defended itself against a grave threat by firm means. Unfortunately little seems to have been done since then to keep up the guard against terror, except for the training of two army regiments for anti-terrorist work. But Pierre Trudeau's firm and successful handling of an ugly situation at a time when few Western governments had yet realized the perils of extremists' bombs and guns set a useful example for the Atlantic Alliance.

The United Kingdom was in the firing line at the same time, for in 1969 a violent new campaign of terrorism conducted by the Provisional Irish Republican Army had begun. The British Army was called in both to fight the terrorists and to protect the Catholics from the Protestants. Two years later suspected terrorists were interned without trial. In 1973 as the crisis grew more serious, and on the recommendation of Lord Diplock, an eminent jurist, the Westminster Parliament passed the Northern Ireland (Emergency Provisions) Act 1973. This draconian measure made it possible to try those charged with terrorist offenses by a judge sitting without a jury. It was a step taken because ordinary courts were unable to function in face of intimidation of both jurors and witnesses. Witnesses were murdered and "knee-capped" by the IRA if they dared to give evidence. It further enabled detention of suspects by the executive—internment—though this power was not used after 1975; and it gave the police powers of arrest without a warrant for up to 72 hours, as well as giving wide authority for search and seizure to the security forces.

This Act provided the legal basis for all security activity in Northern Ireland. But the IRA then spread its terror campaign to the British mainland. After a particularly horrific bomb attack on two pubs in Birmingham in 1974, which killed twenty-one people and roused strong public emotion, the Labor government brought in the Prevention of Terrorism (Temporary Provisions) Act.

It gave the Home Secretary the power to exclude from the UK persons concerned in the commission, preparation or instigation of acts of terrorism. Court procedures were dispensed with on grounds that the decision is taken usually on intelligence information which could not be revealed in court. The second great power given to the Minister is to detain a suspect terrorist up to seven days without bringing him to court after his arrest by policemen without a warrant. It also provides for the proscription in Great Britain of organizations considered to be concerned with terrorism. The Act has proved useful against international as well as against Irish terrorists.

These two Acts show just how far a democratic state was prepared to go in combating terrorism. Successive British governments have been conscious of the conflict between their provisions and the preservation of civil rights. However, in time of crisis extreme measures are necessary, and as Merlyn Rees, the former Labor Home Secretary, has pointed out both the Emergency Provisions and the Prevention of Terrorism Act have to be approved by parliament every six and twelve months respectively. "By this means we hope we can keep alive the realization that these measures are emergency ones only and should be temporary."

For further proof that extreme dangers bring extreme laws in any threatened country, the Republic of Ireland has even harsher legislation against the IRA than the British. The IRA has been a proscribed organization in the Republic ever since 1974, two years before London banned it. And since 1976 the IRA has been denied the right for its spokesmen to be interviewed on television, though they still are allowed to appear on British television, which is popular in the Republic. The Republic also has courts without juries, presided over by three judges, and it is sufficient evidence of IRA membership for a senior Garda officer to state to the court that the suspect is a member of it. In brief, it may be said that anti-terrorist legislation in the Republic of Ireland is probably a greater infringement of civil rights than is tolerated in any other Western democracy.

After careful examination of the British emergency anti-terrorist legislation, Joseph W. Bishop, professor of Law at Yale University, came to the conclusion that despite the safety clauses built in to the American constitution it would not be impossible to impose similar measures in the United States. Theoretically such things would be ruled out by the 5th Amendment and the 6th Amendment which specify that no one shall be deprived of liberty without due process of law, and that the accused shall enjoy right to trial by an impartial jury. But, Bishop argued, the Supreme Court has never treated the commands and prohibitions of the Bill of Rights as categorical. Abraham Lincoln suspended *habeas corpus,* interned those suspected of being Confederate sympathizers, and tried people by non-jury military commissions without interference from the courts. Furthermore he defended his actions by claiming that no government, however democratic and liberal, could be expected to stand by and see itself destroyed by the lawless who place no restriction on their own violence.

These legal matters are mentioned here because the tactics of the struggle against terrorism by the democracies are based upon reasonable and necessary emergency legislation. After Munich, as the minds of governments in the Atlantic Alliance began to concentrate on the new problems, there were changes too in international law as each nation began to work out its policy stance.

The general aim was to make terrorism a crime, and to consider terrorists as criminals. But laws were also modified to help police forces detect and deter terrorists before they committed their crimes.

Each state recognized the need for better intelligence work, and set its security organizations the task of penetrating cells of the international terror groups to discover their plans in advance. Passive defense too was important, and the West used its inventiveness and technical skills to make attacks more difficult by hardening the targets. The United States led the way by tightening airport security, using guards and electronic gadgetry to detect hijackers before they boarded aircraft. Closer working relationships were achieved between different organs of the security forces in the various nations. And some progress was made in international coordination among friends.

The first step was to teach the aggressors that the age of deals and concessions was at an end. Tactics developed by the New York City police in dealing with criminal kidnapping proved that by standing firm it was possible to break down the will of terrorists in a similar situation, and force them to surrender without harming the hostages. Security authorities in the Irish Republic used these tactics in the eighteen-day siege of IRA fanatics holding prisoner a Dutchman named Dr. Tiede Herrema, and demanding release of IRA men held in the Republic. The kidnappers failed and surrendered. The new defense arsenal of surveillance, cameras and listening devices was used to help with timing the final talk-out.

Command and control structures at all levels were set up to deal with emergencies and decision-makers studied the problems and the data, and prepared to deal with terrorist crises.

On the ground there are now specially trained police squads ready for action and equipped with the weapons and the bullet and blast-proof clothing to help them face killers and bombers. Special military units developed their own particular skills to act in aid of the civil power when something more than police expertise was needed.

The Israelis, who live always in a state of emergency surrounded by enemies, went the whole hog in fighting terror with terror, making counter strokes which would not be tolerated in a more secure society.

The British, with long experience of colonial wars and faced with prolonged high intensity violence in Northern Ireland, have bent the rules, and have taken measures not dreamed of in more peaceful times. To watch a search operation in Ulster carried out by the British army and the RUC is to see how the tactics and equipment of anti-terror struggle have progressed. For example, infantry seal off a farm, surveyed by a helicopter reporting all movement, dogs expert at sniffing explosives move in together with a special search team operating mine detectors. A bomb disposal squad with a Goliath miniature radio-controlled tank equipped with TV camera to spy out the land, and hooks to grab bombs or explosives waits with its operators. Army intelligence and police question the people who live there. A whole new tactical concept has grown from such operations, which will be useful in other places.

Unlike conventional wars, terrorist wars do not have a certain beginning nor a decided end. But what can be said now is that the defenders have policies, strategies and tactics to meet the threat. The United States under President Reagan has begun to take a stronger line in using the resources which have slowly been developed. In the succeeding chapters we shall explain how each of the Western nations in its own style and fashion has set up the forces to prepare for the counter assault.

2.

Britain: The SAS against the Terrorists

Few nations have the opportunity to see their elite counter-terrorist forces in action. Mogadishu, Entebbe and Teheran all took place thousands of miles away from the home countries of the attacking forces, their dramas were played out where the television cameras could not reach and where censorship prevented the full story being told. The curious world must usually make do with a "sanitized" version of events and the full story is only told when the counter-terrorists meet to talk shop.

However, on Monday 5 May 1980, a fine brisk day, Britain's 22nd Special Air Service Regiment supported by specialist units of the police carried out "Operation Nimrod," the assault on the

Iranian Embassy in the heart of London which provided a remarkable display of counter-terrorist techniques and the deadly actuality of terrorism. It was a Spring Bank Holiday, so thousands had turned out to watch the show from behind the police barricades and millions more were watching television. But no one quite realized what they were about to see . . . the body of Abbas Lavasani, the Iranian zealot, rolled out of the door of the Embassy . . . the SAS assault squad, clad all in black, hurtling down ropes from the roof . . . one trooper caught in his rope, flames licking at his body . . . the explosion . . . the smoke rushing out of the windows as the building caught fire . . . the crackle of automatic guns . . . the screams of the hostages' relatives.

And, later there was the public inquest on the five terrorists who were killed and the trial of the one who survived, during which the hostages, the terrorist and the security services told their stories and their evidence was examined in open court.

These events provided a unique opportunity to study the tactics, weapons, organization and philosophy of the SAS and their police allies.

Even then, the whole story did not emerge. The SAS soldiers were allowed to keep their identity secret, the finer points of their tactics were not discussed and the verdict of "justifiable homicide" did not erase doubts that the soldiers could have captured, rather than killed, more of the terrorists. It became apparent that the sole survivor is alive—serving a life sentence—only because he was sheltered by the hostages themselves.

What emerged as the drama unfolded was an example of military efficiency of which most Britons felt justly proud, but also a feeling in some quarters that possibly the SAS were too enthusiastic, to eager to kill, and there was a certain disquiet about deploying the army in London. British troops are supposed to fight overseas, not in their own capital.

Britain therefore experienced at close quarters the dilemma of all civilized countries in countering the assault of international terrorism: how to set up and use specialized forces without falling into the terrorist trap of destroying the rule of law; how to fight one monster without creating another.

London, for all its civilized aura, is a city long accustomed to the noise of terrorist's bombs and assassin's bullets. The anarchists of the nineteenth century and the recurring campaigns mounted by Irish nationalists have ensured that the capital has rarely been entirely free from terrorism. But never have there been as many incidents as in the past decade, for not only did the Provisional IRA attack London, the city also became a surrogate Middle Eastern battlefield, where Arabs fought Israelis and settled their own tangled quarrels with bullet and bomb. Londoners became accustomed to Arabs killing each other for some obscure purpose far removed from normal life. It came as no great surprise therefore when Iraqi-backed Arab terrorists from the Iranian province of Khuzestan (sometimes called Arabistan) forced their way into the Iranian Embassy in Princes Gate, a row of fashionable houses mostly converted into embassies, seized a number of Iranian and British hostages and made a series of demands which had nothing whatsoever to do with Great Britain.

To counter the terrorists, however, William Whitelaw, the Home Secretary in charge of the Iranian Embassy affair, had at his disposal the SAS, police units highly trained in the art of counter-terrorism and teams of expert negotiators.

The operation had started six days before when Whitelaw took the decision to summon the SAS within hours of the newsflash that the embassy had been seized at 11:30. By 3 p.m. the "Pagoda" immediate reaction team of the SAS had flown to London by helicopter, installed itself in barracks in St. John's Wood and was "doing its sum." They were in plain clothes, were ordered not to appear in public and their presence in London was denied. All these decisions were taken by Whitelaw acting as chairman of COBRA, the government's crisis committee which takes its name from the Cabinet Briefing Room. (COBRA had last been convened in June 1977 when Idi Amin of Uganda threatened to fly to London to attend the Queen's Silver Jubilee.) It is headed by the Home Secretary of the day, the Secretary of the Cabinet Office, in this case, Sir Robert Armstrong, and 15 others representing the Home Office, the Foreign Office, the Ministry of Defense, the Police Force and D16 and D15. COBRA can also be augmented by specialist advisers. During this operation the Commander of the SAS strike team, by now working from a tactical headquarters set up in the Royal School of Needlework close to the embassy, attended some of COBRA's meetings. While Whitelaw was in general control, Prime Minister Margaret Thatcher took the chair on more than one occasion. COBRA did not go into the operation "cold." Everybody knew what they had to do and where to assemble when the codeword was given.

This expertise came from the realization that such an incident was always likely to happen and the team had conducted its own "wargames" to prepare for the event. One of these games, held in 1979, presumed that a British Air jetliner with a full load of passengers had been hijacked to Dacca in Bangladesh. The game plan also called for one of the passengers to be a political personality and someone in the Foreign Office wrote in the radical politician Dame Judith Hart as the mock victim. Then the game was played out. It was estimated that it would take two and a half "hercs"—the four-engined Hercules (C 130) transports which carried the Israelis to Entebbe—to fly the assault team and their equipment to Dacca. One would be for the technical gear and the two black Ford vans would be needed by the technical people. They tried to foresee every eventuality; for example, land lines would need to be laid and these would have to be flown to the incident because Bangladesh, a backward Third World country, would not be able to supply them. Another Hercules would be needed to fly in the assault part and the half would be for the diplomatic personnel who would carry out negotiations with the host government and with the terrorists. The game was played to the end. Diplomatic difficulties were overcome to allow the SAS team to land. They prepared for a long siege. It became obvious the terrorists would not give in and were preparing a massacre. So the "Sassmen" were sent in. It was estimated that the operation ended in success with only a couple of casualties. We do not know if "Dame Judith" was among them.

The diplomatic practice served COBRA in very good stead because during the Iranian siege the Foreign Office had to conduct the most delicate negotiations with the Arab ambassadors in London, hoping to engage them in the efforts to end the siege peacefully.

The negotiations, carried out by Douglas Hurd, Minister of State at the Foreign Office, were unsuccessful. The Arabs behaved disappointingly, especially, the Jordanians, who insisted that before they could ask the terrorists to surrender they would have a guarantee that they would be flown out of the country to freedom. This was an assurance that COBRA would not give. As the Jordanians were shortly to support the Iraqis in their war against Iran and the terrorists were the tools of the Iraqi secret service, perhaps the Jordanian reaction was understandable. The refusal of the Arab ambassadors to meet the terrorists brought them to the edge of despair. They were reaching the moment, recognized by psychiatrists as the most dangerous in any siege, when after days of negotiation and strain, the terrorists would either surrender or kill.

Shortly after 7 p.m. the body of Abbas Lavasani was put out of the front door and when it was carried away Deputy Assistant Commissioner John Dellow, who was in charge of the police operation, reluctantly handed over command to the Army. Two hours earlier police marksmen had taken up new positions. The change-over was recognition that six days of negotiation and tactics had failed, the terrorists had started to kill and they threatened to continue to kill a hostage every half hour. There was now no option but for the SAS to go in.

One "stick" *abseiled* from the roof and burst in through windows at the back of the house. More men crashed through a wall which had been weakened by the removal of bricks from an adjoining house until only the plaster remained. Two men placed an explosive charge fitted to a wooden framework against the windows of the first floor which had been armored to protect the embassy against attack by terrorists. It was this charge which set fire to the furniture piled against the window and eventually led to the destruction of the building. Once inside, the assault force, wearing gas masks, moved from room to room throwing stun grenades mixed with CS gas, identifying the terrorists, shooting them with their Heckler and Koch MP5s or Browning automatic pistols, and bundling the hostages out of the blazing building.

It could, of course, have gone terribly wrong. The great fear was that the terrorists had explosives strapped to their bodies and would blow everybody up if the SAS attacked. The odds for a successful assault kept changing as the terrorists moved around the house—their movements tracked by the fibre optics, infrared cameras and listening devices, which gave COBRA a picture of what was happening inside the building. It was hoped to get odds of 70-30. But once the terrorists had started to kill their hostages the order was given to go in when the odds were a dangerous 60–40. From beginning to end the operation took only 22 minutes.

The action completed, the SAS handed back control to Deputy Assistant Commissioner Dellow and left the scene in a hired Avis truck.

Could the SAS have taken more of the terrorists prisoner? Some of the hostages insisted during their court appearances that most of the gang had tried to surrender and had thrown their weapons away. But as the assault started several of the terrorists had sprayed the hostages with bullets, killing one man and wounding others. In his evidence Police Constable Trevor Lock, captured while on guard when the terrorists first broke in, told how one of the terroirsts died:

> I was with Salim—the terrorist leader—on the first floor of the embassy. I was told to use a field telephone to tell police outside that they were going to kill another hostage. I told them and a voice at the other end asked to speak to Salim about fuelling an aircraft and arrangements about a bus to take them to the airport.

But as Salim, armed with a Polish-made machine pistol, took the receiver there were shouts from upstairs. "He dropped the phone and walked back from me. I heard crashing glass and a loud explosion." Realizing that a rescue attempt was being made, Lock shoulder-charged Salim.

> He hit the door with such force it flew open. The pistol fell out of his grip and skidded along the floor. We fell on the floor and I struggled with him and managed to contain him. I lay on top of him with my arm holding his head back. He was unable to move and I was shouting at him that it was his fault and that he had created the situation. He said, "It was not me. It was the others."
> I then reached for the gun I was carrying (he had kept it concealed throughout the siege) and pulled it out of the holster and placed the muzzle in Salim's ear.
> I thought of pulling the trigger, but decided not to. If I had shot him then it would have been in anger and I have not been trained that way. Then through the gap in the door, two lemon-shaped objects came rolling in. They were the same shape and same green color as the hand-grenades the terrorists had been carrying. I was expecting them to explode any second.
> When they did go off, if threw me off Salim and when I realized I was still in one piece I realized they were stun grenades. They gave off a loud explosion and a flash and oozed CS tear gas. It hurt my eyes and hurt my skin. It was very painful. When I realized I was going to be okay I saw Salim crawling on all fours towards his pistol under a desk. I then threw myself with all the strength I had on Salim and landed on top of him again.

"I managed to grab hold of his right wrist and pulled it away from the gun." A moment later the door flew open and he heard someone shout: "Trevor, move, away."

"It was a voice that you don't question," said Lock. "I rolled over and heard a burst of automatic gunfire. I looked and Salim lay there apparently dead."

He was indeed. But if Trevor Lock had not tackled him he could well have used his machine pistol with deadly effect on the assault team—especially the man who was tangled in his rope. It was in these conditions that the SAS moved through the house. Their orders were to save the hostages and they were taking no chances in the smoke and flames and hysteria in the embassy that any of the terrorists had hidden weapons. They have lost too many men that way in the past.

They took no chances with the hostages even those who were unmistakably European. They were bundled down the stairs, passed from hand to hand, forced to lie down and had their hands tied until their identities had been checked. Dealing with terrorists, especially those who have already killed, is no parlor game. Surely, in this type of incident, it is better that all the terrorists should die rather than risk the life of another hostage or a member of the assault force.

The operation was absolutely in keeping with the regiment's motto "Who Dares Wins" and its reputation for daring professionalism. The public's feeling was encapsulated in the London *Economist*'s headline: "The Army's Secret Glory Boy." It is the sort of description which makes the regiment wince with embarrassment. They are not glory boys. They do their very best to shun all intimations of glory, insisting that they are highly trained, dedicated soldiers who fulfill a number of functions. Anti-terrorist work or, as they describe it, Counter Revolutionary Warfare, is just one of those functions. They point with some bitterness that the month before they attacked the embassy, one of their troop commanders, Captain Richard Westmacott, was killed storming into a house in Belfast which had been taken over by a Provisional IRA gang armed with an M60 heavy machine gun, one of a number stolen from a U.S. National Guard Armory and smuggled to Ireland. There was no glory for him. And when a Military Cross was awarded to him posthumously six months later, the official announcement mentioned only his parent regiment, the Grenadier Guards. Not a word was said about the regiment with which he died.

"Operation Nimrod" gave a great fillip to British morale and allowed the country to indulge in a rare and rather embarrassing bout of self-satisfaction. Not that the British were alone in this. Congratulations arrived from all over the world and the Americans, depressed by the failure of their own hostage rescue mission in the Iranian desert, were happy to buy drinks for anyone with a British accent just because the British had proved it could be done. But, while pleased that it had given such satisfaction with the efficiency of its work and recognizing that in this instance it had to "go public" the regiment was perturbed by the display of its skills which had been recorded forever on film and available for any potential enemy wishing to study its techniques. They were not identified by the Army—although the commander, Major Jeremy Phipps, stepson of Sir Fitzroy Maclean, who fought with Tito's partisans in World War II, was identified because his mother proudly but indiscreetly let it slip to one of her friends that "Jeremy is going to get a medal . . . " The hoods the storming party wore served as a means of disguise as much a conscious attempt to frighten, and and when it was all over they handed authority back to the police and slipped quietly away to the St John's Wood barracks for a celebration attended by a grateful Prime Minister, before returning to their permanent home at Bradbury Lines in Hereford.

It has always been like that with the SAS. The initials could well stand for Silent Air Service rather than Special. Secrecy is drummed into every recruit and once he has been accepted as a full member of the regiment he is taken into a family which exists only for itself and to gossip about that family is unthinkable. This pact of silence has become one of the regiment's most effective weapons. No one knows where its men will appear next, how they will operate, what new equipment they will use to surprise their enemies. Surprise is their watchword and it has been so ever since the regiment was formed forty years ago. It also suits the government well because there are occasions when the regiment is used in places and circumstances which could be highly embarrassing to the government and the army if the news leaked.

The regiment came into being as one of a number of special units that sprang up during the early years of World War II in the Western Sahara Desert. It adapted itself to fight in every theater of war under every type of condition and because of that it is the only one of the private armies to survive, and is today recognized as the most effective special force anywhere in the world. The regiment sprang from the fertile, aggressive brain of the then Lieutenant David Stirling, a young officer in the Scots Guards who was serving with the commandos. Phillip Warner in his book *Special Air Service* reproduces Stirling's account of the gist of it. In the book Stirling argued:

> There were considerable possibilities in establishing a unit which would combine minimum manpower demands with maximum possibilities of surprise. Five men [he later reduced this to four, the standard SAS stick] could cover a target previously requiring four troops of a Commando—about 200 men. I sought to prove that, if an aerodrome or transport park was the objective of an operation, then the destruction of 50 aircraft or units of transport was more easily accomplished by a sub-unit of five than by a force of 200. Two hundred properly selected, trained and equipped men, organized into sub-units of five, should be able to attack at least 30 different objectives on the same night as compared to only one objective using the Commando technique; and that only 25 percent success in the former was the equivalent to many times and maximum possible result in the latter.
>
> A unit operating on these principles would have to be so trained as to be capable of arriving on the scene of operation by every practical method, by land, by sea, or air. The unit must be responsible for its own training and operational planning and that therefore the Commander of the unit must come directly under the C-in-C.

That was written forty years ago. It remains the basic philosophy of the Special Air Service.

Later, in an article written for *The World History of Paratroopers* Stirling wrote:

> From the start the SAS regiment has had some firmly held tenets from which we never depart. They can be summarized as follows:
> 1. The unrelenting pursuit of excellence.
> 2. The maintaining of the highest standards of discipline in all aspects of the daily life of the SAS soldier . . . We always reckoned that a high standard of self-discipline in each soldier was the only effective foundation for Regimental discipline . . .

3. The SAS brooks no sense of class and, particularly, not among the wives. This might sound a bit portentous but it epitomizes the SAS . . .

It is certainly true that no officer who is not accepted by the men will be allowed to stay in the regiment. For what the regiment has developed is a true meritocracy in which no man can take his place until he has proved himself worthy of it, and cannot retain that place unless he remains worthy of it no matter what his rank or connections. Nevertheless, as in all other regiments, the SAS tends to draw on men from a certain background and in its case this tends to be, especially among the officers, Scottish Roman Catholic. Stirling himself is both a Scot and a Catholic; so is one of the first recruits, now Brigadier Sir Fitzroy Maclean, as is his stepson Jeremy Phipps who is a member of that proud Scottish Catholic family the Lovats. That family produced in Lord Lovat, who went into action accompanied by his personal piper, one of the finest commando leaders of World War II. Roy Farran, who achieved fame in the latter part of the war and some notoriety in Palestine after it, is a fervent Catholic and Robert Nairac, tortured and killed by the Provisional IRA in Crossmaglen, the heart of Provo country, went to the same Roman Catholic public school as Stirling, Ampleforth. Nairac, who owned the kestrel round which the film *Kes* centered, as described as a "romantic catholic."

The reason for the Scottish-Catholic line running through the regiment may well be simply that Stirling, being both, tended to pick men of a similar type to himself, thus establishing a lineage. But we suspect there are other reasons linked to the Scots' long history of expertise in guerilla warfare and the traditions of secrecy imposed on Roman Catholics through persecution by the Protestant English. The combination of both traits in the Scottish Catholics makes them ideal members of the SAS. It is one of the many ironies of Northern Ireland that they should now be fighting the Roman Catholic Nationalists.

It is not the purpose of this book to tell the history of the regiment, fascinating though it is. The SAS ended World War II swollen to a brigade and covered in glory. However, it almost died in the inevitable cut-backs of military strength when the war ended, surviving only as a territorial regiment until it was reformed to fight in Malaya against Communist insurgents during the "Emergency" of the fifties. At first it did badly: too many "cowboys" had worked their way into its ranks. But gradually they were weeded out as successive commanders took drastic action.

As the regiment put itself to rights towards the end of its stay in Malaya the opportunity presented itself for the SAS to prove without doubt that it was needed to provide the cutting edge of the British Army in this modern type of conflict.

The opportunity arose in Oman in 1958. Even then the strategic position of this stark, backward country commanding the Straits of Hormuz through which passes the oil which fuels the industrial nations of the West and Japan was well appreciated. The previous year trouble had been stirred up by the Egyptians— then in their Nasserite revolutionary phase—and the Saudis who were pursuing an ancient claim to Omani territory. But the rebels had been beaten back into their mountain strongholds by a mixed force of British troops and the Trucial Oman Scouts. However, it needed something special to dislodge the heavily armed sharp-shooting rebels from the mountains. The SAS was called in. "D" Squadron made a swift transition from the steamy jungles of Malaya to the arid rocks of Oman, re-equipped—they needed long range sniping rifles instead of short range shotguns—and retrained. They were followed by "A" Squadron with a squadron of Life Guards and a detachment of Royal Signals. Their short campaign culminated in a 9,000-foot night climb to assault the rebels' headquarters. It was a complete success. The men had more trouble with their donkeys than with the rebels who were taken by surprise and fled. This was the start of a long association between the SAS and Oman which continues today. The regiment returned in force in 1970 when the country was in danger of being taken over by rebels trained and armed by its Communist neighbor, South Yemen. They lived and fought as tribesmen and their forays often took them deep into South Yemen. Their commander was John Slim, son of Field-Marshal Lord Slim who had fought the Burma campaign.

The SAS are as much at home now in Oman as they are at their own barracks in Hereford. Sultan Qaboos has a splendid body-guard of warriors in white robes armed with machine pistols and silver khanjas, the curved daggers of South Arabia, but his real protection comes from a group of ex-SAS men. Other serving members of the regiment advise and train his own forces and every now and again they disappear into the jebel and the desert to see "what's going on over the other side." There is not much happening in South Yemen that the SAS do not know about.

The SAS also fought in Borneo and Aden in between the two outings in Oman. Fighting in and around Aden, the Red Sea port and base, between 1964 and 1967 had its political problems. Prime Minister Harold Wilson had already announced that Britain was going to abandon Aden, and yet the army was being asked to fight the Adeni insurgents. The fighting outside Aden, up in the Radfan was similar to that in Oman, except that the enemy was fiercer, with the tribesmen rejoicing in the name of the "Wolves of the Radfan." It was in Aden city, however, that they began to learn new skills and direct their attention towards their present anti-terrorist role. If one exchanges the setting from the hot stinking alleys of Aden to the weeping grey skies and rundown blocks of flats of Belfast, the fighting in the two port cities has a remarkable similarity. Bombings, assassinations, intimidation, sudden fire-fights and "no-go" areas with the troops kept on a short leash for political reasons while the murderers disappear to be protected by their families and supporters: the same rules apply in poth places. When it seemed that the terrorists were getting the upper hand, choking off information by murdering policemen and their informants, the SAS took to the streets, dressed as Arabs and armed with the Browning automatic pistol which has remained one of their favorite weapons, and fought the assassins with their own methods—just as they are doing in Belfast today. These operations were called "Keeny-Meeny," from the Swahili words that describe the progress of a snake hidden in long grass and which developed into a phrase meaning undercover work. The SAS liked the sound of it and adopted it, so much so that when Lt. Colonel Jim Johnson set up his own company to protect VIPs and to advise foreign governments on security he called it KMS—Keeny Meeny Services.

It was from this experience in Aden that the SAS started to think about its possible role as an anti-terrorist unit—without of course abandoning its other roles. Here lies one of the regiment's great strengths. It is a thinking organization, always planning for the next encounter, the next development and yet remembering the lessons it has learned in its various campaigns and believing in the "Bible" of David Stirling's founding memorandum. Only when the regiment has ignored, or been forced to ignore, those principles has it not lived up to its own demanding standards.

These standards start with the selection of the men who want to join. They are all volunteers, mostly from the Parachute Regiment—which is none too happy about losing its best men. Every man who applies is told again and again that if he is not invited to join it is by no means a disgrace. It does not mean that he is not an excellent soldier and a brave man. It simply means that he does not meet the regiment's own physical and mental requirements. It is often more difficult for an officer to be accepted than a trooper, for an officer who may command a platoon in an infantry regiment with skill and dash may be completely out of place in a four-man stick where he is not a commander but a member of a team who are all equally important.

Once that has been made clear to a would-be Sassman the process of selection starts. It is not a "young" regiment. Like astronauts, its soldiers tend to be mature and although no one is accepted over the age of 34 the average age is 27. This means that many of the non-commissioned applicants have already reached the rank of corporal or sergeant. And it is here that the NCO candidate must pass his first test of dedication for, to join, he must give up his rank and the pay that goes with it and revert to the rank of trooper. Once past that first hurdle, the recruit is put through a punishing series of physical tests. He is started on the "boys" trek, a march across the Welsh hills carrying a 25-pound pack on his back, then for four weeks (five weeks for officers) he is driven to the point of exhaustion and beyond.

The packs are weighted with bricks and more are added each time he sets out; the mountain courses get steeper and the tests that he has to do on the way become more arduous. "Sickeners" are thrown in to provide another test of mental and physical fortitude. When the exhausted recruits arrive at their pick-up point they see their transport drive away as they struggle over the last few yards. They are then told that the course has been extended for another five or ten miles. It is at this point that a number of men decide that the SAS is not for them after all. For the final test each man is on his own, setting out with a 55-pound pack to cover 37½ miles of the toughest country in the Brecon Beacons in 20 hours. Anybody unable to complete this test is failed.

But the course is literally a killer. Three men died on the Brecon Beacons during solo treks in appalling weather during a 13 month period between 1979 and 1980. One of them was a most distinguished member of the regiment, Major Mike Kealy, who won the DSO in a fierce little action in Oman in 1972. He died of exposure and exhaustion in the Welsh mountains seven years later trying to prove that he was still fit enough for the SAS. The names of those who die on training exercises and in action abroad—actions sometimes disguised as training accidents—are inscribed on the base of a hideous clock tower set up in the Hereford HQ. And those that return from a particularly hairy operation are said to have "beaten the clock"—a black-humored reference to the fatuous television game "Beat the Clock." The fact that not all of them win the game is proved by a row graves in a nearby churchyard. The clock also bears the inscription (from Flecker's *The Golden Journey to Samarkand*): "We are the Pilgrims, master; we shall go always a little further; it may be beyond that last blue mountain barr's with snow, across that angry or that glimmering sea."

And that is what the SAS does; it goes always a little further. Those that pass the intial tests go further to 14 weeks of follow-up training. The first part of the course is taken up with general training, an extension of the skills they have already acquired as trained soldiers. They then spend three weeks learning combat survival that involves living off the land, surviving in Arctic conditions and swimming fully clothed. The final part of the course takes place at Brize Norton airfield where they undergo specialized parachute training. As many come from the Parachute Regiment and are already trained, what they are taught at Brize Norton is freefall parachuting at night from heights far greater than normal jumps. Through the whole of this 14 week period, emphasis is placed on weapon training, using the SAS weapons, the Heckler and Koch sub-machine gun, also the favorite and the symbol of the Baader-Meinhof terrorist gang, the Browning .45 automatic pistol, with which they are expected to reach an extremely high standard of fast, accurate shooting, the pump action shotgun developed for use at close quarters especially in the jungle, and the Sterling sub-machine gun fitted with a silencer. They also train in various personal weapons, knives and crossbows for silent killing and they go through an intensive program of foreign weapons' training so that they become familiar with weapons likely to be used by an enemy. This knowledge is invaluable because knowing the advantages and weaknesses of an enemy's weapon enables them to make a finer assessment of a situation. It also ensures that if they are forced to use captured weapons, they will not be unfamiliar. During weapon training each recruit uses between 1,200 and 1,500 rounds of ammunition.

Throughout the 14-week course the recruits are constantly watched. They are on trial and the mental tests of suitability are just as stringent as the physical and professional tests. Of all the men who apply only 19 out of 100 meet the physical and mental requirements. Those who suceed in completing the 14-week course are awarded the sand-colored beret with its winged dagger emblem, blue belt, and the SAS parachute wings. But even then the training has only just started. For the next year they are on probation learning the skills that make them Sassmen. They become experts in explosives; they are taught battlefield medicine with particular emphasis on bullet wounds for where they go there are rarely doctors and first-aid stations; they learn how to operate different types of wireless sets. And they learn about jungle and desert warfare.

And then they go on still further, specializing in medicine, languages, skiing, mountaineering and underwater warfare. It is said that each four-man stick of trained men is composed of a "brain surgeon, a university don, a nuclear scientist and an Olympic athlete." This is an exaggeration of course, but each man in a stick specializes to a very high standard in one of four subjects: medicine, demolition, SAS men have climbed Everest and rowed the Atlantic, communications and languages. Individuality is encouraged.

There must, of course, be a framework into which all this individuality fits and occasionally, as in Oman, the stick system becomes subordinate to a larger organization involving some 60 to 80 men. Henry Stanhope provides a neat description of that organization in his splendid book *The Soldiers:*

It is similar to that of an ordinary infantry battalion, but with several specialist offshoots. There are four operational squadrons, each with 72 men and six officers, and each squadron is in turn divided into five troops. There is an amphibious troop, an air troop, a surveillance troop, a mountain troop. Each of these consists of an officer and 15 men, the fifth is a specialized signals troop of 24 men, most of them seconded by the Royal Corps of Signals. In addition to these squadrons there are a number of special sections, including a research cell, an initial training cell and Northern Ireland cell—the most recent addition to the regiment.

There are also links with the 21st SAS, the Territorial unit through which the regiment survived after the war, and a second Territorial unit, the 23rd SAS, that was formed in 1959 and specializes in escape and evasion, taking over from M19, the secret British department for which Airey Neave operated after he escaped from Colditz Castle. Airey Neave, who became a Conservative politician specializing in Irish affairs, was murdered by the Irish National Army.

It is in the special sections that one must look for part of the reason for the success of the regiment in its anti-terror role. When given the anti-terrorist role it entrusted its research cell with the task of developing the equipment needed to fight urban terrorism. The best known of the gadgets is the "stun-grenade" or "flash-bang" which explodes with a loud explosion and a flash of brilliant light to stun and blind the terrorists for some five to six seconds at the start of an assault. CS gas has now been added to the grenade to give it yet another dimension. It was this grenade which was used to such good effect by GSG9 in their assault on the hijacked Lufthansa airliner at Mogadishu. The SAS also developed the all-black top to toe outfit worn in the assault on the Iranian Embassy in London. This, the latest in anti-terrorist fashion, is designed not only to protect the wearer against fire and gas but also to put the fear of God into the terrorists. At the embassy it also terrified the hostages.

However, although the regiment's researchers are lavishly supplied, by British army standards, with funds and equipment, the advances in electronic anti-terrorism are so complicated that they rely on the government's own scientific officers to produce the necessary wizardry. The researchers advise on what is needed and field test the equipment, but leave the scientific development to the experts. Most of it centers round discovering what is happening in a building or an aircraft where hostages are being held. There are infra-red devices that can tell how many people are in which rooms. There are television eyes on the ends of flexible armored leads, fibre optics which can see through cracks and round corners, directional microphones which can pick up the slightest noise.

But what happens when the electronics have done their job, when the talks break down and it becomes necessary for the Counter Revolutionary Warfare team to go in shooting? Tony Geraghty in his recent book *Who Dares Wins* puts the problem in perspective:

> . . . at the end of the road, when all the cunning of "gee-whiz" technology has been exploited, the central problem of the siege is appallingly crude: to save hostages' lives by killing, if necessary, the terrorists holding them. The SAS solution is to train its close-quarter marksmen to an extraordinary degree of skill, honing their reflexes in action . . .

The honing is done initially on the range and then in the Close Quarter Battle House better known as "the Killing House." The marksman goes through the house from room to room at speed "killing" dummy terrorists with two shots in the head while keeping the hostages unharmed. It calls not only for catlike reflexes but instant recognition of the situation and impeccable accuracy. Any mistake could be fatal. On occasions officers of the regiment are used as "hostages" in the killing house. It is said this not only ensures that the marksman hits the right target but that the officer is suitable to remain a member of the regiment.

One unfortunate member of the British Foreign Office who went to Hereford after the Iranian siege to express the Foreign Office's thanks and congratulations was given a demonstration of the regiment's methods. He was taken to the killing house and sat on a sofa between two straw "terrorists." Then the rescuers burst in and with blinding speed riddled the "terrorists" with bullets. He remarked afterwards that it was a good job he was nearly bald otherwise the bullets would have cut his hair off. His "rescuers" however said they had taken extra care with him and showed him how neatly they had positioned the bullets in the floorboards round his feet.

The intelligence center is where the Sassman learns about his potential enemies. It provides background on current affairs, what is happening in those parts of the world to which a stick might be sent, and also an up-to-date account of the various terrorist groups and their members. Bodyguard teams are sometimes sent abroad to guard a foreign head of state friendly to Great Britain and to train his own men to take over the task. It is essential that these teams should know the current state of play in that country and to recognize immediately anybody who might intend harm to their charge. When necessary, the regiment can call on the Secret Intelligence Service (D16) and the Foreign Office for briefings and information. It is here that SAS work starts to slide over into special agent work and the soldiers have to tread the minefield of diplomacy and politics.

It is no less a minefield in Northern Ireland to which Sir Harold Wilson, then Prime Minister, publicly committed the regiment in January 1976. The IRA scoffed at this announcement. Their argument was that the SAS had been in Ireland throughout the emergency. In a way they were right for "D" Squadron had served there during the early days of this present bout of the troubles. They served openly wearing their cap badges and patrolling as a unit. However, they were then withdrawn to fight in Oman and officially the SAS had left Ireland. But what happened was that a number of officers and NCOs were transferred from the regiment back to their parent regiments which were serving in Ireland where they acted as intelligence officers and also set up their own sticks of men trained in SAS methods inside the parent regiment. Some officers, like Captain Nairac, changed their cap badge with every regiment that arrived for its four-month tour of duty. By the time he was murdered the regiment was officially back in Ulster but he had maintained his undercover role and the army strenuously denied that he was SAS. Nobody believed these denials and at the time of his death the handbook of the First Guards Club, the officers' dining-club of the Grenadiers, his parent regiment, gave his extra-regimental employment as "22 SAS Regiment."

The Wilson announcement, so alien to the SAS tradition of "Keeny-Meeny" was made for propaganda effect, to convince the IRA that Britain was determined to fight on in the strongest possible way. Certainly the Provo terrorists fear the SAS more than any other regiment in the army. They hate the paratroopers because of the events of "Bloody Sunday" in Londonderry, when the 1st Parachute Regiment killed thirteen Republican supporters when they opened fire on a protest march which had turned into minor riot. But they fear the SAS. This reputation appeared to have the desired effect in bringing to an end the Balcombe Street siege in London in December 1975 when a Provisional IRA "Action Service Unit" of four men took over a flat and held its occupants, Mr. and Mrs. Matthews, hostage. These men had been terrorizing Mayfair and when Mr. Ross McWhirter, joint publisher with his twin, Norris, of the *Guinness Book of Records,* offered a reward of $100,000 for their capture, they went to his home and murdered him. They also killed the eminent cancer specialist Professor Hamilton-Fairey with a bomb intended for his neighbor Sir Hugh Fraser, the Tory politician. Having taken over the Balcombe Street flat they were surrounded, but held out for six days while the police tried to talk them out. An SAS Counter Revolutionary Warfare, or "Pagoda" team, as they became called, was alerted and made plans to assault the flat. But in an inspired piece of "psywar" it was deliberately reported that the SAS were on the scene and the gang, listening to the radio, heard the report. As Sir Robert Mark, then commissioner of the London police, wrote later: "Thereafter they could hardly surrender fast enough." This may be ungenerous to the policemen who so skillfully conducted the talks which led up to the surrender and it is probable that the terrorists would have surrendered in due course. It does seem, however, that the news that the Sassmen were on the spot convinced the terrorists that if they did not surrender immediately then the SAS would most certainly storm the flat and shoot them dead.

That was one of the few occasions that the SAS has broken cover during its involvement in Ireland. Another took place in very different circumstances in September 1980 when David Stirling organized a gala dinner in aid of the regiment's Benevolent Fund. The dinner was held at Annabel's night club and the tickets were $150 a head. It raised some $53,00 but no serving members of the regiment were present. The Ministry of Defense had expressed concern about their appearance at a public function for security reasons. It was assumed that their presence might have encouraged an attack on the function by terrorists, but the Ministry was really talking about the possibility of members of the regiment being photographed and their identities revealed.

Stirling wrote what seemed to some to be a somewhat indiscreet appeal for support. In it he said:

> The regiment is only a few decades old. In this short time it has not been possible to accumulate the funds normally available to older regiments to cope with even the most rudimentary call on regimental welfare needs—yet the SAS, even more than any other regiment, has always to be in a state of high readiness.
>
> Recently, for example, during a four-week period the Regiment was involved in two operations. The first one you know all about—the Princes Gate operation; the second is one about which you know nothing. The action at the Iranian Embassy, very unusually for the SAS, took place in full view of the television cameras. The other was carried out in characteristic secrecy and silence. The second operation, an unsung episode, resulted in the rounding-up of four much sought-after terrorists in Northern Ireland. It also saw the death of a magnificent young SAS officer . . .

That officer was Captain Westmacott and the operation in which he was killed was a typical SAS enterprise. He was with a plain-clothes patrol keeping "obbo" (observation) close to the junction of Antrim Road and Limestone Road in North Belfast. Each member of the patrol had committed to memory the photographs and descriptions of known Provisional IRA terrorists. They were especially on the look-out for groups of three or four men whose known technique was to move into a house on a familiar army patrol route, hold the inhabitants hostage, set up an ambush with Armalite rifles and one of the heavy M60 machine guns which had been stolen from the National Guard depot in Denver, Colorado, in 1976 and then report an incident—a burglary or traffic accident—which would bring either an army patrol or the Royal Ulster Constabulary hastening to the scene. This ploy has been used on a number of occasions and has resulted in several deaths. The official version of the Westmacott incident is that he and his patrol stopped outside the house because "their suspicions were aroused." It is far more likely that they knew the ambush was being organized. Westmacott could have surrounded the house and called for the Army's Quick Reaction Force to come to his aid. But he knew there were two women in the house and he wanted to make sure they were not harmed. So he made a dash for the door, but was met with a burst of fire and killed. At the same time one of his men was wounded. The house was then surrounded by police and soldiers and the terrorists, with the muzzle of their M60 still poking through the window, waved a piece of white material and asked to talk to a policeman and a priest who had been called to the scene They then surrendered— but not to the SAS. More of the "M60 Gang" were rounded up but seven of them escaped with an eighth man from Belfast's Crumlin road jail in a daring, well-planned break-out the day before they were due to be sentenced.

In an operation similar to the one in which Captain Westmacott died, two houses in the Roman Catholic area of Twinbrook in Belfast were raided on October 1980 by soldiers dressed in helmets and blue parkas with orange armbands. They carried automatic weapons and used sledgehammers to break down the doors. The authorities would not say that the men were SAS but the action bore the hallmarks of one of their raids. A regular army major who arrived on the scene was told to "go away." It transpired that the houses were being used as an advice center for Provo prisoners but that the men watching the houses supected that they had been taken over by the Provos to set up an ambush.

The SAS reviews the different treatment accorded these two incidents with resigned cynicism. Captain Westmacott was killed trying to ensure that two women hostages were saved. He was shot down by a Provo killer group setting up an ambush with a heavy machine gun. And yet his death hardly rated a comment in Ireland. But when another group of Sassmen, believing them- selves to be in a similar situation, break down a door, tie the hands of a woman and her 14-year-old daughter for a few minutes—just as they tied the hands of the hostages they rescued from the Iranian Embassy—and a youth has his hand injured, the Provos and their supporters raise the old propaganda cry that the SAS are psycopathic killers. That is all part of the game in Ireland but the Provos as usual drew along with them politicians who wittingly or unwittingly play their game for them. Gerry Fitt, the independent member of Parliament for West Belfast, announced that he was going to raise a question in the House of Commons demanding to know "who was responsible for this terrorist operation . . . ? " And Michal Canavan, security spokesman for the mainly Roman Catholic Social Democratic and Labor Party, said: "Jackboot tactics of this kind in the present climate of sectarian and political assassinations in West Belfast are unforgivable and must cease forthwith.''

Officially the regiment says nothing about these accusations, it will not even agree that its men were involved, but one member summed up the men's feelings: ''If it had been an ambush set-up and some of us had been killed in the raid I doubt very much if there would have been a word of protest.''

SAS men rarely wear uniform in Belfast and if they do they wear the cap badge of other regiments. Armed with Browning pistols, they operate in civilian clothes, posing as laundrymen, milkmen, melting into the local scene.

Outside the cities, and especially in South Armagh, the so-called bandit country, the Sassmen—a name given to them by the Irish—play the game of watching and waiting, holing up in a hedge or a fold in the ground and spending days there, piecing together the pattern of activity until the picture becomes clear enough for action to be taken. In most cases the information is passed on to a regular unit or the Royal Ulster Constabulary. But occasionally, when a particularly notorious killer is involved, the SAS send in a team to ''lift'' him themselves. If he should show any signs of resistance then he is a dead man. The Provos then make a great propaganda fuss about the SAS murdering an unarmed man. But they know the score and the regiment's reputation goes up another notch among the Provos' hitmen. Sometimes, inevitably, events go tragically wrong. In July 1978 John Boyle, son of a farming family, discovered a cache of arms under a headstone in a cemetery. His father told the police. The SAS was alerted and an ambush set up by five men under the command of Sergeant Allen Bohan and Corporal Ronald Temperley. For some still unexplained reason young John Boyle returned to the cache after dark. Bohan and Temperley, believing him to be terrorist, shot him dead. They were tried for murder before the Lord Chief Justice of Ireland, Sir Robert Lowry. Sir Robert found them not guilty, accepting their pleas that they believed he was a terrorist and had picked up a rifle. But he attacked Bohan for being an untrustworthy witness and argued that it was a ''badly-planned and bungled exercise.'' And he went on to deliver the lesson of the case: that while terrorists could consider themselves outside the rule of law, the army could not. ''I do not intend to give any currency to the view that the army is above the general law in the use of weapons.''

The role of the SAS in Northern Ireland is an undercover one to back up the regular army units, and the Royal Ulster Constabulary which is increasingly taking over security duties from the British Army. The 40 years' experience as a special forces regiment has made the SAS into one of the finest anti-terrorist foces in the world. It has always been something of an international unit, and its officers and NCOs now spend a fair amount of time teaching their methods to the anti-terrorist units of allied countries.

Close relations have been established with the German GSG9 and its commander Ulrich Wegener, and especially with Colonel Charles Beckwith, the hard-nosed commander of the American Black Berets, who was in charge of the assault party during the ill-fated attempt to rescue the American diplomatic hostages from Iran. They also maintain liaison with the Dutch. SAS soldiers provided technical know-how for the Dutch Marines when they stormed a train hijacked by the South Moluccans at Assen, and for GSG9 at Mogadishu.

Although there is some liaison with the Israelis it is not as close at it might be. Both sides remember those days at the end of the Palestine Mandate when Roy Farran formed his Q Squads on SAS principles to hunt down Jewish terrorists. Farran was court martialled for the murder of a 16-year-old boy suspected of being a member of the Stern Gang; he was acquitted but the Israelis were determined on vengeance. They sent a book bomb to his home in England. It was opened by his brother, Rex. It exploded in his face and he was killed. The SAS does not easily forget. The regiment is also involved in protecting the rulers of a number of Arab states who are important to Britain and these are men who could be considered natural enemies of the Israelis. So relations with the Israelis are conducted through Ulrich Wegener.

It would be wrong to leave Britain's military anti-terrorist forces without discussing the role of the Royal Marines. Although the SAS has an amphibious capability and is at all times prepared to counter a terrorist attack on Britain's North Sea oil intallations with helicopters and Hercules transports on permanent stand by—members of the regiment have even sailed on long voyages on super-tankers to plan counter-measures in case one was hijacked—it is the Marines who have prime responsibility for protecting the vital oil platforms.

In the 1970s they trained to cope with the threat of a terrorist attack on the oil fields. They specialize in frogman tactics and assault by fast rubber boats and helicopters. Joint exercises with the Royal Navy and Royal Air Force are held twice a year, codenamed Purple Oyster or Prawn Salad according to their scale. The task force is on instant call from its base at HMS *Condor,* the headquarters of 45 Commando Group, Royal Marines at Arbroath in Scotland. They have planned three ways to reach threatened rigs: by Sea King helicopters which can ferry eight to ten men in under an hour to the nearest oil installations; by Hercules (C 130) for parachuting frogmen into the sea; and by surface craft and submarine from which they would launch their small boats. Plans were coordinated with the Norwegians who have formed their own special unit to deal with terrorist attacks against their installations in the North Sea. And civilian planning was organized through COBRA. In May 1980 the Marines reorganized on the experience of the previous six years and set up a 300 strong "reaction force" which was called Comacchio Company and took over responsibility for the oil fields. In 1981 it was reported that their strength was going to be increased by 25 percent. Their training follows the same principles as the SAS—especially the secrecy with which its members surround themselves. Units are constantly at sea on patrol vessels watching the rigs and they, too, have their own international connections with units such as the Dutch Marines, the Norwegians and the U.S. Navy's SEAL teams. So far they have not needed to demonstrate their skills. Like so many anti-terrorist forces they are prepared for the eventuality that may never come. But they must be ready.

The sharp edge of Britain's security armed forces, the SAS and the Royal Marines, are only called into action when a situation has got out of hand, and when military muscle is considered essential. British law makes it perfectly clear both to Police Chief Constables and to the army authorities in what circumstances the army may provide what is officially known as Military Aid to the Civil Power (MACP). The army may be called in to deal with any threat to security which the police are inadequately equipped to deal with. While the military are undertaking such a role they remain completely under the control of the civil authorities, and they enjoy no extra privileges. As soon as the emergency is over, and the level of violence has fallen sufficiently for the police to take over again, they do so. It is a perfectly sensible and necessary arrangement.

The one area in the United Kingdom where the police and the army work continually together is in Northern Ireland. The Royal Ulster Constabulary, who wear distinctive green uniforms, are continually involved in the struggle against terrorists. The RUC is the only permanently armed police force in the British Isles. With 6,000 men the RUC has an unenviable task, the more so as it is still seen in Northern Ireland as a sectarian force drawing only 11 percent of recruits from the Roman Catholic community. Although training and discipline have improved and equipment is now more up to date the RUC could not keep the peace without the help of the British army, though successive governments have expressed the hope that one day they will be able to manage without military assistance.

The police themselves have considerable resources for dealing with terrorism and they operate a number of specialized units. The first of these is C13, the Anti-Terrorist Sqaud. It was formed in January 1971 when the Angry Brigade anarchist group ex ploded two bombs at the home in Barnet north of London, of Robert Carr, then Secretary of State for Employment. Detective Chief Superintendent Roy Habershon (who retired as Com- mander in 1980) set up a major investigation team in "S" Division. It became the nucleus of the Bomb Squad which was formed on July 29, 1971 following more explosions, one of them at the home of the then Minister of Trade, John Davies. This squad, led by Commander Ernest Bond, who for security reasons was known only as Commander X, was based at New Scotland Yard and was attached to the Serious Crimes Squad led by Commander Robert Huntley.

Its first success came in August of that year when patient and traditonal police work allied to forensic investigation led to the break-up of the Angry Brigade and the imprisonment of most of its leaders. But this was only the start of the Bomb Squad's work, for Britain was shortly to suffer the full blast of IRA and Middle East terrorism. Letter-bombings, shootings and hijackings be- came common-place. Then, on February 22, 1972 the Official IRA bombed the parachute regiment's mess at Aldershot in retaliation for "Bloody Sunday." This remained a specific act of retaliation, however, and the full assault by the Provisional IRA on the mainland did not start until March 8, 1973 when car bombs exploded outside the Old Bailey and New Scotland Yard, killing one man and injuring some 250.

The following year, 1974 was a bloody year. There were Provo bomb attacks on the National Defense College and on a coach carrying soldiers' families along the M62 motorway in February. July saw the attack on innocent tourists by a bomb planted at the Tower of London. There were bombings at Guildford in October and Woolwich in November. The carnage culminated in the Birmingham pub bombings in which 20 people were killed and 180 injured. The same period also saw the emergence in London of the Venezuelan assassin, Carlos, operating on behalf of the Popular Front for the Liberation of Palestine. As the terrorist campaign mounted, so the squad which had been formed in *ad hoc* fashion because of the Angry Brigade grew in numbers and skills. In December 1972 Commander Robert Huntley took over with Detective Chief Superintendent James Nevill as his deputy leader.

The strength of the squad is around 150 but it varies acording to the level of terrorist activities and it can call on the services of experts from a number of different fields. The Fingerprint Branch at Scotland Yard, for example, set up a section to deal specifically with terrorist incidents. Members of the squad have been drawn from the Special Branch, CID, uniformed officers and, during the 1974–5 Provisional IRA campaign, men were recruited from the provincial forces.

The calling in of polce from the regions helped to strengthen the squad when it was working flat out. Then the officers involved were able to take back the knowledge they acquired to their own forces. The Bomb Squad, as its name implied, concentrated on the explosive aspect of terrorism, its explosives officers becoming among the world's most expert in detecting and defusing bombs of an increasing complexity. Only five years ago the typical bomb consisted of several sticks of blasting powder or "Co-op mixture" (so called because its ingredients, individually harmless, could all be bought at Cooperative Stores) exploded by a timing device based on a cheap wrist-watch. Today explosives officers have to cope with bombs similar to the type that killed Lord Mountbatten, a sophisticated device exploded from a distance by a radio switch of the kind normally used to control model aircraft and boats, or the even more complicated mercury-detonated device that killed Airey Neave in which a timer raises a gate, freeing a blob of mercury, and when disturbed rolls onto an electrical circuit completing the circuit and detonating the bomb.

Many of these bombs now have anti-handling devices built into them, photo-electric cells which are sensitive to the explosive officer's flashlight, or trembler devices which explode the bomb if it is moved. Sometimes the bombers leave several small bombs with simple mechanisms that easily defuse and then plant a killer bomb, apparently similar to the others but with a booby-trap built into it.

In that year it became obvious that the Bomb Squad would have to change to keep up with the increasingly complex develop- ments in international terrorism. Commander Habershon, who had returned to take charge when Commander Huntley retired in March 1975, saw the change through. In February 1976 the squad was reorganized into C13, the Anti-Terrorist Squad, and was given a wider field to cover and greater powers with which to do it. It has had a great deal of success. The Balcombe Street Siege became a text book example of how to handle an operation where known killers arc holding hostages. Sir Robert Mark, then Commissioner of Metropolitan Police, brought in a team of psychiatrists, and under their guidance Chief Superintendent Peter Imbert took over the nerve-wracking job of maintaining contact with the terrorists through a field telephone. Peter Imbert handled the "talking-out" process with skill and sympathy.

At the same time the tall, handsome Jim Nevill presented the public face of the siege. His calm presence on the television screen during the siege made him renowned as the representative of the fight against terrorism. He never really enjoyed the limelight. By appearing so often he made himself a target for terrorist reprisals. But he accepted his television role as one of the essential weapons in the fight against the bombers. He said: "We needed to reach the public. Our means of informing them is through the media, and I accepted it as part of the job."

When there is an incident such as Balcombe Street or the Iranian Embassy and a shoot-out becomes likely, the Anti Terror- ist Squad can call on its own police equivalent of the SAS before asking the army for assistance. It is D11, the "Blue Berets," which is in fact Scotland Yard's firearms department, and the squad is formed for emergencies by bringing together some 20 men led by the Yard's own weapons instructors.

Their appearance in action for the first time at Balcombe Street wearing the uniform they chose for themselves—blue berets and blue battle dress—caused apprehension among those who are suspicious of elite armed police units. This apprehension grew when it was learned that they had chosen their own weapons and adopted their own methods of training. The weapons form a strong armory. They are:

1. The Enfield Enforcer rifle, a 7.62 sniper's rifle with telescopic sights for "precise hits."

2. The same Heckler and Koch sub-machine gun used by the SAS, but with the automatic fire selector blocked.

3. The Remington pump action shotgun with fixed and folding butt.

4. The Webley and Scott gas gun for firing CS tear gas.

5. The short Smith and Wesson five-shot revolver which is also carried by all policemen on bodyguard duty.

6. The .38 Smith and Wesson special with either five- or six-inch barrel which is the normal weapon issued to police officers from their stations when authorized by a senior officer.

7. The 9mm Browning pistol as used by the SAS. It is only issued to specialist officers facing "high risk" targets.

The basic training for the Blue Berets who were formed in the early seventies is a four-day course on the Metropolitan Police range or one borrowed from the army. Targets are set at various distances and at the end of the four days a candidate for the squad must be able to put nine out of ten shots into each target. Those that do not measure up to this standard are, like SAS recruits, "returned to unit." After the basic training the instructors set out to turn the new men into marksmen. They are trained in shooting moving targets, in street fighting, and night firing in the countryside. Because this involves physical demands not usually made on policemen they are also given a modified form of commando training with assault courses, camouflage and close quarter combat exercises. On operations they are linked by radio earpieces to a "firemaster" whose order to fire is the only one they are allowed to obey. When an operation ends they return to their normal police duties. Senior officers have pledged that they will never be summoned automatically, but only when their armed presence is deemed necessary.

Another important adjunct of the Anti-Terrorist Squad is C7, the Technical Support Branch, the scientific wizards of the police who develop their own surveillance and monitoring devices and communications techniques. They have developed some remarkable eavesdropping equipment, some of which was used by the

Republic of Ireland police in October 1975 when the Dutch industrialist Tiede Herrama was being held hostage by the wildcat Provos, Eddie Gallagher and Marian Coyle, in their attempt to obtain the release of Rose Dugdale. She had been imprisoned for, among other things, trying to bomb a police station with a milk churn full of explosives from a hijacked helicopter. Using this equipment, a version of which was also used at Mogadishu, the Irish Garda were able to build up an accurate picture of what was happening in the besieged house.

Heavy back-up is provided by the Special Patrol Group, formed in 1965 as a mobile reserve available to assist divisional police in the Metropolitan area where and whenever required. Scotland Yard says its primary function is to provide saturation policing in areas where crime is rife. The group also furnishes a manpower reserve for demonstrations and disturbances, major incidents, large-scale searches or inquiries and road blocks. It is formed into six units under the control of a chief superintendent. Each unit has an inspector in charge, three sergeants and 29 constables—including at least one woman. The units are based strategically throughout the Metropolitan Police district. Each has three personnel carriers capable of seating 12, and a car for an inspector. All the vehicles are on the information room radio net at Scotland Yard and they also have their own individual net. All SPG officers are volunteers who have completed the two-year probationary period. More than 80 percent of them are trained to use firearms.

It was the SPG that provided the cover force at Balcombe Street and the Iranian Embassy. But just as with the "Blue Berets" there are misgivings about this group with it evocative name. There have been many demands for its disbandment following the accusations that members of the SPG bludgeoned a school-teacher, Blair Peach, to death during the London National Front riot of 1979. The SPG were labelled "shock troops" and it was said that their real purpose was to crush left-wing demonstrators. Scotland Yard argues, however, that the SPG is used on all marches, labor disputes and festivals where serious public disorder is anticipated and they are therefore bound to be drawn into any violence that breaks out. The Yard adds: "It must be remembered, however, that the central task of the SPG is routine patrolling on foot and in vehicles in areas where street crimes, burglaries and hooliganism have reached a high level. Such is the success of the group in this role that each year up to 4,000 arrests mainly from crime are made by the 'SPG.' "

Other units involved with the Anti-Terrorist Squad in the fight against terrorism are A11, the Diplomatic Protection Group, which was formed in 1974 to protect foreign embassies and diplomats in London; the Special Branch Protection Squad which provides bodyguards for Ministers and important visitors; and the Royal Protection Group which looks after the Royal Family.

Police Constable Trevor Lock, on duty at the door of the Iranian Embassy when the terrorists struck, was there as a member of the Diplomatic Protection Group. As we have seen, PC Lock behaved extrmely well during the siege and was later awarded the George Medal for his gallantry. However, there was some disquiet that he should have been left alone to guard what was obviously a vulnerable target. Providing guards for all such potential targets is a tremendous burden on the Metropolitan Police. In the House of Commons Home Secretary William Whitelaw said the "the embassies themselves have a considerable duty to look after their own protection, which many of them do. They should carefully consider it." Among those that do, of course, is the Israeli embassy. It would take a very brave terrorist to attack the well-protected Israeli embassy in Kensington and the chances of success would be very slender. The only defense at the Iranian Embassy was PC Lock. One armed officer was obviously not enough. Had police resources been greater to mount more effective guard the great siege need never have happened.

While all these forcs are ranged on the anti-terrorist side to react to acts of terrorism, they are absolutely useless without a good intelligence organization which enables them to forestall attacks, arrest terrorists or react quickly if an incident does take place. The Anti-Terrorist Squad therefore relies heavily on the Special Branch for information. The Special Branch was formed out of the Irish Special branch following the campaign of bombing by Irish revolutionaries from 1883 to 1885. Scotland Yard became more active in investigation of bombings only after the cast-iron toilet in the center of Scotland Yard was blown up by the Fenians on May 30, 1884. Paul Wilkinson in his *Terrorism and the Liberal State* maintains that "the most appropriate body for the tasks of intelligence-gathering, collation, analysis and coordination is the police Special Branch or its equivalent: it is normally the case in a liberal state that the police service enjoys at least some degree of public confidence, and cooperation.''

That remains true, but such is the complexity of international terrorism that the Special Branch must also be able to draw on the Secret Intelligence Service and other specialized agencies for information about terrorists arriving in this country to carry out operations. It is possible, for example, that the murder of former Yemeni Prime Minister Abdullah al-Hejiri, his wife and the Minister of the Yemeni Embassy in London on April 10, 1977 could have been prevented along with the Mogadishu hijack if a proper evaluation had been made of Zohair Akache, who murdered the Yemenis and later commanded the hijack gang. Akache was well known to the London police as a Palestinian fanatic with a penchant for attacking the police. He appeared at Marlborough Street Court on December 15, 1975, charged with assaulting a policeman, and was sentenced to six months' imprisonment and deportation. But a year later he had sneaked back into Britain and he was spotted by an alert policeman in a Wimpey Bar in the Earls Court Road. On February 2 he was seen going into 86 Inverness Terrace, a road of cheap rented rooms, and the Special Branch was informed. Apparently no action was taken and two months later Akache carried out his triple murder outside the Royal Lancaster Hotel, drove to Heathrow Airport and, using a forged passport, boarded a Kuwait Airlines plane for Baghdad.

Six months later, after killing Lufthansa pilot Jugen Schumann and forcing the co-pilot to land at Mogadishu with 79 passenger hostages, he was killed by the GSG9 assault team. A series of errors due to a misrouting of information prevented Carlos's arrest in London, and enabled him to carry out his spectacular series of terrorist crimes culminating in the kidnapping of the OPEC oil ministers in Vienna in 1975. The Special Branch has learned a lot since then; it is making use of the National Computer linking its information to that of the German anti-terrorist computer at Wiesbaden. Once a terrorist or somebody with terrorist connections is logged on the computers it is difficult for him to make a move without a policeman somewhere feeding the information back.

The increasing use of computer data banks by the police is a source of worry to liberal minded people both in Britain and elsewhere. There is anxiety about the use to which information stored in order to fight back at terrorist organizations might be put. Already there have been distressing cases of people being mistaken for terrorists who suffer from over-enthusiastic police investigation. Also, the operation in Britain of special police groups such as the SPG, and the calling in of the SAS to perform commando operations in the heart of London is a worrying new development. Although the general feeling is that these measures are necessary, public opinion keeps a watchful eye open for any serious threats to the old established rights of freedom and privacy.

3.

Reagan Rearms against Terrorism

It was precisely at the time when the world-wide terrorist threat was developing that the strongest weapon in the American armory against it, her internal and external intelligence capability, was itself under close scrutiny. In the aftermath of the Vietnam war and of the Watergate affair both the Central Intelligence Agency and the Federal Bureau of Investigation were under a cloud. The Senate and the Congress kept a suspicious eye upon them and curbed their activities.

In the declining years of J. Edgar Hoover the FBI had greatly exceeded its brief in lawful counter-intelligence against groups suspected of preparing for violent acts. Under his direction in

1961 it launched the notorious Counter Intelligence Program (COINTELPRO) against such groups as the SWP, the Socialist Workers' Party, using such unsavory methods as disruption and harassment. Details became public when court action was taken against the Bureau, which itself later admitted that the program was "abhorrent in a free society."

The CIA too had gone far beyond the acceptable small-scale covert operations and moved into grandiose activities of a para-military nature, such as the Bay of Pigs and the Chile plot. Both President Johnson and President Nixon used the Agency for ambitious interventions overseas. After Watergate came an un-dammed wave of allegations about CIA plots, some true, others false; some came from genuine democrats and others from those exploiting the affair as a lever against democratic society.

In the mid seventies Congress passed a number of measures which placed restrictions upon the activities of both organizations. The amended Freedom of Information Act gave greatly increased public access to classified information, and it was made mandatory for agencies to reply to requests for information within ten days.

The Privacy Act allowed individuals to "determine what records pertaining to him are collected, maintained, used or disseminated" by government agencies. It banned the keeping of records on people belonging to revolutionary or subversive groups. These two acts mostly affected internal security.

But the Ryan Amendment was more concerned with external affairs and forbad the President to authorize any covert operation without informing six Congressional committees.

The McGovern Amendment made it possible to deny a non-immigrant a visa to enter the US simply because the applicant was alleged to be a Communist Party member.

The Levi guidelines issued by the then Attorney General, Edward H. Levi, circumscribed the activities of the FBI, the traditional guardian against subversive and terrorist organizations. The guidlines not only banned them from "harrassment" of such groups, but also laid down that they must not make illegal entry into their premises. The FBI was only to investigate and carry out surveillance on organizations suspected of mischief when it could show that the organization was committing violent acts or was about to do so. Two years later the FBI Director, William H. Webster, reported that the bureau was practically out of business in the domestic security business.''

In 1978 the Foreign Electronic Surveillance Act required the Executive Branch to seek warrants before bugging any US citizen, or even a permanent resident alien, even for purposes of national security. Until then it had been deemed that the powers of the Presidency were sufficient to approve such surveillance without a warrant.

These measures, taken in the commendable cause of creating a freer and more open society, nonetheless lowered America's guard at a crucial time, both internationally and domestically. The Freedom of Information Act inhibited the cooperation between the CIA and European and Israeli intelligence. For the military intelligence services, which do trade information on terrorism, fear that whatever they pass to America may quickly become public. This discourages not only the services concerned, but also their informants who are terrified of reprisals against them should their intelligence role be discovered.

In 1980 Ambassador Anthony Quainton, Director, Office for Combatting Terrorism, told the Senate Committee on the Judiciary: "I have had expressed to me by a number of foreign governments their concern that the provisions of the Freedom of Information Act will result in the unauthorized disclosure of information, which they have provided us in confidence through a variety of liaison channels which exist . . . I am afraid we have received less information that we otherwise would have because of that concern."

The political scandals of the seventies and the new controlling legislation were followed by the mass dismissal of CIA officers, including many senior officers. Two thousand were fired from CIA headquarters at Langley, Virginia, and this further weakened an already demoralized service. The same effect was discernable in the FBI, and at state and local levels police counter-intelligence units were affected by these developments.

For example, when the New York Police Department was investigating a Puerto Rican bomb attack on a tavern it had to ask for information elsewhere because it had already destroyed its own files on Puerto Rican militants.

When the Hanafi sect of Black Muslims attacked three buildings in Washington, D.C. and held 134 hostages for 36 hours special police squads did well in containing the raid. They succeeded in talking out the gunmen. But the incident might have been prevented altogether had not the flow of information about militant Hanafi organizations dried up as a result of libertarian legislation which forced the withdrawal of their undercover men, who had succeeded in infiltrating the groups a year before.

In their enthusiasm to curb excesses and restore freedom of the individual, it can now be seen that the legislators had gone too far. The fine balance between safeguarding the rights of loyal and decent citizens, while at the same time maintaining the defenses to prevent mischief by those who want to overthrow the democratic system favored by the majority, had been upset. In the first year of his Administration, President Reagan has taken various measures to strike a better balance between the rights of individuals and the need for intelligence agencies to collect information on terrorists.

Although they did not operate on the same scale as similar groups in other parts of the world, the United States did have its home-grown terrorists. In imitation of the European anti-capitalist groups, the New World Liberation Front bombed offices, hotels and clubs frequented by the rich on the West Coast. For a time the Weathermen, the Weather Underground Organization, formed in 1969, became active in the preaching of solidarity with ethnic minorities and the Third World by carrying out bomb attacks—some 30 in all.

The most exotic of the American terror bands and the one attracting most publicity was the Symbionese Liberation Army which gained notoriety by kidnapping Patricia Hearst. It was a small militant "loving" group with anarchist aims and a high proportion of women members. It faded away after FBI agents and Los Angeles police killed its leader, Donald De Freeze, and five others in a shoot-out.

More dangerous are the various Black Muslim factions still active, like the Hanafis. In addition there are the imported terrorist clashes on American territory. Jewish extremist organizations bomb the homes of Arab diplomats, Cuban exiles attack pro-Castro Cubans. Croatian émigrés seized the West German consulate in Chicago, hijacked an airliner bound for New York and took it to Paris, while others attacked Yugoslav government offices. Like Europe, America may still become the cockpit for other people's terrorist battles.

Ethnic groups have recently become more active. For example, Omega 7, a small organization of anti-Castro Cuban exiles regarded by the FBI as the most dangerous militants in the United States, has accepted responsibility for a number of bombings and murders. One of their devices exploded at Kennedy International Airport in luggage about to be loaded aboard a TWA flight to Los Angeles. They twice bombed the Cuban mission to United Nations, and injured eight in an attack on the Soviet mission of the same organization.

The Armed Forces for National Liberation (FALN), a Puerto Rican terrorist and nationalist group demanding independence, is still an active force, small in number but a continuing threat by way of its connections and the help it receives from Castro's Cuba.

Domestic terrorism has by no means reached the seriousness of terrorism in other parts of the world but the figures issued by the FBI for the decade ending in 1980 show that in each year some 100 law enforcement officers were killed in terrorist and politically motivated crimes.

The CIA inventory of international terrorist incidents for the year 1980 carried the warning that citizens of the United States, expecially businessmen, were still primary targets for terrorist attacks, particularly in the Middle East and Latin America. During the year six Americans were killed in El Salvador, two in Turkey, one in the Philippines and one on the occupied West Bank. Ninety-four others were wounded. Favorite targets for the preceding year were American, British and French. Drawing attention to the new development of terror attacks carried out by national governments, the same report stated that, "our records list 14 attacks by Libyan assassination teams in Europe and the United States."

One of the early acts of the Reagan administration was to expel the entire staff of the Libyan embassy in Washington after denouncing the hitmen of President Qaddafi for planning to kill more Libyan exiles in the U.S. And it was a welcome sign of a new toughness in the American style of government when the CIA report plainly described Qaddafi as: "The most prominent state sponsor of and participant in international terrorism 'giving aid' to almost every major international group."

The report also signalled new thinking in Washington by revising its statistics upwards and by stating that previous data had been too dependent on U.S. sources, but that the Agency was now satisfied that its records were "complete and current," replacing statistics in all their previous surveys. As a result they catalogued 6,714 incidents of international terrorism between 1968 and 1980, including 760 during the year 1980. There was little doubt that the revision was a sign of new emphasis within the administration on the worldwide dangers of this kind of warfare.

It was the terrorist seizure of the American Embassy in Teheran which had concentrated the country's attention on the scale and nature of the problem. That event helped to win the presidency for Ronald Reagan, and he began taking firmer action to use the tools already at hand within the U.S. to redress the balance.

Despite their difficulties with intelligence gathering, the Americans had responded to the growing threat by creating special forces, and with tactical innovations. For several years the FBI has been running instruction courses at its academy in Quantico, Virginia. Special Weapons and Tactics Teams (SWAT) were set up at all levels of law enforcement agencies. American inventive skill was used to provide them with weapons, transport and technical devices.

Special Weapons and Tactics Teams consist of five men usually organized to consist of the leader, a scout, an observer, a marksman and a rearguard. In an ideal unit all are interchangeable. In the case of the FBI teams and those in large U.S. cities, one team is always on alert and ready for any emergency. The equipment varies but the sniper always has a special rifle with vision amplification sights. Grenades and tear gas grenades are always available.

The New York City Police Department pioneered the techniques of kidnap siege and negotiation. This was a logical development, for so far as the police are concerned there are many similarities between counter-measures against terror and their long term war against heavily armed criminals. And in that field it has great experience.

As long ago as 1972 they formed a special unit under the command of a flamboyant and devoted officer Lieutenant Frank Bolz, (now Captain) and they named it the Hostage-Negotiating Team. The team consisted of 70 officers, including women, who were all members of the Detective Bureau, specially selected after psychiatric tests for steadiness. It was Commissioner Patrick Murphy, then head of the Police Department who changed police thinking on how to handle hostage situations. He gave his reasons for abandoning the idea of police assaults in such circumstances: "There can be no more use of firepower, considering the carrying strength of the average bullet. It can travel further than the limits of where the problem exists and is a serious danger in the crowded urban conditions under which we live."

The commissioner's aim was to dispel the idea of New York cops as trigger-happy officers always ready to attack, and to seek other ways of dealing with the increasingly widespread tendency to seize hostages, both by terrorists and by armed robbers surprised by the arrival of police. About the same time a New York Police Inspector, named Simon Eisdorfer, was considering the lessons of the Munich affair. Conscious that great harm had been done by the over and hasty reaction of the West German police he began working on the problem of how to cope with similar incidents in the United States. After handling his first case in August 1972 when a 19-year-old gunman seized a woman clerk he recognized how clumsily the police had gone into action. During a failed getaway attempt the young man was shot dead. Eisdorfer said later: "We did everything wrong."

It was at this stage that after consulting with the Commissioner he began to make a study of earlier hostage affairs including the one upon which the film "Dog Day Afternoon" was based. In the course of his research the Inspector was in touch with Harvey Schlossberg, a police detective who also held a master's degree in psychology. This was the officer who laid down the first guidelines for negotiating with hostage takers, and who first trained Frank Bolz.

Using Eisdorfer's tactical suggestions and Schlosberg's psychological guidelines the Department started a six-month training course for police captains and above in how to handle hostage situations. Before the first course ended they were confronted by just such an event. Four members of a militant sect of Moslems barricaded themselves inside a sports store in Brooklyn with 13 hostages.

The officers, still under training and developing their techniques, had to learn in action. It was Bolz's first case. Although there was a great deal of anxiety about the many decisions that had to be taken on the spot during the three-day siege, it ended well. The gunmen surrendered and none of their hostages were harmed. The policy of talking and waiting had proved itself a success.

Frank Bolz, then a young looking 46 year old with long experience, had shown the qualities of mind necessary for this type of operation. He is a burly figure of Irish and German extraction with a voice like William Bendix, who has the natural policeman's gift of talking and persuading people to talk.

Between 1974 and 1977 he personally handled 80 talk out cases and not a drop of blood was spilled. Still enthusiastic, he continued to run the negotiating team until 1981. He wears a dark blue baseball cap with the insignia of the Team upon it and has a passion for gadgetry. Even though negotiators do not make arrests, he has handcuffs strung to his waist, and although the negotiating aim is not to open fire he wears a revolver, as all New York cops must. In addition he carries a bleeper, a pencil flashlight, lock picks and a small dental mirror on a stick so that he can see round corners.

"What we try to do is to change their thought patterns," says Bolz speaking about hostage takers. "If they say we want the release of a prisoner, we change the subject, and ask if they need something to eat. We try to bore them to death." Like many other people he disapproved of the action of a colleague in Washington who, faced with the demand from the Hanafi Moslems for the release of their leader without bail, agreed to it. He believes negotiation is fine, but compromises must not be made with the principles of criminal justice.

The New York guidelines for dealing with hostage takers are divided into three phases: Phase 1, The Emergency Service, a heavily armed police unit equipped with riot guns and sniper's rifles is brought to the scene to contain the incident. Voice contact is established between the police negotiator and hostage taker. Meanwhile detectives research records to discover the psychological background of the terrorist. Crowd control is supervised by a police field commander.

Phase 2: If necessary, an escape vehicle is provided for the hostage-taker and police pursuit vehicles are brought up. Police clear the route to airport.

Phase 3: Similar arrangements to those made in Phase 1 come into operation. Containment is organized at the new scene and negotiation is continued.

In all these phases everything depends upon the skill and

timing of the negotiator. For he alone, even though he may consult with psychiatrists and other informants, must decide when the hostage-taker is ready to give in. It is a golden rule not to confront the terrorist or criminal with wives or close friends and relations, for this only heightens emotional tension. The records show that these tactics have worked on numerous occasions and for this reason the New York Hostage-Negotiating Team was widely consulted by police forces both with the U.S. and abroad.

By the seventies Western governments were still literally putting their money on hostage negotiation as a panacea for this kind of terrorism. But the scene changed drastically in 1977 after the incidents involving the South Moluccan terrorists, and then after Entebbe.

Once again it was the Israelis who made the running. For although when the Air France airliner was first hijacked in Athens they began a process of negotiation, they were really more intent on working out the feasibility of a long-distance assault. To the outside world it appeared that because of the large number of hostages and the remoteness of the place to which they had been taken negotiation was the only possibility. But in fact while negotiations continued, the task force to release the hostages by force was already on its way. Indeed, Idi Amin, then President of Uganda, was at the time convinced that Palestinian prisoners whose release had been demanded by the international terrorists were in the aircraft which actually contained Israeli troops. Negotiation had been demoted as a tactic. It had become a ruse used by the Israeli government to gain time to prepare a counter assault on the terrorists. Negotiation was simply an initial tactic in the assault strategy.

From Entebbe onwards it was the governments under attack which took the initiative and used dirty tricks to a good end. The era of the professional assault teams ready to strike back over great distances had begun and their existence provided governments with new flexibility in the terrorist wars.

This development made negotiation less fashionable internationally, and led to other notable victories. It was also heartening proof that Western countries under provocation could develop their own techniques to deal with the changing patterns of hostage-taking.

Less spectacular though equally important tactics were already making their mark upon aircraft hijacking, which may be viewed as one branch of hostage-taking activities. Hijacking can be used either in order to employ the seized aircraft as a bargaining counter, or to use it as an escape route for a failed, or even for a successful, piece of hostage-taking.

At first it was all too easy for terrorists to get on board aircraft with weapons and explosives. The key date in the reawakening of Western governments to the danger was September 1970, the date of the multi-hijacking of aircraft to Dawson's Field in Jordan, an event which demonstrated that no Western country's aircraft were free from the threat of attack.

It was after that event that President Nixon appointed a retired Lieutenant General, Benjamin O. Davis, as Director of Aviation Security. His father had been the first black cadet at West Point and became the first to attain the rank of Major General. The son went even further in military advancement. His task was to coordinate anti-hijack measures throughout the nation at airports handling 150 million passengers a year. At that time there were 15,000 domestic flights a day.

At first the President had called for the installation of sky marshals on U.S. aircraft and the Treasury Department provided a temporary group 500 strong. Eventually they recruited, in cooperation with the Bureau of Customs, some 1,500 agents, known as Customs Security Officers, to ride, as it were, shotgun, on the nation's airliners. Airline carriers were far from happy with this development, not least because they feared the effect on flight bookings of news of high-altitude shoot-outs aboard their airliners. In addition there was the embarrassing incident of the hijacking of an aircraft which was under the protection of a sky marshal and of a FBI agent. The carriers asked for the sky marshals to be disbanded.

From the start General Davis had been less than enthusiatic about armed guards on flights for he believed that they were useful only as a deterrent to terrorists. For by and large aircraft and their passengers, once off the ground, were too vulnerable for real in-flight resistance. To his way of thinking the only effective tactic was to make sure that terrorists were prevented from getting aboard aircraft and the way to do this was to institute 100 percent searches at every boarding gate. But even when special equipment—magnetometer arches and magnetic and electronic hand searchers—became available everything still depended on the men handling them and of the willingness of passengers and airport authorities to cooperate.

It was in 1973 that the search of all passangers became mandatory and in the next two years there were only three hijack attempts in planes flying from U.S. airports. At the 531 airports in the U.S. only 300 people refused to be searched and were turned away during 1973. Over 3,000 were arrested and the authorities seized 2,000 guns, 3,5000 lbs. of high explosives and vast quantities of knives and other offensive weapons.

Within ten months in 1975, 165 million passengers were screened, as were 125 million non-passengers, at airports but the number of handguns confiscated had fallen to 1,600. General Davis's tactics had succeeded, for the number of hijacks dwindled again. Of course, this success was won at the price of some sacrifice of human dignity, for no one likes being searched and forced to wait in line.

In the single year 1974 the searchers confiscated 2,400 firearms and 25 potential hijackings were prevented. The Western European nations quickly followed the American lead. This process of "target hardening" by physical security measures certainly made the task of the terrorist much more difficult, though at a cost which was counted not only in terms of a sacrifice of personal freedom and the humiliation of body searches. Security is an expensive business. For example, the international airport at Schipol (Amsterdam) in the Netherlands reported that it employed 500 security people and the cost of security measures was $10 million a year. Inevitably when hijackings became less common the authorities had to be on their guard against complacency and slackness in the security procedures.

The Israelis, whose national airline El Al was an obvious target for both Palestinian and internatioal terrorists, had taken even sterner measures. They not only put armed sky marshals nicknamed "the 007 squad" on every flight, but also divided the flight deck from the passenger cabin with bullet-proof locked doors and made the cargo holds bomb-proof.

Few airlines were ready to take such stringent precautions. Nor was there any eager response to a hard line plan of action to defeat the hijackers put forward in 1976 in a memorandum from Mordecai Ben-Ari, Executive Chairman of El Al to IATA, the International Air Transport Association. It proposed the establishment of a Central Security Committee of airline presidents to work out unified defense measures. He also advocated creation of an airline security intelligence center at IATA Headquarters to collect and disseminate information and data on terrorist groups in order to make possible preventive action by governments.

An IATA security enforcement authority was suggested to supervise arrangements and security measures by airlines and to give a security rating for each airport and airline. The Israelis also wanted airline presidents to lobby their respective governments and give active mutual aid to other airlines. As usual when such firm actions were suggested some did, and some didn't. Nonetheless defensive measures taken—careful passenger and baggage searching, either physical or by means of X-ray devices, magnetometers and closed circuit TV screening—have certainly helped to reduce the number of hijackings.

Analyzing hijacks attempted between the successful storming by the SAS of the Iranian Embassy in London in April 1980 up to the end of May 1981, the London *Economist* drew this conclusion:

> Since the splurge of hijackings in 1969–70, tougher government action in resisting hijackers' demands has led to a steady fall in the number of hijacks . . . In the past year, there have been only two direct surrenders to hijackers; by the governments of Pakistan and Honduras. Where troops have decided to take on the terrorists by force, they have been pretty successful.

In the eight hijack attempts logged for this period the hostages were released unharmed in almost every case. It is significant that in most of these cases the seizing of aircraft took place in Third World countries—Turkey, Colombia, Afghanistan, Honduras and Thailand. Firmness is beginning to pay off in terms of airline security against terrorism.

But when America and the European countries first began tightening their defenses against the hijackers, terrorism was stll booming. It became necessary for governments to set up infrastructure to combat it in all its manifestations.

The Munich affair prompted the U.S. government to establish the State Department's Office for Combatting Terrorism in September 1972. Its Director, Ambassador Anthony C.E. Quainton, firmly declared its policy, "We make no concessions to terrorists' blackmail.'' Working from the principle that to give in to such blackmail could only encourage further acts of terror, the government decided not to pay any ransom, release prisoners, or make political concessions to obtain the release of captive government servants.

In the early 1970s President Nixon took this stance when two U.S. diplomats were seized by Black September terrorists who stormed the Saudi Arabian embassy in Khartoum. The two men were murdered. Ambassador Quainton has set down the principles of U.S. government strategy thus: ''We condemn all terrorist acts as criminal. We make no concessions to terrorist blackmail. We will not pay or negotiate a ransom. We will not release prisoners. We look to host governments to exercise their responsibilities under international law when Americans are abducted abroad, but we do not offer advice on how to respond to specific terrorist demands. In the case of private Americans who are abducted, we assist their families and employers, short of negotiating terrorist demands. We do not counsel them on how or whether to meet these demands.'' He added that although the primary concern must be the lives of those taken hostage tactics must be tailored to the situation.

The strategy to cope with terrorism was based on the idea that prevention was more satisfactory than cure, and therefore good intelligence must be built up on terrorist activities. As we have seen, legislation to ensure the accountability of the intelligence services both domestic and foreign complicated this task. For the essence of acquiring precise information about terrorist plans is to penetrate their organization by means of covert operations.

An easier task was to provide sound protective measures for obvious targets. We have seen how such precautions succeeded in thwarting hijackers. The government spent $100 million on improving the physical security of its embassies and other properties abroad. Government staff were given instruction in security measures and offered members advice about how to reduce risks of abduction, and help was also given to private business to improve their precautionary measures. But despite all these efforts, terrorists still succeeded in seizing people, aircraft and buildings.

It became necessary to improve command and control structures for dealing with emergencies, and in 1977 the National Security Council carried out a review of the government's anti-terrorist program. The Office for Combatting Terrorism was then given the task of coordinating response to both domestic and international terrorism with one structure for incident management and another for policy making and contingency planning. It is composed of senior officials from the Departments of State, Defense, Justice, Treasury, Transportation, Energy and the CIA. Lower-ranking representatives of these agencies make up the Working Group to Combat Terrorism, which exhanges intelligence and coordinates programs of the various agencies.

The Office was made responsible to the Special Coordinating Committee of the National Security Council under the Chairmanship of the President's National Security Adviser. Under this system of control works a "lead agency" concept, so that for international incidents the State Department has operational responsibility, while for domestic ones coming under Federal jurisdiction it is the Department of Justice and the FBI which take the lead. Other Federal agencies are drawn in as needed.

The Department of State now has an Operations Center on duty round the clock in instant communication with other Federal agencies and with diplomatic missions around the world. Whenever it is faced by a major event the Office for Combatting Terrorism sets up a task force or working group of the agencies concerned, as well as the regional groups concerned within the Department. This task force handles the American reaction and manages the crisis.

In the case of internal terror incidents responsibility falls upon the Justice Department and the Federal Bureau of Investigation in conjunction with state, and local law enforcement agencies. The FBI headquarters in Washington has set up a terrorist crisis control center with up-to-date communications so that it can be in touch instantly with its offices throughout the country and with the other agencies. The system worked well in one of the few big internal incidents when a militant Serbian nationalist group seized an American Airlines flight and tried to get the release of a comrade held by the authorities in Chicago. The crisis center was in a position to react within minutes of announcement of the hijack.

At a tactical level the FBI have highly trained teams ready for fast deployment. They can also call upon the U.S. Marshal Service. And ultimately the President has the option of calling in the armed forces to aid the civil power. The FBI crisis center is staffed by agents with special knowledge of kidnappings, hijackings and civil disturbances. It has even set up a Behavioral Science Unit which has established a computerized terrorist threat dictionary for analysis by psycholinguistic experts in an attempt to use the words spoken to provide a description of the terrorist and his likely behavior.

The dictionary, compiled over a period of four years, has established 350 categories of threats. It was used to analyze the tapes sent by Patricia Hearst when she was kidnapped and the specialists rightly predicted that she would join her kidnappers.

American authorities have relied heavily upon the FBI's SWAT teams and those of the various police forces. Whether in national or more local incidents, these are the men seen on television and in newspaper pictures at the scene of the action, helmeted, visored, wearing flak jackets and bearing automatic weapons, such as the Ingram M10 or the M21 sniper rifle, to hold down terrorists. They have tear gas and masks to protect themselves from it; they have riot guns and the whole panoply of law enforcement weaponry. They are trained either to hold the situation while negotiation is carried on, or to attack if negotiation breaks down.

SWAT teams exist at all levels of law enforcement from the top FBI ones ready for instant deployment to a critical area, down to local police forces where their services are rarely called upon. Some are trained at the FBI academy, which also offers courses on negotiating, and others at local level. National squads have operated outside the United States, either training security police in Latin American countries or giving the benefit of their advice and training to, for example, the Saudi Arabian National Guard.

One of the busiest teams, though usually with criminals rather than with terrorists, is the tough Los Angeles City Police SWAT team. It is a force less tolerant than the New York Police under the influence of Frank Bolz and Harvey Schlossberg, for it believes in forcing the pace in sieges. It dislikes what it calls hold and stall situations, preferring to employ its own formula of the "Three T System"—time, talk and tear gas. Its men take their time setting up a cordon and posting snipers, and then try to talk to the captors. If that fails, then comes the tear gas—but only if there are no children or old people involved because they are particularly vulnerable to the gas. Then, if that does not work, the sharpshooters, each capable of hitting a coin at 200 yards, open fire, for it is the belief in Los Angeles that if one captor is killed it sharpens the mind of his companions and persuades them to surrender. SWAT officer Dennis Tipps, who travelled the country training other SWAT teams said: "We learned our way in the school of hard knocks. It's no good having a stand-off, you must control the situation. You learn to bargain, but let's face it, you need a hell of a lot of luck."

SWAT, with its action orientation, has been criticized by Professor Stephen Sloan as a result of simulated terror attacks he has conducted with students and police at the University of Oklahoma. He reproaches them for over reliance on sophisticated weaponry as the basic means of "defeating" terrorism. Sloan feels that to become obsessed with tactical assault on terrorists is to forget longer term aims in the strategy of anti-terrorism. There is also the danger of "militarization" of the police. Over-spectacular assaults on militant groups in sieges can serve the cause of terrorists by drawing attention to their aims, and over-reaction produces on occasion a public feeling of hostility to the police who in these circumstances may be seen as the aggressors.

The reaction of American police forces at various levels to the terrorist threat was enthusiastic, indeed in some cases overenthusiastic, in the matter of weapons and formation of tactical units. There are some 20,000 agencies involved at the state and local level, plus another 50 at national level. So it is natural that many different standards should apply, and that rivalry between the various police forces sometimes pushed them into a scramble for control of fashionable new elite strike forces. In this they were encouraged by sales pressure from the manufacturers of security equipment.

The level of training remains uneven. For example, the tactical teams in New York and Los Angeles are outstanding for their high standard of efficiency, even though they have more experience of dealing with armed criminals than with terrorists. It is also clear that training has by no means been standardized.

A survey recently carried out in Oklahoma showed that although police teams were well equipped with grenades, tear gas grenades, automatic weapons, night vision devices and special frequency radios to prevent terrorists monitoring their communications, they lack sufficient training in hostage negotiation and crisis management. Nor did they take part often enough in training exercises.

It is important that units at the local level should be well prepared for the task because they are the first to respond to a crisis within their jurisdiction before more specialized outside help can arrive. Indeed it is the local officer who must assess initially the nature of the incident, and to what extent it must be considered an act of political terrorism. The successful conclusion of anti-terrorist operations must often depend upon the initial judgments and action of those first on the scene. In many cases it would be better for local units to understand their own limitations and simply to act as holding forces.

For handling dangerous and large-scale terrorist operations the U.S. relies upon the tactical teams provided for national use by the FBI. But, although the FBI was involved in the Hanafi siege in Washington, it was the District of Columbia Metropolitan Police which controlled the operation. And it still appears that the question of who controls operations on such occasions has not been resolved.

The FBI began training its agents several years ago, and there are now first-class tactical teams with helicopter and aircraft capacity to rush elite units from Washington and other key areas to the scene of action.

One further organization which might have a role to play in the fight against terrorism is the National Guard. So far as the Federal authorities are concerned, the National Guard functions as a reserve for the armed forces. But it also has the task at the state level of providing support services in times of local emergency. In a serious terrorist incident the unit could provide logistical support to the police and undertake a variety of tasks such as perimeter security, or offer transport and medical facilities.

As European countries step up their defense capability against terrorists it seems quite likely that the open society in America may attract more foreign terrorists. If the epidemic does spread more alarmingly to the United States there is no doubt that the specialized police groups will give a good account of themselves, and that more experience in action will improve their skills and efficiency.

What was lacking in the United States for several crucial years was a special military force, ready to be called upon when military muscle and skill was needed for critical operations. But it was not until 1977 that President Jimmy Carter gave orders for the formation of a special anti-terrorist force to begin training at Fort Bragg under the command of Colonel Charles Beckwith. It was a decision long overdue.

Project Blue Light, as it was called, was surrounded with great secrecy. Indeed when the army was asked for the biography of Colonel Beckwith, the only details forthcoming were of the "name, rank and number" variety which prisoners of war are allowed to give their captors. "Colonel Charles Beckwith, born January 22, 1929. Attended college. Commissioned 1952. Assignment 'classified.' Serial number 258-364046." In fact rather more was known about his military record as an aggressive, successful soldier in Vietnam, and what was publicly available confirmed that he had the right qualifications for building the new force. Charles Mohr of the *New York Times* had come across him in South East Asia, and wrote:

> In October of 1965, the small garrison of a United States Special Forces camp at Plei Me in the South Vietnam highlands was besieged by several thousand North Vietnamese regular infantrymen. A special 250 man rescue force was landed by helicopter into the forests a few miles from the triangular shaped camp. Charles Beckwith, then an army major, led his rescue force through the brush, through the North Vietnamese lines and —at a run—into the front gate of Plei Me. He then characteristically tried to take the offensive. He ordered three counterattacks in the first day, discovering after each sally had been forced back into Plei Me that major units of North Vietnamese regulars had for the first time been committed to the war in South Vietnam.
>
> When a newspaper reporter arrived at Plei Me a few days later on a medical evacuation helicopter and asked a grizzled sergeant how to find Major Beckwith, the sergeant answered: "When you see a real big man yelling, Press on!, that's him . . . " At that time Beckwith was commander of "Delta Force," a tough unit composed of several hundred Indo-Chinese mercenary riflemen recruited and paid for by the Special Forces with CIA funds.
>
> On another occasion in action with this unit he was badly wounded when ground fire raked his helicopter. An army surgeon found him sitting upright on his litter shouting that he needed immediate treatment because he was bleeding to death. "He was right," said the surgeon, "for a few minutes later he would have been dead. Beckwith is one man who saved his own life.

The Blue Light Project got under way in November 1977, a

month after its fully operational German equivalent, the GSG9 squad, had gone into action in Mogadishu, Somalia, to set free a hijacked Lufthansa airliner.

Fort Bragg is now the headquarters of Rapid Deployment Airborne troops and also the command center for army Special Forces. The Special Forces School at the Fort had been set up as direct result of President John F. Kennedy's belief that insurgencies were a new kind of warfare and that they could only be fought successfully by a new type of soldier. A great deal of research into guerilla war and the best ways of countering it was carried out there by officers of the armed forces and by psychiatrists specializing in military affairs. The emphasis of all this training was naturally upon the areas of greatest interest to the United States at that time, namely Vietnam and Latin America. CIA training in covert operations in conjunction with military units was also heavily involved at Fort Bragg.

One of the difficulties facing Colonel Beckwith and his Blue Light project was where to find suitable officers and troopers for the skilled and disciplined new unit. At first he naturally turned to the Green Berets he had known in the Delta units in Vietnam. The army was not short of experienced men who had taken part in small unit raids. But what the new unit needed most was young men with new talents, rather than those of experience, but also with more years behind them. Their task was to learn the tactics and methods of anti-terror operations with their emphasis on rescue rather than on fighting. That involved careful selection techniques devised by the Fort Bragg psychiatrists and special operations experts, for in addition to the qualities just mentioned the recruits, although aged no more than 28, needed to be mature and highly disciplined. There was no place in the unit for motion picture heroes. What the unit was looking for were fairly extrovert men, self-sufficient, cunning and not over-trusting. All volunteers—and only senior NCOs and above were accepted— were put through a number of psychological tests, including the well known 16 PF personality test.

Special Forces recruits according to Fort Bragg specifications had needed 25 basic skills, which included navigation, firearms expertise, explosives and grenades aptitudes, not to mention mission procedures, leadership and knowledge of sensors and first aid. To these the soldiers of the Blue Light formation needed to add instruction in handling the new weapons of counter terrorism, stun grenades, special firearms for use in the enclosed space of an airliner, and the techniques for entering hijacked aircraft, and for disposing of terrorist bombs.

Colonel Beckwith started with physical training and small arms perfection training. This was followed with combined physical and initiative tests. During this training it was possible to weed out the less capable entrants before too much time had been wasted on further instruction.

No official figures are forthcoming either for the size of the present force or for the percentage of volunteers rejected in training. But it is known that the original call was for up to 300 volunteers and by mid 1978 there were not more than 60 or so interim trained troopers at Fort Bragg working as Blue Light. An official statement in 1978 made it clear that a complete new unit would be formed within a year and it would take five years to muster a fully-trained unit. It is likely that the fully trained unit would consist of not more than 150, with a high proportion of officers.

Fort Bragg, spreading over forest, plains, hills and lakes, has seven dropping zones for parachute training, which all anti-terrorist troopers must have. There are field firing ranges, close fire "killing" ranges and aircraft fuselages for hijack release practice. Helicopter work is a feature of the place for training on helicopter assault tactics and so is secrecy. Colonel Beckwith chose for his training center and headquarters the stockade, or military prison, which had recently been completed in a secluded part of the base at a cost of $1.5 million.

The actual unit is now referred to simply as Delta group, which is the only one capable of emulating other Western anti-terror forces, though the Defense Department once claimed that there were 18 such units comprising 6,702 men. The fact is that this total includes two Ranger light infantry regiments and other special forces formations who, though equipped only with the usual light forces weapons (the basic M16 automatic rifle, for example), have been given some training in the protection of nuclear and other facilities against terrorist assaults, and the basic principles of how to combat guerillas. They are not really specialized troops.

The Delta unit deploys special weapons, such as the Beretta modified by the Israelis to fire low powered .22 slugs, for use against terrorists in hijacked aircraft. They have M21 sniper rifles equipped with Laco Laser target acquisition devices, and they also use Heckler and Koch MP 5s. Stun-grenades are available for anti-hijack raids together with more homely equipment like aluminium ladders for reaching aircraft doors. The unit also has electronic surveillance devices. All these weapons and special gadgets are highly useful, but the main attribute of an anti-terror team, usually not more than five men to a storming party, is its training and frequent practice at carrying out simulated operations.

Before the five years, which was estimated to be necessary for welding together the Delta anti-terrorist units, had run its course, they were called upon to take part in a long range, hazardous mission. In April 1980 Colonel Beckwith led 90 of his men on "Operation Eagle's Claw," planning to rescue the 53 American hostages held in the U.S. Embassy in Teheran that had been seized by the mob and was under the control of Iranian terrorists.

The seizure of the American Embassy was in fact a new form of terrorism. The militants who took over the compound in an act which showed their contempt for all international practice was at least partially under the control of the revolutionary government of Iran. It was an act of official state terrorism carried out upon the national territory of the government responsible for it. It had to be recognized from the start that any large scale operation to free the hostages might be regarded as an act of war with far-reaching consequences.

The relieving force needed to be small. It had to operate with helicopters from a carrier in the Indian Ocean fleet at extreme range, and relied upon the support of military aircraft flying long distances over largely hostile air space.

President Carter was well aware of the risks when he gave orders for the operation. They had been spelled out for him by Cyrus Vance, then Secretary of State, who warned that the operation would be "immensely complicated and difficult." He argued that even if the rescue teams reached the U.S. Embassy in Teheran some of the hostages would be killed during the rescue, and in any case once the diplomatic hostages had been released, the Iranians could easily replace them with other American expatriots.

By April 1980 the U.S. had in the Indian Ocean the largest fleet it had ever maintained in that part of the world. There were two aircraft carriers, 12 warships and an amphibious task force of

1,800 Marines. On April 24 six C130s took off from Egyptian airfields on their circuitous route to the Iranian desert rendezvous near Tabas, with 90 men of the Delta force under the command of Colonel Beckwith. The following day eight Sea Stallion helicopters RH 53 Ds flew off from the USS *Nimitz* to meet them at the base designated as Desert 1.

"Operation Eagle's Claw" had begun. The plan of action was a multi-stage one. After the first rendezvous between the helicopters and the fixed-wing force, the helicopters were to ferry the task force to another base, from which they were to move into and seize the Teheran Embassy compound and hold it while another team freed Bruce Laingen and his foreign service colleague from detention in the Iranian Foreign Ministry. Then the helicopters were to fly in, ferry them back out to the C 130s for the flight back to freedom.

But in warlike raids things rarely work out as crisply as planned. The story of the failure of the mission is now well known. The helicopters ran into trouble with mechancal defects and sandstorms. The raiders, once on the ground, were spotted by a busload of Iranians and a bunch of smugglers, who had to be grabbed and held, and tragedy came with the collision during refueling between a Sea Stallion and a C 130 which cost the lives of eight servicemen. President Carter aborted the mission.

On the ground Colonel Charles Beckwith, the officer who had devoted so much energy for so long in training his Delta squad, was surrounded by burning wreckage and soldiers scrambling to get airborne before first light. "My God, I'm going to fail," was the thought running through his mind as he recalled the event later at a Pentagon briefing in Washington. "I sat down and cried," and the tears were of frustration and rage.

His doubts had begun early in the operation when the helicopters were delayed and when only five of the eight expected arrived at the rendezvous. He said that the decision to call off the operation and evacuate was given at 2:10 a.m. and the collision between a Sea Stallion and a C 130 took place 42 minutes later. The Colonel did not know what had caused it but the heat from the ball of fire was so intense that helicopter pilots alongside had to leave their aircraft. Unfortunately the blaze was not enough to destroy other helicopters that had to be abandoned in the hasty departure, still containing detailed and annotated operational plans which fell into the hands of the Iranians who exploited them for their own propaganda.

Americans and their friends in Europe were shocked and horrified by the failure of a brave rescue attempt, but there was little desire to condemn an attempt which reasonable people believed was entirely justified. In these circumstances criticism centered on the planning and execution of the mission, and a slightly hysterical search for scapegoats began.

It was not until several months after the abortive raid that the Joint Chiefs of Staff received a definitive evaluation from a committee of six senior officers headed by Admiral James L. Holloway, retired Chief of Naval Operations. Only parts of the report were made public, but it found no evidence of culpable neglect or incompetence. The report denied allegations which had been flying about that the helicopters were not properly maintained, but considered that three more helicopters ought to have been available. It also thought that more attention should have been paid to prepare for bad weather conditions. More interesting was their conclusion that one important reason for the failure was that preparation for it had been hampered by excessive secrecy. Because of this factor a number of military officers had not even been told the aim of the mission they were preparing for. It is understandable that the President, for political and diplomatic reasons should have kept preparations under wraps, but there was evidence that security had gone too far, interfering with training for the attack. For example, the commanders had not been able to provide their officers and troopers with a mock up of the desert rendezvous even for the dress rehearsal of the operation.

Fascinating though the tactical criticisms may be, what is even more important in a survey of how the military option must be exercized in organizing the counter assault on terrorism were the detailed remarks about the organization of anti-terror operations in the U.S. armed forces. The Chiefs of Staff were told that the crucial error was in planning which was *ad hoc* and did not have the advantage of using an existing command. This seems to show that the work done at Fort Bragg by Colonel Beckwith, in selecting and training his Delta force, had been wasted because it was purely low-level tactical preparation. In the rush to create an anti-terror force insufficient attention had been paid to the mechanism of command and the role of higher command when it went into action.

Part of the trouble was lack of inter-service cooperation. On the ground in Iran were Delta special forces, Marines and Army soldiers, as well as Air Force personnel, and the Navy in the Indian Ocean. An army officer, Major General James Vaught, was in overall command, Colonel James Kyle of the Air Force had responsibility for fixed-wing aircraft, and was on site commander in the desert, while Colonel Charles Pitman of the Marines also had command responsibility and Colonel Beckwith controlled the Delta squad.

Officers on the spot were not clearly identified, and there was no easily identifiable Command Post for the Commander. In these circumstances confusion was inevitable, more so as the report revealed that training for the raid had not been properly coordinated between the different units. It was the kind of military action which only stood a chance of success if the training had been thorough enough to develop speed and precision in execution. Individual training was fine but it had not been coordinated despite the several months of preparation.

The conclusion drawn from this detailed examination of "Operation Eagle's Claw" was that a special new counter-terror unit had to be set up, and that its personnel should be drawn from all the armed services. It was reported in Washington that the then Defense Secretary Harold Brown had approved the formation of a joint task force for anti-terror work with the aim of bringing such a force under a single unified command to be reviewed by an advisory panel consisting of seven members. But since then little has been heard of further plans for this formation, either because of secrecy, or because of the elections and the emergence of a new President beset by other problems. Yet creation of the unit outlined is of great importance if the country is to be ready to face new emergencies in the field of terrorist warfare.

The task of creating such an ambitious force is complicated by a number of considerations. Traditional inter-service rivalries loom large. The Marines were involved with the original Delta unit and would very much like to develop their own anti-terrorist capability, though military observers do not think that they will finally be allowed to have it. They may have to be content with their traditional role guarding embassies abroad. Already improved training and tactics for this defensive duty are being seen to, which is most important. For, if the Marine guard at the Teheran compound had received orders to defend it, opening fire on the mob if necessary, the embassy might never have fallen into the hands of the hostage-takers.

Within the Navy, the SEALS have important protection tasks and they too want to develop techniques for seaborne, deep penetration, hostage rescue attempts. They will probably be allowed to specialize in swift and relatively uncomplicated operations against hostage-takers in Third World countries with a coastline.

The Coast Guard already have an agreement with the FBI, where they would be involved in any maritime coastal incident. They have conducted various exercises in the protection of offshore oil facilities, though with their limited manpower they are unlikely to assume a greater share of the anti-terror task.

The Air Force too, apart from its essential support job for providing air transport for the other services, is sensitive to terrorist threats. One of their tasks is to protect vital installations, both airfields and nuclear centers, and they would like to use this as a way of promoting their Special Operations which again were involved with Delta.

The trouble is that for their own reasons all these specialized units are displaying too much zeal in their attempts to secure for themselves a position in the elite anti-terrorist units, a fashionable field of enterprise with a great deal of glamor attached. The further lure is that, as President Reagan puts a high premium on meeting such threats, it is certain that he will channel more Department of Defense money into the specialized units. Glamor and money are irresistable to the armed services which always have to keep one eye on the enemy and the other on the budget.

At the present moment it is still not clear what will be the fate of the Delta unit. Colonel Charles Beckwith has retired, and a struggle is already taking place within the Special Forces and the Rangers over who will inherit the anti-terror role. To some extent it is a clash of interest between Fort Bragg, where Delta was formed, and the War College of the Americas in Panama. This brings us back to definitions, for the Panama school is oriented towards the preparation of Black and Green Beret units of Special Forces for intervention in guerilla wars, particularly in Latin America, and sees terrorist activity in those terms; Fort Bragg, which was originally in the anti-guerilla line of business in Vietnam, now considers it can offer special expertise for combatting strictly terrorists of the Baader-Meinhof and PFLP variety. So do the Rangers, the light infantry commando units which have also been training in the anti-terror field.

Much ink will be spilled and harsh words exchanged between senior officers and the Defense Department before these inter-service clashes of opinion are genially resolved. But it seems increasingly likely that as the lessons of the Teheran raid sink in the counter-insurgency mission of the military will be redesigned to include a counter-terrorism mission geared to the protection of diplomats and embassies in foreign countries.

4.

Israel: An Eye for an Eye

It is laid down in the Talmud, the holy book of Jewish law, that "If someone comes to kill you, rise and kill him first." And that, under the impact of centuries of oppression and the attempt to wipe out the Jewish race in the Holocaust, has become the watchword of the Sayaret Matkal, the razor-sharp cutting edge of Israel's counter-terrorist forces.

Sayaret Matkal is an organization about which the Israelis are so secretive they do not even mention it by name. As was Yahweh, the ineffable name for God, it is known to all but uttered by none. It is spoken of only as Ha Yehida, "The Unit," and its men as Ha Hevreh, "The Guys," which all seems a bit unnecessary because everybody, especially its Arab enemies, knows it is the Sayaret Matkal, the General Staff Reconnaissance Unit.

Almost every branch of the Israeli army has its own Reconnaissance Unit of specially trained men. The Sayaret Zanhanim is the Paratroop reconnaissance team and the Sayaret Golani a similar team belonging to the Golani Infantry Brigade who are among the toughest infantrymen in the world. But it is the Sayaret Matkal which raids Beirut to kill Palestinian leaders and flies to Entebbe to rescue hijack hostages from the joint clutches of Palestinian and German terrorists and Idi Amin.

The story of specialized anti-terrorist units in Israel starts with the formation of the joint British–Jewish Special Night Squads in the 1930s by Orde Wingate, that eccentric, brilliant guerilla leader who later became famous as commander of the Chindits operating behind the Japanese lines in Burma, only to die in an air crash in 1944 as he prepared a new campaign. He obtained permission from his British superiors to teach the Jews how to protect themselves against marauding Arabs. But Wingate, a Talmudic scholar, believed wholeheartedly in its teaching to kill rather than be killed and he turned his squads into efficient guerillas who were happier striking at the Arabs in their own villages rather than waiting to be attacked. Moshe Dayan was one of the young men he led on these operations. Dayan recalled that when they returned at dawn after a night's fighting and prepared breakfast, "Wingate would sit in a corner, stark naked, reading the Bible and munching raw onions as though they were the most delicious pears."

The British authorities tolerated Wingate's activities for a time—they helped protect the Iraq Petroleum Company's pipeline from Arab sabotage—but he was eventually transferred out of Palestine. However, his aggressive doctrine and tactics imbued the Israelis who fought first the British and then the Arabs for their independence.

They fought with odd lots of weapons scraped together from the cast-offs of armies all over the world, while their opponents fielded regular trained troops equipped with up-to-date weaponry, so it is not surprising that once the War of Independence has ended and the State of Israel had been established, Zahal, the Israeli Defense Force, concentrated on establishing a regular army. Tanks, jets and submarines became more important than guerilla warfare. But the paraphernalia of modern war could not stop the small parties of Arabs who slipped across the border from the Lebanon and Jordan and the Gaza Strip to kill, blow up water pumps and set fire to crops. In 1951 these terrorists caused

137 casualties, mostly children.

In 1952 that figure rose to 147 and in 1953 rose again to 180. Mot of these casualties were caused by infiltrators from the West Bank of the Jordan which had been occupied by King Hussein's forces in 1948. The Israelis' initial reaction to these incidents was to mount reprisal raids by regular units of the army. They were not always successful, the army's morale sagged, and so did that of the civilian population which realized that it could not rely on the army to protect it. It became obvious that a special unit, something on the lines of Wingate's Night Squads, would have to be formed. In August 1953 Mordechai Makless, who was then Chief of Staff, decided to set up "Unit 101" under the command of Ariel Sharon, a battalion commander in the reserves who was studying at Israel's School of Oriental Studies. Sharon, later to become famous as "Arik," the general who crossed the Suez during the Yom Kippur War and brought Egypt to the verge of defeat, toured Israel looking for the men he wanted, aggressive and intelligent fighters who had fought, guerilla style, in the War of Independence. He gathered about forty of them together in what became his private army. They wore whatever they wanted, sported no badges of rank and carried whatever weapons suited them best. And they never, ever saluted. They specialized in night-fighting, infiltration, sudden lethal swoops on the enemy. In this original form however, Unit 101 lasted only a few months. It was almost disbanded after it retaliated to the killing of an Israeli woman and her two children by attacking the Jordanian village of Khibye, blowing up 45 houses and leaving 66 villagers dead. This led to a condemnation of Israel by the UN Security Council and it was felt in Israel that the policy of retaliation was becoming counter productive.

However, Sharon was saved by the appointment of Moshe Dayan as Chief of Staff. Dayan, who had originally opposed the formation of a special unit, but had been won over by Sharon's ability to infuse fighting spirit into his men, sanctioned the merger of Unit 101 with the Paratroop Battalion with Sharon in command. The paratroopers had become rather staid, parade ground soldiers and so there was useful cross fertilization between the two. Sharon's brigands taught the Paras guerilla warfare and the Paras' administration taught Sharon how to run a properly controlled army formation. It was this combined unit which fought most of the anti-terrorist and reprisal battles in the escalation of violence which led up to the outbreak of the Six Day War in 1967. The officers believed in the "follow me" school of fighting. As a result many died. Sharon was wounded and so were most of his colleagues. But among the survivors were three men who were to become generals, Motta Gur, Yitzhak Hoff and Rafael Eytan.

The immediate reaction to the victory of 1967 was that Israel would be safe for ever, but it soon became apparent that the Arab raiders were operating even more fiercely than before. What had happened was that with the Arab armies shattered and the Arab world in a state of shock, the task of carrying on the fight against Israel fell to the Palestinians. They began to operate in small parties on the West Bank of the Jordan and the Gaza Strip, both now occupied by the Israelis. On the West Bank they would cross the Jordan and hole up in the caves and gullies in the hills leading up from the river, and in Gaza they would emerge from the teeming alleys of the refugee camp to throw grenades, murder and lay mines. The terrorists did not achieve much because they mostly confined their activities to Gaza and did not operate in Israel. But the exploits of men like Mohammed Mahmoud El-Aswad, the "Che Guevara of Gaza," provided a much needed fillip to Palestinian morale. The task of clearing up Gaza fell to Arik Sharon and he did it with his customary panache. He followed the technique used by the British during the Mandate of blowing up the houses of people who helped the terrorists. He drove bulldozers through the refugee camps, opening up broad avenues so that his quick reaction forces could seal off areas with mathematical precision. The Arabs of Gaza talk of this period with awe. Sharon will never be forgotten in that ancient city. He killed off the terrorists one by one and broke up the cells. By the beginning of 1973 he had Gaza under control.

The West Bank operations were different and more difficult because the terrorists could slip across the Jordan and either hide in the caves or in safe houses in the Arab villages, complete their missions, and return to Jordan or travel north to cross the Lebanese border. At first the Israeli army reacted in the flamboyant style which had spread throughout the army from the cross-fertilization of Unit 101 and the Paratroopers. Senior officers who had survived the war led small parties of troops in assaults on terrorists holed up in caves and a number of invaluable leaders, among them a full colonel and two lieutenant colonels, were killed. It became so costly that new tactics were devised. The Jordan was sealed off by a fence and minefields, and the paths along it carefully raked so that early morning patrols could tell if marauders had managed to slip through during the night. Behind the patrols were artillery batteries and aircraft ready to rake the hillsides if terrorists were discovered. The troops involved were mainly Druse Border Guards. Along the Lebanese border the Israelis took more aggressive action sending armored patrols over the border to prevent the guerillas even approaching the wire.

The naval commandos whose frogmen had raided Alexandria and Port Said during the Six Day War were already carrying on their own private fight with the terrorists based along the Lebanese coast. The Golani Infantry Brigade and the Paras had also built up their own elite sections with their Reconnaissance Units. But it was decided that while they were first-class fighters within their regiments, another completely different style of unit, based more on the traditions of Unit 101, was needed. And so the Sayaret Matkal came into being.

The Sayaret Matkal is not part of the ordinary army and answers only to the Chief of Intelligence although, unlike Unit 101, its members normally operate in uniform. It is based on the edge of an airfield in the center of Israel and its normal strength is around 200, although it can draw on experts from other specialized units for specific tasks. It can also call on reservists if it needs older men with unique qualifications. Unlike most comparable special units, the Sayaret Matkal does not rely on trained volunteers but draws raw recruits from the extraordinary establishment called the Kelet, the recruit depot just outside Tel Aviv, to which all young men report when they are called up for military service. It is like a great employment exchange where the representatives of the various commands and regiments try to seize the cream of each intake to mold in their own particular image. The Paras have a sign on their hut in the depot which reads: "The Brave to the Paratroops." The Golanis dispute this. Certainly for years the Air Force and the Naval Commandos took the best of the recruits. Now it is Sayaret Matkal which laps up the cream. The procedure is for an officer, a team leader, to go to the Kelet and select 15 to 20 volunteers to form a team. There is great competition to get into the unit and generals tend to try to put their sons into it—two of Dayan's young relatives are senior members. After they have been chosen and the task of the unit explained to them they start their training. It follows the arduous pattern of elite force training with exhausting marches across the desert and the mountains. But there is this difference: the Sayaret Matkal does much of its training in enemy territory and the recruits learn very quickly when they know that real enemies with real bullets may be behind the next sand dune. Fort Bragg and Bradbury Lines may be tough, but this is actuality.

Apart from being superbly fit and able to navigate and live in the desert they become marksmen in the weapons they are most likely to encounter. They use the Uzzi, the Israeli invented machine pistol which has been adopted by most of the world's security services. They also use the Kalashnikov, the Russian assault rifle which the Israelis have captured in great numbers from the Arabs. They are trained on the Galil, another Israeli-made automatic weapon which can do anything from launch grenades to open a bottle of orange juice but which tends to be cumbersome for special operations. Pistol shooting ranks high in the curriculum and here the Israelis use an unusual weapon, the .22 Beretta pistol. They train with this pistol because some of them move on to become members of the hit teams which eliminate Israel's enemies abroad and the "007 Squad" who fly with El Al. The technique when used by the hit men is for them to get as close as possible to their victim and them pump a full magazine into him at the shortest possible range.

The recruits are trained in close combat fighting with particular emphasis on the knife. Explosives also receive much attention with training in how to use plastic explosive to blow in doors, and to make booby-traps and car bombs. Most of the recruits speak Arabic and English as well as Hebrew and other languages are taught. But more often than not it is possible to pick men for specific jobs who are already fluent in the necessary language because immigrants to Israel come from so many different countries. Parachuting, both static line and free-fall, communications, cross-country driving in wheeled and tracked vehicles, camouflage—they acquire all the skills which help to make an anti-terrorist fighting man. Special attention is paid to helicopter-borne missions with the use of abseil ropes and joint operations with the naval commandos who probe the Lebanese coast virtually every night.

The emphasis in all training is on secrecy and speed. They are taught not to fire until it becomes necessary but then to attack with power and speed, winning the fight while the enemy is still off balance.

By the time the team has finished training it will have shrunk from 20 to under ten. It will then be phased into operations for, it must be remembered, Sayaret Matkal is on active service the whole time. The newly-qualified team starts its work with simple reconnaissance missions into neighboring Arab countries—extensions of their training exercises. But then, as it gains confidence and experience, it is given more difficult tasks, until, if it proves itself, it may be given a "spectacular."

Teams may be augmented for a particular job, or, if it is of a special nature, only one or two men will be chosen. The best men are posted away to take an officer's course from which they will emerge to go to the Kelet to pick their own teams and start the process again. However, service in the Sayaret Matkal is not necessarily the way to the top. A degree of jealousy surrounds all special units and officers who have served in them have a question mark put against their names by more orthodox soldiers.

The Sayaret Matkal does not believe in negotiation and will not use the extended "talk-out" techniques favored by other countries. The Israelis believe that these rarely achieve success and that the danger to the hostages and the counter-terrorist forces grows greater the longer a siege continues, with the gunmen becoming more alert and trigger-happy as their deadline approaches. They prefer to attack as soon as they are in a position to do so and will use negotiations only as a blind under which to prepare their assault. They would rather attack with speed and decision and overwhelm the opposition. No siege in Israel has lasted more than 24 hours.

The Israelis argue the case for pre-emptive strikes: it is better to kill their enemies in their own bases and so prevent them mounting their operations, rather than conduct elegant sieges inside Israel. While appreciating the excellence of other forces' pieces of electronic wizardry and the skill of the talk-out experts their aim is to prevent the need for such expertise arising. Such a policy has its attractions, especially for a beleaguered, small nation like Israel under continual attack from the enemies based round its borders. When national survival is at stake all manner of actions become permissible that would not be countenanced in more secure societies.

General Shlome Gazit, the former Director of Military Intelligence, insists on the correctness of the principle of pre-emption. He argues that: "Whoever adopts a defensive, passive strategy against insurgency is almost doomed to failure. You cannot fight and win any war by defensive means only." His doctrine is one of permanent counter-offensive, attacking the leaders, bases and support systems of terrorist groups. He believes in covert paramilitary operations to attack such targets. "Such operations," he says, "are supposed to be designed in such a way as to avoid leaving any marks and evidence as to the attacking force. They will not be formally acknowledged even after the operation has taken place, even if the evidence leaves little doubt as to the identity and origins of its performers."

But when does counter-terrorism itself cross the border into terrorism? When Mossad sent a Hit Team to Lillehammer in Norway in 1973 to kill Ali Hassan Salameh, the organizer of the Munich massacre, they got the wrong man and shot down an innocent Moroccan waiter in front of his pregnant Norwegian wife. The international embarrassment was so great that under cover of the Yom Kippur War the Hit Teams were recalled and they have not operated in Europe since. However, Salameh who, under the codename of Abu Hassan was Fatah's Head of Special Operations, was one man the Israelis would not allow to live. They blew him up with a radio-controlled car bomb in Beirut in January 1979, turning his car into "a pile of melting metal." With him died four bodyguards and five innocent people who happened to be passing by. One of them was Susan Wareham, a British woman, secretary for a construction company. One can have few regrets for Salameh. But what about Susan Wareham and the other innocent dead? Did they deserve to die because the Israelis were determined to kill the men responsible for Munich? Was Salameh's crime any greater than that of the men who set off the bomb? Officially, in accordance with the Gazit doctrine, the Israelis have never admitted responsibility. Unofficially, they say: "We are desperately sorry, we had no intention of killing them. They were in the wrong place at the wrong time . . . " And the Israeli satisfaction at finally getting Salameh outweighs their regret at the deaths of the people who died with him.

The Sayaret Matkal was described to the authors as being rather like a thoroughbred racehorse stable full of nervy, high-strung performers, who respond brilliantly to leadership but react strongly against poor leadership. They have a fierce form of self-criticism in which the absolute fundamental is the truth. The one crime which is never forgiven any man or officer is to lie. The result is that everyone is then encouraged to speak his mind which, of course, they do and there tends to be more argument over an operation than there is in the other elite counter-terrorist units.

The major difference between the unit and similar anti-terrorist formations is that Israel lives in a state of war and believes in the policy of retaliation. It operates in a different political dimension. One of the first of the major operations carried out by the Sayaret Matkal was mounted in October 1968 in an attempt to convince the Egyptians to stop the shelling of Israeli positions on the Suez by proving to them that Egypt was wide open to attack. The unit flew into Egypt in helicopters, blew up two important bridges across the Nile and destroyed the new power station at Naj Hammadi, deep inside Egypt and hundreds of miles behind the artillery batteries on the Suez. The next raid was even more spectacular and it marked a significant development in the unit's role.

The result of such retaliatory operations was that the Israelis had been so successful in curbing terrorism inside Israel that the Palestinians had been forced to turn to international terrorism, striking at the Israelis abroad, not only to harm the Israelis but also to involve the rest of the world in their struggle.

On July 22, 1968 the Palestinians carried out the first of their hijacks, taking over an El Al airliner flying from Rome to Tel Aviv. On December 26, 1968 two men attacked another El Al plane at Athens airport with automatic fire and grenades. It was proved that both incidents originated in Beirut. Two days after the Athens attack the Israelis retaliated in an attempt to force the Lebanese to prevent the terrorists from mounting their attacks from Lebanon. A 40-strong force of "The Guys" landed on the main runway at Beirut International Airport at 9:30 p.m. In their book *The Israeli Army*, Edward Luttwak and Dan Horowitz describe the scene:

> Panic broke out in the crowded passenger lounges. Arabic-speaking Israeli soldiers controlled the crowds, giving instructions via hand-held loud speakers. At the same time another group of commandos [because of Israeli military censorship they were

unable to name the Sayaret Matkal] escorted passengers who had already boarded Arab-owned aircraft back to the passenger lounge. Thirteen Arab aircraft, including nine jetliners, were blown up after being thoroughly searched to ensure that no passengers were left on board. Although there were vast secondary explosions from their fuel tanks when the TNT charges were set off, no other aircraft parked on the tarmac was damaged and there were no casualties. Even when some Lebanese policemen opened fire, the Israelis managed to intimidate them by firing in the air and refrained from shooting back.

The airport is only two and a half miles from Beirut and motorized units of the Lebanese army were sent to the scene of the raid almost at once. The Lebanese column was intercepted by another squad of commandos which had set up a road block on the way to the airport. Again, there was no shooting and no casualties. The Israelis released some smoke canisters and this was enough to stop the Lebanese from advancing any further. At 10:30 p.m., one hour after they had landed, the commandos returned to Israel.

The raid was led by Brigadier General Rafael "Raful" Eytan who had been one of Sharon's combined Unit 101-Paratrooper squad and he has a bullet-furrow in his scalp to remind him of those days. Throughout the raid he sat in the airport lounge drinking Arabic coffee at the bar. When the time came for him to leave he paid for the coffee with an Israeli note and for some time afterwards that note was kept behind the bar. Eytan went on to command the Northern Front during the Yom Kippur War, withstanding the full power of the Syrian attack and then mounting the counterattack which took the Israeli army as close as they dare go politically towards Damascus. He later became Chief of Staff of the army.

The raid was an undoubted tactical success and did demonstrate that the Jews were no longer the people who had marched, unprotesting, into the gas chambers. They had given notice to the world that they would strike back ferociously if they were attacked. But the long-term results were less satisfactory. The Lebanese were of course powerless to prevent the terrorists operating from Lebanon. President de Gaulle had used the raid as an excuse to cut off all arms' shipments to Israel at a time when the Defense Forces relied heavily on French equipment. The United States was displeased. The Palestinians acquired more publicity for their cause. And Middle East Airlines was able to buy a whole new fleet of jetliners with the insurance money.

The unit continued to raid inside Egypt during the War of Attrition and its prestige grew as news of its exploits spread through the highly-efficient Israeli grapevine—along with the jealousy of other units. The next spectacular in which the unit was involved was their assault in May 1972 on a hijacked Sabena airliner at Lod Airport in the heart of Israel. The aircraft, a Boeing 707, flight 517 from Brussels to Tel Aviv, was seized by two men and two women belonging to Black September. They boldly ordered the pilot to fly on to Lod where they announced that they would blow to smithereens the plane, its 90 passengers, ten crew and themselves unless the Israeli government released 317 Arab prisoners.

The Israelis played along with the hijackers and even with the Red Cross official who was negotiating between the two sides— he was afterwards to complain bitterly that he had been deceived and compromised—but throughout the negotiations a team of Sayaret Matkal men were practicing on a 707 in a nearby hangar. When they had perfected their assault technique they told the hijackers they would give in to their demands. The men in white overalls who could be seen approaching the aircraft, said the Israelis, where mechanics who were coming out to inflate the tires which had been let down when the aircraft first landed. The mechanics were the assault party. They burst in through the doors. The two male hijackers were shot dead but not before one of the attackers was wounded. A woman passenger was also shot dead while one of the female hijackers and the commander of the assault were wounded.

This as the first time that a hijacked airliner had been success-fully stormed and its lessons were applied five years later when GSG9 performed its similar feat at Mogadishu. The Sabena incident also introduced for the first time the name of Jonathan Netanyahu, the Sayaret Matkal commander who was to die at Entebbe. He was at Lod and was furious that he was not included in the assault party.

After Lod came the massacre at Munich in 1972. Although the world threw up its hands in horror and Palestinian became a dirty word in the West, it was in every sense a victory for the Palestinians. They had shown that they were capable of carrying out a well-planned international operation and of being ready to

die for their cause. They had finally, irrevocably, forced the
world to take notice of them. At the same time the Germans had
shown themselves desperately vulnerable to terrorism, without
the specially-trained men needed to fight this esoteric form of
warfare. And the Israelis were bitterly frustrated. Moshe Dayan
wanted to fly a Sayaret Matkal team to Munich but he was
refused permission. He was allowed to send two advisers but no
assault party. But one consequence of the German failure at
Munich was that when GSG9 was given the anti-terrorist role it
turned to the Israelis for advice and there has been close cooperation between the two units ever since.

The Sayaret Matkal's frustrations at being excluded knew no
bounds and from the moment the Israeli athletes died it was
inevitable that the Israelis would strike at the men responsible for
the massacre. The war of kill and counter-kill erupted with Israeli
and Arab agents murdering each other in the streets of Europe's
cities. Some men of the Sayaret Matkal were seconded to Mossad
to form the hit teams that set out to destroy the Palestinian
terrorist network in Europe. It was also decided to stike a
devastating blow at the men who organized the Munich operation.

On the night of April 10, 1973 teams of the unit were carried
up the coast to Beirut in fast patrol boats. They wore casual
civilian clothes and when they landed from rubber dinghies they
walked directly to cars that had been hired for them by Mossad
agents operating in Beirut. Mossad had also briefed the teams
before they set out. One of Mossad's welcoming committee,
posing as an Englishman, had stayed at the Coral Beach hotel and
had gone out every night at dusk to fish off the beach. He was a
good fisherman too: he kept the hotel kitchen supplied with fresh
mullet. But on the night of the raid he had other fish to fry. The
raiding parties knew exactly where they were going. Netanyahu
was with one team that drove to an apartment block in the Rue
Khaled Ben Al Walid, which housed most of Fatah's leaders.
Their task was to kill Abu Youssef, Yasser Arafat's deputy and
Chief of Intelligence of Fatah, one of the men who had planned
Munich. When they burst into his apartment he fled into the
bedroom and locked the door. They raked the door with Uzzi
sub-machine gun fire and when they broke it open they found
him dead and his wife mortally wounded. By this time the alarm
had been given and the five-man team had to fight its way out. A

70-year-old Italian woman who looked out to see what was going on was killed, so was Abu Youssef's body guard and the apartment block's watchman. And then three truckloads of Lebanese gendarmerie arrived. They were shot up and the team drove furiously to the beach clutching Fatah files which they had seized from Abu Youssef's flat. Two other teams killed Kamal Adwan and Kamal Nasser. Adwan was in charge of operations in Israeli-occupied territory and in Israel itself and was responsible for a number of deaths.

That night the Sayaret Matkal also blew up part of the headquarters of Naif Hawatmch's organization, the Popular Democratic Front for the Liberation of Palestine, and killed a number of his men in a bloody little battle. They also attacked three other terrorist offices in Beirut and a diversionary force blew up a terrorist bomb-making workshop and ammunition cache at Sidon, south of Beirut. When the Beirut raiders left, leaving their hired cars parked neatly on the foreshore, they took with them the Mossad agents who had organized the operation. The agents left their luggage behind and their bills unpaid. The Israeli's had, of course, murdered. But as Mrs. Golda Meir told the crowded Knesset: "We killed the murderers who were planning to kill again."

The business of terror and counter-terror halted momentarily in 1973 while the Arab States and Israel went to war again and the Sayaret Matkal fought in the Golan Heights and the Sinai as part of the units which were thrown in piecemeal to stem the Arab advance. Netanyahu fought through the first desperate week on the Golan Heights and was awarded the Distinguished Conduct Medal. By this time he had become a symbol of bravery in Israel—a biblical hero. He seemed to embody all those fighting qualities which the country needed in order to survive. Max Hastings has told his story in his most perceptive book *Yoni, Hero of Entebbe*. Netanyahu had been born in the U.S., the son of Professor Benzion Netanyahu, editor-in-chief of the *Encyclopaedia Hebraica*. Yoni was a scholar too. He gave up a brilliant career at Harvard after the Six Day War when he became convinced that it was his duty to return to Israel to serve his country. Twice wounded, he conducted his exploits despite a partially crippled right hand. He was a complicated man, an introvert cast in the same mold as Orde Wingate. His men described him with an old Hebrew phrase which means "the man of sword and Bible." He was a natural guerilla fighter and a gifted leader. But the demands of fighting with the Sayaret Matkal were great. The strain broke up his marriage. The war fought by Netanyahu and his men was personal. They looked their enemies in the eye before they killed them. It is not for nothing that the unit has its own staff of psychiatrists.

By the time of his death at the age of 30 Netanyahu was a tired man. He had spent virtually all his adult life at the sharp end of war and was longing for personal peace, a peace which he could not grant himself while he felt Israel was threatened. His death, shot through the heart while directing his assault team from an exposed position on the tarmac at Entebbe, was predictable. The pitcher had gone to the well once too often. The only strange thing about his death was that it had not happened earlier.

He had just two years, 1973 to 1975, away from the unit when he was posted to the Armored Corps, becoming commander of a battalion of Centurion tanks. It was during this period that the Sayaret Matkal was involved in a disaster. It happened at Ma'alot, a new town of mainly immigrant Jews in the Upper Galilee. On the night of May 13, 1974 three men belonging to Naif Hawatmeh's PDFLP slipped across the Lebanese border. The next evening they shot up a pick-up truck taking Arab workers home and killed two Arab women. On May 15, Israel's Independence Day, they broke into an apartment and murdered a family of three. Then they seized a school in which 100 children belonging to Gadna—a cadet organization—and four teachers were spending the night on a holiday hike from the holy city of Safed. The terrorists released one of the teachers and several of the children to carry their demands to the Israeli authorities. They wanted 26 prisoners—one for every year of Israel's existence—to be released and flown to Damascus. When they received a codeword broadcast from Damascus they would release the hostages. The incident, coming only a month after a similar incident at nearby Kiryat Shemona which cost the lives of 16 civilians—eight of them children—and two soldiers, caught the Israelis at a time when their determination appeared to be flagging.

The terrorists had chosen their targets well. Not only were the towns close to the Lebanese border but their occupants, mainly from North Africa, were more excitable than the longer-established European Jews. They showed their anguish and they were fearful. The government was caught in a terrible dilemma. Ever since the first successful hijack when the Israelis had surrendered to the terrorists' demands they had vowed "never again." But now, with so many children involved and the people of the district verging on hysteria, the government agreed to accept the terrorists' conditions. The French and Rumanian ambassadors were engaged in the negotiations. But the Israelis could not agree to the terrorists' stipulation that they would not release the children until the freed prisoners had reached Damascus, and the time ticked on towards the deadline after which, the terrorists threatened, they would blow up the school and everybody in it. Moshe Dayan argued that it was the government's decision to attempt to negotiate which led to the disaster because it meant that the army could not take immediate action.

Dayan was there and so were his two nephews. When the deadline approached with no agreement reached, the unit stormed the building. They killed all three terrorists but not before the Palestinians had killed 22 of the school children and wounded more than 60. In his book "Story of My Life," Dayan wrote: "The attempt to rescue the children was not the most successful military action ever undertaken. One reason can be attributed to delaying the attack until the last minute. During the morning it was still possible to find moments when the terrorists were not alert. However, as the final hour approached they were tense, cautious and careful not to move about as freely as they had done earlier. The second error involved the actual execution of the operation. Our men advanced too slowly using an inappropriate weapon. They mistook the floor, went up to the third and had to come down to the second, when they threw a phosphorus grenade and had to wait until its smoke cleared. By that time the terrorists carried out their massacre of the children." Using hindsight, the Israelis should have used their electronic devices to pinpoint the position of the terrorists and a stun grenade to immobilize them. The phosphorus grenade was too crude for the task. It was a case for an elegant solution.

Dayan was mobbed by grief-stricken parents when he tried to console them. It became known that there had been a major division of opinion between Dayan, the Defense Minister, and General Mordechai Gur, the Chief of Staff, on how the incident should be handled. There was recrimination and blame enough for everybody. It was in tune with the unease which was debilitating the country. Mrs. Golda Meir, shattered by the losses of the Yom Kippur War, and bearing ultimate responsibility for the nation's lack of preparation at the start of that war, had already announced her resignation. The economy was in a mess. There was evidence of corruption in high places. The morale of the nation, so high after the Six Day War, had never been lower. And now it had been proved that even "The Guys" of the Sayaret Matkal were fallible. Like Munich, Ma'alot was a great victory for the terrorists.

Netanyahu returned to Sayaret Matkal in the summer of 1975. He found it much changed. The Yom Kippur War had taken such a toll of the best of the tank corps and regular units like the Golani that many of the unit had to help in what amounted to completely rebuilding the Israeli army. Priorities had changed. After the Egyptian infantrymen had shown what they could do to tanks with their Sagger anti-tank missiles, it became imperative for the Israelis to turn their own mechanized infantry forces into a far more important arm of Zahal and to integrate them into the tank force. The Egyptians had demonstrated that the Israelis could not win by tanks alone. All this, plus the memory of Ma'alot, had infected the unit with the national epidemic of loss of confidence.

Netanyahu set about remaking the Sayaret Matkal in his own image, honing the men for the day when he knew their sharp edge would be needed. That day came on June 27, 1976 when a mixed gang of German and Palestinian terrorists of George Habash's PFLP hijacked an Air France Airbus, flight 139 from Tel Aviv to Paris. It landed at Entebbe where it became obvious that the odious Idi Amin was in on the plot. The rest is history: the separation of the Jews from the other passengers . . . memories of the German executioners at the gas ovens . . . the demonstrations by the hostages' families in favor of giving in to the demands of the terrorists . . . the planning of the rescue mission . . . and the dramatic swoop out of the night of the Sayaret Matkal in their Hercules transports under the overall command of Brigadier General Dan Shomron, the General Officer Commanding Paratroopers and Infantry, with Netanyahu leading the storming party.

The Israelis killed a number of Ugandan soldiers who opposed the assault and then wiped out the terrorists guarding the hostages. They killed the Germans, Wilfrid Böse and Brigitta

Kuhlmann, both seasoned terrorists, and five Palestinians. Three hostages died and the 74-year-old Mrs. Dora Bloch, who was in the hospital when the rescue took place, was dragged out and murdered on Amin's orders. And there was Netanyahu. The raid restored Israel's confidence in itself and dealt a shattering blow to the terrorists.

Shomon Peres, then Minister of Defense, spoke passionately at Netanyahu's graveside when he was buried in Jerusalem's military cemetary: "There are times when the fate of an entire people rests upon a handful of fighters and volunteers. They must secure the uprightness of our world in one short hour."

It has been a long hour for the Sayaret Matkal since then for, while they have not been involved in any more comparable operations (up to the time this book is written in early 1982), they have been engaged in a long and bloody struggle fought out in Southern Lebanon against the Palestinians who have set up their bases in "Fatah-land." The Israelis have pursued the doctrine of pre-emptive strikes by mounting raids on Palestinian bases almost as far as Beirut.

Members of the unit have also operated with the Christian Lebanese in their civil war with the Moslem Lebanese and the Palestinians. They now know Lebanon almost as well as their own country and have won a reputation in Lebanon similar to that of the SAS in Ireland. They have also had to contend with a number of attempted infiltrations of Israel by Palestinian terror squads.

In this harsh and unremitting war "The Guys" have suffered a number of casualties. Not much is written about their exploits. Publicly, they still do not exist as a unit. The most that will be reported is that troops went ashore at a certain point and attacked a terrorist headquarters. But behind those bare announcements lies the dedication, the expertise and the blood of the Sayaret Matkal, a counter-terrorist force which is always in action.

5.

West Germany: Technology against Terrorism

"We are no killer troop," argued Colonel Ulrich Wegener, commander of West Germany's GSG9. "What we need is disciplined, sober-minded men who by speed and decisive action make their weapons superfluous." In that one paragraph he summed up both the strength and the dilemma of his anti-terrorist unit. For, while his men have shown themselves to be capable of that speed and decisive action in dealing with the Federal Republic's urban guerillas and their Arab allies, they have to be extremely circumspect when taking such action in order to avoid raising the spectre of military elitism.

The need to create the unit arose partly because post-war Germany has been organized specifically to prevent the reemergence of Nazi-style army groups. Government powers were devolved to semi-autonomous *Länders* (states) on a federal principle, as opposed to the centralization of Nazi Germany. One consequence of the constitutional re-organization was that when the storm of terrorism burst after the student riots of 1968 and the Arab defeat in 1967 Germany was unprepared. Reactions were inhibited, and the independent police forces of the states could not match the organization of the terrorists. And so, when sharpshooters were needed to deal with Black September hostage-takers at Munich, the task fell to the Bavarian State police who were insufficiently trained for it. As a result of this failure the *Grenzschutzgruppe 9* (GSG9) was formed. Wegener, addressing a symposium in London on ten years of terrorism, explained how his new command came to be formed:

This attack showed a gap in the security system designed to ensure public safety within the Federal Republic. We had at the time to ask what was unusual about this new threat . . . In this first place, it was not a matter of an individual criminal of the normal type. The terrorist groups were fully prepared for their assignment; they were tightly controlled, well equipped and in most cases heavily armed. They had received extensive paramilitary or military training, and, planning and execution of the attacks followed basic principles and methods of guerilla warfare. Their political goals and ideological motivation were apparent. Many of these attacks, especially those of the Palestinians, had, as at least one of their goals, the focusing of the world public attention on their particular political problem and they were very effective.

If one stood back and studied the efforts of the German security forces to combat terrorists, the following points were apparent. First, there was the lack of an intelligence organization especially designed to combat terrorism, which is absolutely necessary. We know that today, but at the time there were no special untis with unconventional, highly trained and selected personnel highly motivated by their mission, and there was a lack of equipment and weapons and an absence of tactical concepts.

. . . In my own view and in that of my comrades and the officers who had the exciting mission of forming a special group at the time, we could not permit the old conventional mistakes to be repeated.

The Federal Border Guard was the ideal parent unit for the GSG9 because, apart from the army, it is the only force in West Germany which is directly under the control of the central government. It was set up after the war to guard the country's borders without provoking the Russians by having army units stationed along the frontier. It also protects federal agencies such as the Chancellor's Office and the Ministries in Bonn and can be called upon for support in particular circumstances by the various provinical police forces. It is armed and has its own transport. So it provides, both legally and structurally, the basis for an anti-terrorist work, having mounted searches at its frontier posts for cars carrying terrorists and explosives from the Middle East to targets in Europe—often acting on tip-offs from the Israelis. So when Wegener presented his report on the need for a specialized anti-terrorist unit it was decided to add one more group to the eight comprising the Border Guard. The new unit, based at St. Augustin just outside Bonn, was formed very much along the same lines as the SAS—counter-terrorist work dictates the way in which these units are orgainzed in just the same way that formal warfare dictates the make-up of an army. GSG9 consists of a headquarters unit, a communications and documentation unit and three fighting units. It has three technical groups dealing with weapons and research and equipment and back-up supply and maintenance services. Each of the three strike units consists of 30 men, and they are broken down into a Command Section and five Special Tactical Sections of four men and an officer. Command was given to Wegener, variously described as "whiplash tough . . . lanky, craggy-faced . . . trim as a ski coach." Wegener, who covers a large part of his face with dark glasses, was called up to serve with the Luftwaffe at the age of 15 at the end of World War II. Captured by the American army, he learned to speak English and then joined the fledgling border guards.

While he was examining the response of other nations to the problem of terrorism, he spent six weeks in America with the FBI, and then a period in Israel. He got on well with the Israelis. One account says they liked him so much, that he was invited to join them on the Entebbe raid, and he was wounded in the arm during the raid. His men, average age 25, are hand-picked volunteers from the Border Guard and the armed forces who have already completed their basic training. They serve with GSG9 for a five to six year period and then usually join one of the police organizations or go the the intelligence agencies. They undergo tough mental and physical weeding out tests—half of them are eliminated in the initial two-day selection course—and then embark on a three and a half month initial training period, followed by three and a half months of special training.

"The aim," says Wegener, "is to create a motivated, confident member of the unit. The first training scheme seeks to make the individual fit in every aspect for his assignment in the group. Special emphasis is placed on making him psychologically fit."

He will not go into details of his unit's tactics, but says: "The tactical concept of the group is based on tight control, flexible leadership, high mobility, surprise, the careful utilization of weapons of all kinds, self-discipline of each member of the unit, and resourcefulness and cunning. The hallmark of Group 9 is the coordination of airborne and motorized forces in accomplishing a joint mission."

Where the group differs from Delta, the SAS and the Sayaret Matkal is that it is a civilian police force and much of its early training is devoted to knowledge of the law, especially as it applies to anti-terrorist operations. But beyond that, the training follows much the same pattern as for the U.S., British and Israeli units. Weapons-training occupies an important part in the syllabus. When Wegener says that he wants to make weapons superfluous he adds: "But when needed, they can shoot straight from every position." They train in unarmed combat—140 hours are devoted to karate—scuba diving, explosives, communications, battle-field medicine and do a great deal of helicopter work. They ski, parachute, climb mountains and are taught hair-raising driving techniques by professional racing drivers on car-makers' test tracks and racing circuits.

In fact every man becomes his own James Bond. To bolster that image—although unintentionally so—GSG9 is equipped with the most modern weaponry and electronic devices. Because the poor shooting at Furstenfeldbruck Airport triggered the Munich massacre, every man of GSG9 is taught to be a marksman, using the Mauser 66 sniper's rifle, each of which costs nealy $2,000. They use infra-red sights and light intensifiers for night shooting. And, they favor Heckler and Koch MP5 sub-machine guns and automatic pistols for their normal work. They are also armed with the .357 Magnum revolver, one shot from which can shatter a car's crankcase. One of their requirements is that they should be able to reach any part of West Germany in "working order" within two hours. In order to do this they are supplied with Mercedes-Benz cars built to Wegener's specifications and BO 105 type helicopters fitted for all-weather operations. They are expert at descending by rope from hovering helicopters and when Wegener, a perfectionist, found the rope unsuitable—one man died in a fall—he had special ropes made for the task.

They also study the origins, ideology and tactics of the various terrorist groups and train in the "dirty tricks" needed to fight them. Each man learns how to pick locks and because so much terrorist activity centers round airports, every member of the operational unit is trained in the handling of airport equipment such as catering vehicles, while the unit always has ten men trained as stewards so that they can pose as airline employees in order to deceive the hijackers of an airliner.

They also train on mock-ups of aircraft and, by courtesy of Lufthansa, on the aircraft themselves. They practice listening to what is happening inside the cockpit and fuselage, using electronic listening devices. They then plan a mock attack, knowing where the "hijackers" are positioned inside the aircraft. And then they mount the attack, using specially developed gadgets to open doors, throwing "flash-bangs" (magnesium-based, cardboard-cased grenades) and entering the aircraft according to a pre-arranged drill. This is precisely what happened at Mogadishu.

"The raid was perfect," a rescued passenger remarked to one of the commandos. "It ought to have been," he replied, "we've practiced it often enough." In fact the Mogadishu operation was not all that perfect. Wegener, who now spends a lot of his time lecturing to police groups about the rescue, ackowledges two moments of worry, one when it was discovered that the ladders they had brought to reach the doors were too short, and the other when one of the doors jammed and took three and a half minutes to open.

The success at Mogadishu came at a vital time for GSG9 becuase in its five years of existence it had only been into action once before and that was to assist the ordinary police in the round-up of an international gang of criminals in Frankfurt. This was an involvement which pleased neither the GSG9 nor the police. The anti-terrorist experts felt they were being used incorrectly while the police forces resented the intrusion of the elite unit into their affairs. In fact there had been a great deal of jealousy of GSG9 from its birth because it members, although still officially policemen working within the same career structure as other policemen, were paid extra money for the skills they acquired—a powerful reason for resentment. Also, the individual *Länders* had formed their own special assault groups in the wake of Munich.

Bavaria, for example, set up a unit which could have been the prototype for GSG9. It consists of four sections, the first comprising four "sticks" of crack shots armed with sniper's rifles; the second section has three *Eingraf Kommandos* (Action Squads) of about 30 men each; the third is composed of six Observation Groups whose task is undercover work, infiltrating suspect organizations and watching suspects; and the fourth is the Special Technical Group.

With forces like these at their disposal it was natural that the states, jealous of their rights, should look on the Federal body with disfavor, especially as it had done nothing to justify the large amounts of money being spent on it and the special status being accorded its men.

Possibly the worst example of this attitude occured in November 1974 when GSG9 was asked to take part in a nationwide sweep for wanted terrorists. The unit's officers took part in the planning of the sweep, but at the last moment were told they would not be wanted. What had happened was that one of the State Ministers of the Interior—independent of the Federal authorities—had objected to the use of GSG9 on the grounds that "all they can do is shoot."

The unit itself was suffering from its inactivity. There was nothing for it to do, or rather nothing it was allowed to do, except train again and again. The men lived in virtual isolation in their barracks and the problem, said Wegener, was in maintaining interest and standards, and not allowing the men to become bored and lax. He had his own doubts about the future of the group and was considering resigning when, on September 5, 1977, Hanna-Martin Schleyer was kidnapped and five weeks later Zohair Akache's terrorist team hijacked the Lufthansa Boeing 737 with its eighty-two passengers—including six German beauty queens—in support of the Baader-Meinhof gang. From the moment his 28 hand-picked men stormed the airliner all was changed. The GSG9 became the darlings of Germany. The bands played for them, they were showered with flowers and the grateful government hung the Cross of Merit round Wegener's neck and promoted him to full colonel. The government had good cause to be grateful, for Interior Minister Werner Maihofer had bungled the search for Schleyer and the German public was demanding action against the terrorists and the head of a political scapegoat.

Maihofer's misery was compounded by the suicides in Stammheim jail—supposedly ultra secure—of Andreas Baader, Jan-Carl Raspe and Gudrun Ensslin, the Baader–Meinhof leaders whose release was among the hijackers' demands. Eight months later he resigned following the report of an independent investigation of the Schleyer affair which blamed the lack of coordination between the various political authorities and the police. In his letter of resignation Maihofer gave as his reason the fact that a tip-off which might have saved Schleyer was delayed.

Schleyer's death, and that of the murdered captain of the aircraft, Juergen Schumann, who was shot in the mouth by Akache, and also the shock caused by the suicides, soured the heroes' welcome given to the commandoes. But criticism of GSG9 itself was silenced. Wegener, who enjoys the limelight, was accepted by the world's security forces as a master of the art, and his advice was sought by many countries. Following the occupation of the Moslem Holy of Holies, the Grand Mosque in Mecca, by Saudi Arabian rebels, the Saudi authorities invited him to send a team of his men to train their special forces in anti-terrorist work.

He was also consulted on the formation of a new German force which, unlike Group 9 does not have to wait for terrorists to commit an outrage before taking action, but goes in search of terrorists wherever they can be found. The new unit, formed by the *Bundeskriminamt* (Federal Investigation Department), was initially composed of 90 investigators operating in small teams on *Zielfahndung* (Target Searches). Its working method is for each team to take one terrorist and immerse itself in his life, using the Wiesbaden computer, whose data banks contain ten million pages of information about terrorist suspects, to provide information about a target which even he does not know. No item of information is too trivial for the target search teams. If they know that a suspect always telephones his mother on her birthday, her telephone is tapped; if he supports a certain football team, investigators will travel to the team's matches inside and outside Germany. Using these methods, 15 major terrorists were tracked down in one period of six weeks in 1978.

Four of them, Till Meyer, Gabriele Rollnik, Gudrun Sturmer and Angelika Loder, were grabbed by a target search snatch squad while they were sitting in a café at the Bulgarian holiday resort of Sonnenstrand in June 1978. According to their lawyer, who accused the government of kidnapping them, four hired cars containing heavily armed German police drew up outside the café and overpowered Meyer and the three women. They were taken to a nearby bungalow, tied up and made to lie on the floor for several hours. At 2 a.m. they were transported to Bourgas Airport in a minibus with German Customs number plates and put on a Lufthansa aircraft which contained another 25 armed German police. The aircraft took off immediately without formalities. It landed at Cologne and the four were taken to prison. Meyer, who had escaped from the top security Moabit Prison in Germany a month before, appeared before a judge who asked him: "Back from vacation?" He was later sentenced to 15 years imprisonment for the kidnapping of the West Berlin Christian Democrat Union leader, Peter Lorenz.

The German authorities refused to comment on the lawyer's accusations. Their version was that a prison warder who knew Meyer had spotted him sunbathing on the beach and had alerted the authorities. Everything that had happened after that, said the Germans, had taken place with full cooperation between the Bulgarian and German authorities. The use of armed German police had been cleared at diplomatic level. The affair provided a rare but welcome example of a communist government cooperating in an anti-terrorist operation.

In another incident with less happy results another target search unit alerted the Yugoslav police about the imminent arrival in that country of Carlos, giving them every detail of is documents, appearance and even what he was wearing.

But, instead of arresting him the Yugoslavs allowed him to stay for four days and leave without being arrested. There were reasons for this behavior. The late President Tito was an out and out supporter of the Palestinian cause and as Carlos was working for the Palestinians, his arrest would have caused embarrassment all round and so he was allowed to slip quietly away. German – Yugoslav relations sufered another blow when Yugoslavia turned loose four of Germany's most wanted terrorists. One of them, Rolf-Clemens Wagner, was wanted for the Schleyer kidnap-murder and the other three, Sieglinde Hofmann, Brigitte Mohnhaupt and Peter Boock, for the murder of banker Juergen Ponto. A search team found them in Zagreb in May 1978 and the Yugoslavs arrested them but refused to hand them over unless the Germans gave them in return a number of anti-Tito Croatian nationalists, some of whom were serving sentences in German jails for acts of terrorism against Yugoslav officals and property inside Germany. The legal and moral complexities were too difficult for the Germans to overcome and so, in retaliation, the Yugoslavs turned the four loose "for lack of adequate evidence" after having held them for six months. But in May 1980 the target search teams had a stunning success, this time with the cooperation of the French police. They tracked down Sieglinde Hofmann and Ingrid Barabas, one of West Germany's most wanted terrorists, to a flat in the Rue Flatters on the Left Bank in Paris. When the police raided the flat Hoffmann tried to draw the pistol tucked into the belt at the back of her trousers. She was overpowered and Barabas put up no resistance. The police then set up an ambush outside the flat and three more women wanted by West Germany walked into it.

All five were sent to Germany. There were no problems with complicated extradition procedures. This doe not mean that there is now complete international cooperation in the fight against terrorism. If a government thinks that it will suit its national purposes to release a known terrorist then it will do so—as the Yugoslavs did and as the French did with the Black September chief Abu Daoud. But what it does mean is that where no overriding national interest is involved, joint cross-border actions can be mounted by national forces and anti-terrorist units, with foreign units being allowed to carry arms and operate on another country's soil. And, when terrorists are arrested, they can no longer hide behind the cloak of political sanctuary.

At the same time it is becoming more and more difficult for hijackers to find airports willing to allow them to land. That change came about between Entebbe and Mogadishu. When the Air France plane was hijacked to Entebbe with its Jewish passengers, a number of countries—Libya, Yemen, Somlia and Uganda—actively connived in the hijacking either in its planning or active stages. But when the Lufthansa aircraft was hijacked, it was forced to tour the Middle East looking for places to land. Nobody wanted it and its cargo of certain trouble. Then, when it eventually reached Mogadishu, the Somalian authorities not only gave the GSG9 commandos permission to attack in West Germany's first overseas military operation since 1945, but also helped in every way, putting its own troops at the disposal of the Germans. There were, of course, good political reasons for the Somalis' willingness to help: they desperately needed weapons to continue the war in the Ogaden against the Ethiopians and they needed financial help to compensate for the Communist money lost when they kicked out the Russians. Nevertheless, their willingness to help defeat an Arab operation was, in Middle East terms, highly significant and it was one of the factors which convinced the Palestinians that hijacking had become unprofitable.

The other lesson to be learned from the series of foreign successes of the German "hit teams" is the supreme value of intelligence, of knowing your enemy.

This is where the Wiesbaden computer, nicknamed "The Komissar," plays such a vital part in the battle against terrorism. Everything is grist to its electronic mill. It is controlled by the Federal Criminal Investigation Department (BKA) housed in a cluster of glass and concrete buildings on a hilltop in a suburb of the peaceful spa of Wiesbaden. In older, cruder times the law solved its criminal problems with a rope on this very spot. Now it relies on data banks which are the envy of the BKA's European colleagues. The Federal government has poured resources into this project. The staff was increased from 933 in 1969 to 3,122 in 1979 and in the same period the annual budget was multiplied ten times, from 22 million to 200 million marks (some $80 million). The heart of the system is an index of information called the PIOS. It takes its name from the categories of information it provides: *Personen, Institutionen, Objekte, Sachen* (Persons, Institutions, Movable and Immovable Objects). It stores—ready to disgorge at the touch of a button—every clue: address, contact, movement and every other item of information not only about terrorism but also about other serious gang crimes such as gun-running and drug-trafficking. Every address found in a suspect's possession, every telephone number and the name of every person who writes to him in prison, and information about every object found at the scene of a terrorist attack or in a place where terrorists have been is stored among the computer's ten million data sheets. They include, for example, nearly 200 addresses in London that are in some way, however remotely, connected with West German terrorists.

When the five women were arrested in the Rue Flatters apartment in Paris the BKA's "servants of the computer" were on the spot disguised as removal men. They stripped the flat and carried everything back to Wiesbaden. Kitchen utensils, railway timetables, empty bottles, cigarette ends, fingerprints, everything was removed to be fed in to the computer. Similarly, when Wolfgang Beer and Jualiane Plambeck, two notorious terrorists, were killed in a road accident near Stuttgart in July 1980, the 2,500 items of information gathered from the crash enabled the computer to demonstrate that they were engaged in the planning of a new terrorist spectacular. Plambeck was a member of the gang that kidnapped Schleyer and she was also believed to have been involved in the Peter Lorenz kidnapping as well as the murders of Juergen Ponte; the Federal Attorney, General Siegfried Buback; and Judge Gunter von Drenkmann, President of the West German Supreme Court.

The computer matched up what was known about her, particularly her close terrorist connections, with the evidence found in the crashed car and within days Horst Herold, head of BKA, was able to announce the seizure of four stolen cars fitted with French licence plates which were to be used in the operation. He also stepped up the search of Adelheid Schulz—the logistics genius behind the Schleyer kidnapping—and Christian Klar who at the end of 1980 remained at the head of the most wanted list because the computer pointed to their invovlement with Plambeck.

Horst Herold says "the most important thing in the fight against terrorism is to be systematic" and describes his data banks as "the material which gives us superiority over the terrorists." Terminals tapping into the computer are now installed in police stations, border points, airports and some police vans. Just how well the system works is illustrated by the case of Stefan Wisniewski, one of West Germany's most wanted men. He was picked up by the French police in the transit lounge at Orly while he was waiting for a flight to Zagreb. They questioned him, then handed him over to the Germans. There were no hearings, no formal deportation order, and no appeal. It was the information fed into the computer because of Wisniewski's arrest which led a target search team to the four terrorists arrested in Yugoslavia. PIOS is not the only function of the computer. A new development is the analysis of handwriting. In a series of tests the computer got the answers 99.6 percent right.

Another development, called *Projekt Sprechererkennung* KT7, analyses the compositon of a recorded voice and then projects on the screen the sort of face which normally produces that type of voice. The value of the computer on "Hangman's Hill" in Wiesbaden is fully appreciated by the other European police forces. Now, instead of contacting Interpol in their search for information, not only about terrorists but also about criminals, the police forces are telephoning Wiesbaden where Herr Herold, delighted to show off his wizardry, puts "the Komissar" at their disposal. The results are instantaneous and often startling. However, Federal Interior Minister Gerhart Baum, who took over from Werner Maihofer, is conscious of over-reliance on electronic wizardry. At a BKA seminar in October 1978 he pointed out: "Computers are necessary and useful, but that is all. We must make sure they do not lead us to over-confident, rash judgements, or stereotyped thinking."

There is one more agency in West Germany concerned in the fight against terrorists and that is the *Bundesamt für Verfassungsschutz* (Federal Office for the Protection of the Constitution). It operates from Cologne, has its own computer which is linked to "Komissar," but also tackles the problem of terrorism by classical counter-espionage procedures, using covert methods such as infiltration and close surveillance. This can be highly dangerous to the agents for the terrorists are aware of their activities and have set up their own professional counter-espionage system. The agents concentrate on acquiring advance knowledge of operations and on tracing the supply lines and logistic centers of the terrorists.

The Germans have also established their own version of the British COBRA. The German version works from the situation control center at the Ministry of the Interior. It has a permanent operations team and when an incident occurs representatives of the Ministry of the Interior of the province join the team. Then, experts in various fields are drawn into the team as the situation develops and special needs appear.

These developments represent a belated, but in the end immensely powerful, response to the threat posed by terrorism to the Federal German Republic. There are those who argue that the threat was never great and that the response has been overwhelming and now poses greater dangers than the terrorists.

Certainly the laws passed to facilitate the work of the security forces have given the government powers which most Germans thought had disappeared forever with the death of Hitler. For example, in a package of anti-terrorist laws passed in February 1978 in the wake of the Schleyer kidnapping and murder, the police have powers when armed with a warrant to search not just a single flat in an apartment block, but the whole block. They can set up control posts wherever they like to carry out checks and searches and can hold for up to 12 hours anyone who cannot give a satisfactory account of himself.

The measures also provided for glass partitions to be erected between jailed terrorists and their visitors to prevent the smuggling of weapons and other forbidden objects, such as parts to make radio transmitters. However, the most sensitive piece of new legislation concerned lawyers' rights of access to their clients and was passed in September 1977 after it became evident that lawyers were acting as couriers for their clients. They were involved not only in the defense of terrorists but also in the planning of prison escapes and subsequent terrorist crimes. The lawyers were part and parcel of the terrorist movement, and some of them are still. Under this legislation lawyers with known terrorist sympathies may be banned from taking terrorist cases. The incident which proved the necessity for this measure was the suicide of the three Baader–Meinhof leaders in Stammheim. Their cells were found to contain an astonishing quantity of forbidden objects, including guns. There is strong evidence to suggest that they were smuggled into the jail piece by piece by the lawyers, the "fellow travellers of terrorism." This was possible because under German law convicted prisoners have unrestricted access to their lawyers until their final appeal has been settled. That can mean for many years. The three Stammheim suicides and Irmgard Möller, who failed in her suicide bid, received 2,200 legal visits in two years.

Chancellor Helmut Schmidt has spoken of the need to maintain "a just balance between the need for security and the need for freedom." And, indeed, given the terrorist problem that the Germans faced, the anti-terrorist laws passed in the 1978 package were mild. Nevertheless, there was much opposition to them and they scraped through the Bundestag by only one vote. One who voted against the laws, the writer Dieter Lattman, explained why he had voted against his own party. To maintain basic rights and liberties, he said, "we need not only the courage to be obedient, which in Germany comes without effort, but sometimes also the courage to be disobedient." One of the problems the government faced was the the public associated the new laws with a much disliked law which was not originally designed as an anti-terrorist measure. Called the Berufsverbot, or Employment Ban, it grew out of a piece of cold war legislation passed in 1953 requiring all civil servants to give active support to the constitution. It was designed to prevent infiltration of the civil service by Soviet supporters. But in 1972, following the student turmoil of the late sixties and the start of urban terrorism, the then Chancellor Willy Brandt was pressured into formulating a new regulation to keep political extremists out of the civil service.

The government now recognized that it went too far for the law was applied to all public employees, involving millions of jobs, including, for instance, teachers and railwaymen.

Under this regulation anyone belonging to a political party regarded as extremist can be banned from employment by the public authorities. It is therefore open to abuse and a case in point is that of railway engineer Rudi Roder who was fired in 1974 after 12 years service when it was disclosed he was a member of West Germany's miniscule Communist Party. Willy Brandt now says of the measure, "Looking back, I have to confess that I was wrong." In fact the Federal government and some of the *Länders* under Social Democratic control no longer apply the regulation. But it is still in existence and is applied particularly in the Christian Democratic Union strongholds of Bavaria and Baden-Burtemberg.

The slogan of the supporters of Berufsverbot is "no freedom for the enemies of freedom," an understandable sentiment but one that gives rise to much bitterness and is counter-productive in the fight against terrorism. "Dear God let me cower so I can get into public service," read the banner carried by one young man protesting against the Berufsverbot. It is in this context also that fears are expressed about the omniscient computer at Wiesbaden for when a man applies for a public service job the computer is fed his name. If it comes up in lights then a deeper investigation of his background may be ordered and the feeling, according to one student, is that "if your name comes up the suspicion is that something must be wrong with you." Interior Minister Gerhart Baum summed up the general feeling about the Berufsverbot: "We always call for new laws when what we really need is more composure."

However, despite all the doubts and worries, the German people in general remain willing to sacrifice some of their freedom in order to ensure their greater freedom of overall liberty and the maintenance of what remains one of the world's most democratic states.

There are also welcome signs that the Federal government under Chancellor Schmidt is making progress in a careful campaign if not to win the "hearts and minds" of the terrorists, at least to bring them to a sense of reality.

Hans-Joachim Klein, who was wounded as a member of Carlos's gang during the kidnapping of the OPEC ministers in Vienna in December 1975, sent his .38 revolver to *Der Spiegel* magazine, escaping from terrorism because of what he heard of his comrades' plans for revolutionary violence: "What I heard in one single month . . . was enough to make me puke, but above all, it made me think . . . I haven't changed from Saul to Paul, but from Saul I have changed back to a person with sensible political thinking and behavior. And even more sensible than before. For this I had to pay a hell of a price." Later he was asked if he felt guilty. He replied: "Guilty is not a strong enough word. I feel that I shall be covered in shit for the rest of my days. It is my own shit because I believed blindly in what I was doing."

Astrid Proll, who escaped to London while being sought by the German police for jumping bail on charges of bank robbery and of attempting to murder two policemen, worked as a mechanic for two years before being caught. She abandoned the hysterical campaign which was being waged against her extradition by "The Friends of Astrid Proll," a zealous combination of left-wingers and extreme feminists who were claiming she would be killed if she were sent back to Germany. She stood trial and was treated leniently, being sentenced to five and a half years in prison, but the three years and ten months she had previously spent in remand custody were counted against the sentence and she walked out of the court a free woman—and an inducement to her former colleagues to abandon terrorism.

Horst Mahler, lawyer, foundling member of the Baader-

Meinhof gang, and once the gang's chief ideologist, was sentenced to 14 years imprisonment in 1972 for robbing banks to finance terrorist operations and then, two years later, got another 12 years, to run concurrently, for forming a criminal association with Ulricke Meinhof. But by 1980 he was being allowed out of prison by day to work in an architect's office, returning to prison every night. Mahler had an early change of heart in prison, deciding that terrorism was the wrong way to achieve political and social reforms, and now, at considerable risk to himself from his erstwhile comrades, he is trying to dissuade young people who might be tempted to join the terrorists.

The German authorities realized these were minor successes and the remaining hardcore of terrorists, some 40 of them at the end of 1980, were not only capable of mounting fresh outrages but at that time were actively planning them. The French police, in the follow-up raids after the Rue Flatters success, had found a laboratory set up in an apartment by two Red Army Faction scientists who had been experimenting with botulism, an often fatal form of food poisoning caused by a toxin. Nevertheless, there was a promise of reconciliation in the government's attitude, a carrot to tempt the terrorists threatened by the big sticks of the search teams, the "Komissar" computer and the hard men of GSG9.

Despite the successes of German counter measures the RAF terror group provided clear proof during 1981 that it was still operational. The Baader-Meinhof gang was born of anti-American fervor because of the war in Vietnam and its successors made a come-back in the late summer to exploit increasing West German hostility to American plans to base more missiles in Europe. At the end of August they placed a car bomb in the headquarters of the USAF in Europe at the Ramstein base near Kaiserslautern which injured 20 including two senior American officers. It was the third such attack in less than a year. Then in the following month the same group ambushed the armor plated car of General Frederick J. Kroeson, U.S. Army Commander in Chief, Europe at Heidelberg. He was wounded when a rocket projectile from Soviet made RPG 7s was fired from wooded hills at his car. Ominously the West German police announced that one of the old hardline RAF leaders, Inge Viett had been reported in the area of the attack with a number of others still on the wanted list.

6.

Holland: The Reluctant Commandos

The Netherlands became a front line state in the subversive terrorist warfare of the seventies and the Dutch government was among the first to make a methodical study of the problem and to prepare defenses against the new form of violence.

Even before Munich the Palestinians had used Dutch territory for anti-Israeli operations. They were small scale attacks on oil and industrial installations with Israeli connections and they were mounted by joint teams of Palestinian and French terrorists. The attacks, interspersed with a couple of hijackings, remained at a low level until, in September 1974, the Japanese Red Army, whose members had carried out the Lod massacre on behalf of the Popular Front for the Liberation of Palestine, seized the French Embassy in The Hague in order to force the French government to release Yoshiaka Yamada. He was the Red Army's currency courier and had been arrested at Orly Airport, his baggage stuffed with $10,000 in small notes. They were to have been used to finance the kidnapping for ransom of Japanese industrialists in Europe but they were forgeries of such poor quality that customs officers spotted them immediately.

Carlos, then the PFLP's chief hit man in France, helped plan the attack on the embassy and put up the money for it—facts recorded in his expense account—and he reinforced the Red Army's demands by throwing a bomb into Le Drugstore in Paris which killed two innocent customers.

The siege at the embassy where the French Ambassador was held hostage was marked by the lack of cooperation which existed between European governments in the fight against terrorism at that time. The French wanted to use their special forces to storm the embassy, claiming it was French territory, but the Dutch refused, arguing that it was their responsibility. In the circumstances there was little the French could do but free Yamada and he, along with his comrades who had seized the embassy, were provided with a plane and vanished into the Middle East. The incident marked the disappearance of the Japanese from the European terrorist scene—they carried out two further operations in the Far East—and the pitchforking of the Dutch into it.

But while the Dutch were sorting out the implications of an attack in their capital on the French Embassy by Japanese supported by a Venezuelan working for the Palestinians, another brand of terrorism was simmering inside Holland. It had its roots in the nation's colonial past but few people outside of Holland knew of its existence until a group of South Moluccans seized a train at Beilan and the Indonesian Consulate in Amsterdam in December 1975. They cold-bloodedly murdered three people in what is probably the world's most obscure and hopeless cause.

When the conglomeration of islands now known as Indonesia won its independence from Dutch rule in 1949, some 12,500 South Moluccans, mostly former soldiers in the Dutch colonial army and their families, chose to settle in Holland rather than risk life under the revolutionary régime. Twenty-five years later, with a population grown to 40,000, their sons and daughters, feeling themselves treated as second-class citizens in grey, cold Holland, and fired by tales of the homeland they had never seen, demanded that the Dutch should force the Indonesians to disgorge South Molucca so they could return to what they imagine is a tropical paradise.

It is and was an impossible dream but the South Moluccans were prepared to kill and hijack for it. The Beilan train hijackers were given heavy prison sentences, but five months later their friends returned to the offensive. They seized a train at Assen and a school full of children at Bovinsmilde, and demanded the release of their comrades. It was to become a classic siege and the Dutch found themselves sorely in need of the security forces they had so presciently set up.

From the first the government had taken the view that the fight against terrorism was in fact a fight against crime in special circumstances. It was logical therefore that the Minister of Justice should be made responsible for anti-terrorism and his department was instructed to organize a Crisis Center in The Hague. This did not make him a "supremo," for the Dutch are by nature people who tend to run things by committee, a necessary institution in a country with so many political parties, where all governments are coalitions. So it was arranged that during serious incidents the Prime Minister, the Minister of Defense and the Minister of the Interior would sit in on the Crisis Center's deliberations. Nevertheless, the Minister of Justice was given the power to make decisions in terrorist affairs. They also became his parliamentary responsibility.

Beneath him in the tactical chain of command is a team of five men under the chairmanship of the Attorney General. The other members are the Queen's Commissioner; the Burgomaster of the locality where the incident is taking place; the local Public Prosecutor; and the local Chief of Police.

However, despite this insistence on dealing with any form of terror as a police matter, the government realized that in serious cases it would be necessary to use the superior fire power and more aggressive tactics of the armed forces under carefully controlled conditions.

The Dutch police are divided into two categories: municipal police of 19,000 men in the big cities, under the control of the Burgomasters; and the State Police Force of 12,000 men administered by the Minister of Justice which polices the rest of the country. Backing up these groups in case of emergency are the 3,500 men of the Royal Military Police, who are also responsible for frontier control.

It was decided that in special circumstances such as terrorist attacks, the Police authorities acting under the Police Act might call upon the services of what were described as "other military personnel." To deal with attacks on airports and the seizure of hostages the government decided to earmark a Royal Marines unit, along with two battalions of armored infantry to be used in assisting the police to seal off an area during a serious incident.

The government made a careful study of the lessons of the Munich affair, and concluded that disaster had come because the West Germans relied upon sharpshooters alone. Thus, when the Dutch established two sharpshooter units one of the State Police and one of Marines, they also began training special squads in assault tactics to work with them. Each sharpshooter unit consisted of 40 men trained to shoot as a team, and to open fire only when radio instructions were received from a fire controller through their earpieces. The men were equipped and trained with Fal rifles and with Heckler and Kochs for shorter ranges. Tactically they were instructed that three marksmen should be assigned to one target and if ordered to kill, they were to make sure of killing. It was the ruling that the security forces might use their weapons in two circumstances: if terrorists began putting to death one hostage after another, or if the government should decide to put an end to a siege dragging on too long, and thereby causing excessive suffering to the hostages.

In brief, the Dutch went about things in a very sensible fashion. The Ministry of Justice also reorganized police resources by setting up a permanent squad of 17 police officers to specialize in the detection of terrorist acts of national importance, as well as a special detective team to investigate people who aroused suspicion that they were planning terrorist acts. This use of the police for preemptive intelligence work proved most successful. In the summer of 1975 a conspiracy by Moluccans to take hostage the Queen of the Netherlands was uncovered. The conspirators were arrested and convicted. In the same year the police arrested and convicted four Syrian terrorists plotting to hijack a train. Unfortunately, it was probably the discovery of this plan and the publicity it attracted that inspired the Moluccans to try their hand at hijacking the train at Beilen only a short time later; for, as we have seen terrorists tend to follow a fashion in their acts.

The Steering Committee, charged with the repression of terrorism, set down general guidelines for the conduct of defensive operations. It also established sub-committees to study technical means and logistics, analysis of incidents at home and abroad, and the training, equipping and tactical use of special assistance units, respectively.

Police officers and soldiers chosen for anti-terrorist groups were all volunteers. They were to serve on short engagements in the case of police units, and would then return to normal law and order duties. These guidelines still control what came to be known as Special Support Unit of the Police. Commander J. Stokreef, Coordinator of the Special Support Unit, speaking at a seminar, explained the philosophy behind this arrangement.

"We think that this is a good way, because the policeman who is involved in anti-terrorist operations can just go back to the everyday situation that he knows and works in afterwards . . . We like them to stay anonymous so that they can go back to their own villages as policemen. We do not want a man to go back to his village and say that he has killed a terrorist."

A careful selection system sifts the volunteers with a psychiatrist examining each man. A psychiatrist also serves with the unit, keeping a watchful eye on the men's behavior in action and checking their stability under stress even after an operation has ended. One peculiarity of the Dutch counterattack on terror is that volunteers in the police, and even in the army, must get permission from their wives before they are accepted. The men also have a right to volunteer out of the special unit, though it is up to the coordinator to decide when they leave.

The second stage in building up the anti-terrorist forces involved choosing an existing military unit to undertake these duties. It had to be a first-class military organization but one that would not frighten Holland's "peaceniks." The choice fell on the Royal Netherlands Marine Corps. NATO commanders have not always been kind in their assessments of the military skill and bearing of Dutch soldiers who tend to wear their hair at an unmilitary length, to be organized in trade unions and fail to display the outward manifestations of martial discipline. But no one makes these criticisms of the Dutch Marines.

Certainly the anti-terrorist unit of the Marine Corps has acquitted itself most professionally. Each man is a volunteer who has completed his basic training. He must be over 18 and in order to qualify has to undergo the same one day psychiatric test as those in the police squad. The unit is organized as a rifle company with 113 men. There is an HQ of 14 officers and men, and three platoons each 33 strong. They are on stand by 24 hours a day, ready with their special equipment to go into action at any time.

For anti-terrorist operations the platoons are split into five-man teams under group leaders. They are armed with machine pistols and revolvers. Two platoons are always operational and the third one is normally used as a training unit giving its recruits a 16 week course. The Marines do a great deal of range work and small-arms training, favoring as their special weapons the Israeli-made Uzzi 9 mm machine pistol and the American-made Police Lawman Mark III, a .38 weapon. Standard NATO machine guns are also available if further firepower is needed and the force also has the by now customary infra-red and image-intensification gadgetry.

The Marines have a good supply of radio equipment, for close communication contact is essential for this kind of work. They train in cooperation with police, army and naval units. For obvious reasons they make a specialty of exercises at Schipol International Airport, the biggest in Holland, and are familiar with the layout of other airports that might be in danger of terrorist raids. Like GSG9 and the SAS they practice methods of forcing entry into airliners. The rest of their training also follows the normal anti-terrorist pattern: street fighting, storming of buildings, and close combat work. They also, unusually, practice riot control.

Apart from this specialized training, a high standard of physical fitness is built up by speed-marching, assault courses, and climbing. At the end of his 16 weeks in the third platoon the marine goes into an operational unit where he maintains his training for 32 weeks, learning the art of working in a team using specialized tactics. Captain R. E. Kloppenberg, a commander of a Royal Netherlands Marine Corps unit, reports, "after a year, we have at our disposal a man who is very well trained and motivated to fight against terrorists from anywhere in the world. He stays in the unit for at least two years."

The Marines first went into action in their anti-terrorist role at Scheveningen Prison on October 31, 1974, just a month after the authorities had been forced to capitulate to the Japanese Red Army terrorists holding the French Ambassador hostage in The Hague. The Scheveningen incident started when four prisoners produced pistols and knives during the regular weekly service in the prison chapel, and seized 22 hostages, among them the priest who had celebrated Mass and the choir which sang at the chapel.

Nine prisoners refused to take part in the affair and were allowed to leave the chapel. It was then discovered that the four who remained were two hard-nosed Dutch criminals, an Algerian convicted of robbing an arms dealer, and Adhan Ahmed Nuri, a 23-year-old Palestinian terrorist who had been sentenced to five years in March 1974 along with his comrade, Sami Hussein Tamina, for hijacking and burning a British Airways VC 10 at Schipol Airport.

It was Nuri who led this cosmopolitan gang. His first demand was that Tamina, who was recovering in the prison hospital after a rather unconvincing hunger strike, should be brought to the chapel. He also wanted to speak to an Arab ambassador and eventually demanded a plane to fly them out of the country. The Dutch authorities, however, were determined that there was going to be no repetition of the Japanese Red Army's success. They started the process of wearing down the kidnappers. They supplied food, blankets, a telephone and packs of cards. Some of the hostages were set free as the siege progressed and then the authorities decided to allow Tamina to talk with Nuri. But when Tamina was taken to the chapel, he refused to meet Nuri and in an emotional telephone conversation told Nuri that he had decided to stay and serve his sentence. From that moment the convicts' will-power began to crumble.

The authorities waited nearly five days, until 3:40 in the morning of October 31, before sending in the Marines in an assault which has become a pattern for rescue missions. The early hour was chosen to take advantage of the convicts' sleeping routine. The two Arabs were asleep and the Dutch were on guard. It was also decided to go in with the maximum of noise and light in order to confuse them. With split-second timing the Marines broke windows all round the chapel and threw in small flare grenades which exploded into brilliant cascades of light while the lock of the chapel door was burnt out in six seconds with a termic lance. A portable siren was turned on at full volume. The Marines then stormed into the chapel firing their automatic weapons into the ceiling. The convicts, stunned by noise, light and fear, tried to run into the sacristy but they were quickly overpowered by the Marines. There was not a single casualty.

It was a brilliant little operation which did not receive proper recognition for the way in which it was planned and carried out, using a nicely balanced mixture of psychology, force and technology. But the Dutch learnt lessons from it and made their plans for future incidents on the lines of the Scheveningen technique. The talk-out worked well at the Indonesian consulate in Amsterdam and the train siege at Beilan where, despite the fact that three hostages were murdered, the negotiating team kept cool, and the South Moluccans were talked into surrender after a 16 day siege. The Marines had been deployed at Beilan and had made their plans for an assault. But they were not needed.

However, they did have to go into action when the South Moluccans struck again at Assen and Bovinsmilde, and this time there was bloodshed. The Dutch were fortunate that the school children held hostage at Bovinsmilde began to collapse with a stomach virus and the terrorists, unable to cope with the situation, relased the children after four days and surrendered. The authorities were thereby freed from the dilemma of having to decide whether or not to storm the school. They had before them the appalling example of the Ma'alot incident.

With the children safe, the Crisis Center was able to concentrate on the train at Assen, perched out in the countryside in the May sunshine with meadows full of sleek cattle on one side of the line and dark woods on the other. It all looked very rural and peaceful. But on the train, it was far from calm. The 85 hostages, most of them commuters on the way to work, were being threatened by Max, the terrorist leader. He made it plain to his captives that he had no intention of surrendering and he and his 12 companions held out day after day while the world watched and the Marines made their preparations. Few of the correspondents who covered the story were particularly impressed by the young Marines. They looked rather as if they were better suited to the disco dance floor rather than serious soldiering. But they proved the journalists wrong.

While they prepared, every effort was being made to persuade the Moluccans to surrender, for the Dutch had no wish to make martyrs and they recognized that an assault on the train against heavily armed, dedicated terrorists was certain to prove a very different affair to Scheveningen. But as each day passed the situation on the train became more and more dangerous with both the terrorists and the hostages showing signs of cracking under the strain. The authorities knew this because Marines had crept up to the train at night and planted listening devices on board.

Finally, when it became apparent discipline on the train was collapsing and open conflict was at the point of breaking out between the gunmen and their hostages, Dr. Dick Mulder, the psychiatrist in charge of the talk-out operation advised that he could do no more and that the Marines should go in.

The Scheveningen technique was to be used, with the Marines attacking in the early hours so as to catch the terrorist off guard. The British SAS, who had studied the Scheveningen operation carefully and had arrived at the same conclusion as the Dutch on the use of blinding light and stunning noise to disorientate their targets for the first moments of an assault, sent two emissaries to Assen with a box of anti-terrorist tricks. Among them was the flash-stun-grenade which the Germans were to use so effectively at Mogadishu. But the Dutch, while appreciative of the proffered help, turned down the grenades. Instead, at zero hour, a flight of Starfighter jets dived at the train and as they pulled out a few feet above the carriages they switched on their afterburners. The impact was devastating. The train shuddered from the blast of noise and jet turbulence and the terrified passengers threw themselves onto the carriage floors. As the Starfighters vanished and the Marines burst into the train from the positions along the line to which they had crept, undetected during the night, two of the passengers stood up and were killed in the crossfire. In a sad vindication of scientific methods they were the two hostages whose background and mental make-up had led the psychiatrists to believe that they were the most likely to crack.

The Marines concentrated their fire on the front coach where the listening devices had indicated that the terrorists were gathered. When it was all over that coach looked like a colander, riddled with bullet holes. Max and five of his gang were killed while the remaining seven were taken prisoner and eventually sentenced to terms of imprisonment of between six and nine years.

In a grim broadcast just after the siege ended, Joop den Uyl, the Prime Minister, declared, ''That violence proved necessary to put an end to the seizure of the hostages, is something that we feel as a defeat." He went on to say, "We saw no other way." That in a nutshell is the attitude of European governments: action may be necessary but it is only taken with great reluctance.

Whatever was the view of the Dutch government at the time, it is now clear that the assault by the Marines was not only justified but inevitable. It was also successful. Athough South Moluccan gunmen perished in the attack they have not become martyrs, and since then a good deal less has been heard from the Moluccans or the terrorist leaders. Indeed such criticism as has been made of the operation concentrates on the failure of the pyschological persuasion practiced by Dr. Mulder.

Twenty days is a long time to allow armed men to hold decent citizens prisoners in their own country, however noble may be the cause of saving life. In that time the siege became institutionalized. Commuters took it for granted that their train would stop at a station on one side of Assen and a bus would take them round the besieged train at a safe distance to a station on the other side. Police settled down in the area, a press corps 200 strong descended on Assen and made its headquarters at a Church Hall. To pass the time the journalists organized a ping-pong championship and the profits from their drinks and food paid off the money outstanding for the building of the hall. Dr. Mulder himself established a routine in his headquarters close to that he followed normally. He even caused some surprise by having a few dozen bottles of wine delivered so he could have a glass or two when things were quiet.

After Assen Dr. Mulder explained his techinque. He attaches great importance to building up a psychological picture of the terrorists, not an easy task in the initial stages of an incident when they are in their most violent and uncontrollable phase. After making it clear to the terrorists that they can expect no quick surrender to their terms he will allow them to speak to the press and appear on television. His reasoning is that this gratifies their egos and by granting them this small success he draws them into a talking, rather than a killing frame of mind. His next step is to organize matters so that there is only one line of communication between the terrorists and the outside world and that is a direct link between the leader of the group and the psychiatrist in charge of the talk-out. Mulder himself maintained constant contact with Max at Assen. Once this link has been established and the terrorists are settled into a routine, there then begins a battle of wits whereby the psychiatrist gradually asserts his control over the leader, guiding him through the depression phase which comes to terrorists when they realize they are losing the game. This phase is most dangerous because it can lead them to despair and the shooting of hostages—precisely what happened at the Iranian Embassy in London. But if the man in charge of the talk-out overcomes these dangers successfully, he should be able to persuade the terrorists to surrender.

At Assen, despite all his undoubted skill, Dr. Mulder failed to reach his final objective and the troops had to be unleashed. Other experts in the field have since criticized Dr. Mulder for conducting the whole operation himself. There is a body of opinion that believes a psychiatrist cannot be authoritative enough to put sufficient pressure on the terrorists. It is better for the negotiator to be a police officer or a soldier, even though he has a psychiatric adviser on hand, as a reminder that if the worst comes to worst force is available to crush the gunmen.

Since Assen, what might be called the psychiatric anti-terror technique has become rather less fashionable. The main reason is that terrorist groups are now aware of its subtleties and the most professional of them have studied the technique and evolved ways of defeating it. Training schools for terrorists now include courses in defeating the psychiatrists in their curriculum.

In earlier sieges talk-out methods had succeeded, notably as practiced by the London Police in the Spaghetti House affair when criminals held hostages in that restaurant, and in the Balcombe Street siege.

When the Iranian Embassy was seized in Princes Gate in 1980, it was recognized very early on that the talk-out procedures were likely to fail because the terrorists were obviously unstable and fanatical.

The truth of the matter is that at Princes Gate and Assen the negotiators did their best but it was not good enough. The lesson to be learnt is that in this particular field of endeavor nothing stands still. Terrorists learn from their mistakes and in order to fight them techniques and tactics must be constantly adjusted to cope with their ever-increasing sophistication. The fact is that when dealing with violent men who refuse to surrender, despite the most expert and devoted efforts of the negotiators, there comes a time when the talking has to stop and the troops have to go in. And when the shooting starts the Dutch Marines have proved themselves as brave, dedicated and professional as any other anti-terrorist unit.

7.

France: Old Methods, New Enemy

France is a country of so many police forces that when the decision was taken after Munich to set up special forces to cope with the wave of terrorism the government was faced with an embarassment of choice. In terms of sheer numbers France has more police officers and officials than any other West European country. At the last count in October 1980 there were more than 105,000.

But that gives a false picture of their striking power in terms of the war against terrorism, for many of the thousands have a purely administrative role and are no more fit to take on terrorists in a street battle than any other group of civil servants. They also moved into the terrorist era completely unprepared for this specialized form of duty. The operational units were still badly equipped even for normal police work at the beginning of the eighties. It had not been until 1979 that the Ministry of the Interior embarked upon a four-year plan to improve this state of affairs. And it was calculated that not until 1981 would new weapons, notably 3,500 "Manurhin" .357 revolvers, 2,000 modern French-made rifles and 1,500 bullet-proof jackets be available for service. Many of the cars in service were outdated and needed replacement. Even more harmful to effective anti-terrorist work was the fact that at the beginning of the eighties radio networks were not up to date and only a beginning had been made in the task of providing the forces of law and order with a comprehensive computer network, starting with 200 terminals.

The difficulties of the French government in creating a really effective force up to the standards of other Western European countries may be judged from the fact that eight years after Munich awakened the Common Market countries from their security topor only 10,000 French police officers were equipped with modern revolvers. At least 30,000 such weapons would be needed to bring the force up to date.

The great problem in these circumstances lay in the choice of unit to specialize in anti-terrorist work from all the forces available. Ever since Napoleonic times France has relied on a number of different forces of police controlled by the Ministry of the Interior.

This Ministry operates both national and municipal bodies through the Prefects, one of each of the ninety-five *Départments* of France. In addition, there are the CRS, the Republican Security Companies, a special force set up to cope with industrial troubles during the insurrectional strikes in the northern coal-fields in the late forties. Specialized training and increased recruitment has turned these companies into intervention units to deal with street rioting. They were used to great effect during the student revolution of 1968. Useful and well trained though the CRS and the mobile police squads are, they did not provide an ideal answer when a highly specialized anti-terror and anti-hijack squad was needed.

Nevertheless in their haste to show they were doing something to prevent a repetition on French soil of the disastrous affair at Munich the government turned first to the police. In 1972 they appointed a senior officer, Chief Commissioner Robert Broussard, to set up what was called the "Anti-Commando Brigade." It was composed of volunteers, with some units working in Paris and others in the provinces.

These so-called BAC squads were set up in profusion, but they were usually *ad hoc* squads without very much training who were brought together from their normal duties only when necessary. They were equipped with Uzzi sub-machine guns which they sometimes used with too much zeal. Initially they received an issue of rifles with infra-red sights but as these were costly, a parsimonious Ministry of the Interior soon decided they could be dispensed with. After a while the BAC squads faded into history except for one composed of 50 Paris policemen which still occasionally swings into action. They receive special training once a month.

In the inter-ministerial struggles which always break out in France when something new has to be done, the first round had gone to the Ministry of the Interior. But in 1974 another decision was made at Cabinet level. The task of providing a crack force for intervention in serious terrorist incidents was given to the Gendarmerie Nationale which is under the Ministry of Defense. The Gendarmerie Nationale proudly bears the title of the oldest regiment in the French army. It is 60,000 strong and its highly-trained officers and men are equipped with small arms and operate as normal infantry units.

In addition to that, however, they have another role as a mobile and armed police force for the rural areas of France where they have the responsibility of keeping law and order from their garrisons in small towns. They also undertake traffic duties and some are organized in mobile teams to act in riots.

From this respected force the Defense Ministry began recruiting volunteers to form a specifically terrorist intervention unit, to be known as "Gigene," the National Gendarmerie Intervention Group. The unit was placed under the command of an enthusiastic officer. It had two bases, one at Maisons-Alfort on the outskirts of Paris, and the other at Mont-de-Marsan, in western France.

The Intervention Group consists of 54 men. There are four officers and 50 NCOs and are divided into three squads so that one is permanently on alert 24 hours a day. The duty squad must be ready to move anywhere in France or to leave on an overseas mission within half an hour, and the reserve groups within two hours. The group, known as GIGN, comes under the direct control of the General Direction of the Gendarmerie and can be used only on government orders after receiving a request for help from a department *préfect*.

To help with their task, the special squad of gendarmes is lavishly equipped with electronic gadgetry. They have radar equipment in their high-powered though anonymous looking cars which enables them to tail cars from a distance. They also have the array of gadgets common to all modern security forces with which they can listen through walls and monitor conversations at long range. And they have the night sights, light amplifiers and electronic spy endoscopes for keyhole watching that have become standard equipment with the SAS and GSG9.

Every officer and man has to be a marksman and they are all particularly good with the Manhurin .357, either long or short barrelled, the standard French police weapon which is comparable to a Magnum. They are required to hit a man in the shoulder in two seconds at 25 meters, and to reach this standard they use 200,000 cartridges a year on the range. Using the French FRF1 rifle with telescopic sights they can split an orange at 200 meters.

In training they simulate terror raids and practice the best ways of freeing hostages in every possible situation and simulating attacks and counterattacks using live ammunition. Before being accepted into the squad, the young gendarmes—most of them married men, all aged between 23 and 30—undergo medical, psychological and initiative tests. If they are accepted after six days of tests they embark on a tough eight month training course. "When I recruit a man I test him for everything," says Captain Prouteau, who has commanded the group since its formation.

Each man is a trained parachutist, and all are skilled climbers and abseilers. They can all swing down a 120 meter rope from a hovering helicopter, and most go in for the martial arts. Explosives are a speciality and claim to be so precise that they can stop a car by blasting off its axles with four pre-set charges.

After many years of effort and training the GIGN is still waiting for its first big prestige operation. Their most publicized chance to prove their quality internationally came in 1976 in Djibouti, the former French colony flanked by Somalia and Ethiopia in the Horn of Africa. After a police raid on a shanty town, four terrorist gunmen seized a school bus with 31 mostly

French children on board near the French air base, and tried to drive it across the Somali border. It was stopped in no-man's-land.

The terrorists, who were joined by two comrades from Somalia, threatened to shoot the children and slit their throats unless the territory was immediately declared to be independent. The gendarmes, aided by troops of the Foreign Legion, went into the attack when negotiations broke down. Marksmen shot all six of the hijackers. One of the children was wounded but the rest were freed and a Foreign Legion officer was wounded in the fighting that broke out around the bus when it came under fire from Somalia.

In the summer of 1981 GIGN dealt expeditiously with what might have been a dangerous hijack situation. A former Trappist monk, Lawrence James Downey, threatened the captain of an Aer Lingus Boeing 737 flying from Dublin to London, and planned to hold the aircraft until the Pope had given in to his eccentric demand that the Third Secret of Fatima should be publicly revealed. The Secrets of Fatima concerned revelations made to a Portugese girl in a vision.

The aircraft was diverted to Le Touquet in Northern France, and a task force of gendarmes cordoned off the airfield. A GIGN team from Paris was rushed there by helicopter and took charge of the operation. It was they who negotiated with the hijacker and were able to persuade him to leave the aircraft, and to surrender his weapon. The fact that a highly professional force was available for swift action prevented bloodshed.

There can be no doubt about the efficiency and enthusiasm of the French counter-terrorist squad which on numerous occasions has proved its capabilities on home soil. They acted promptly and bravely in 1980 when, under fire from Corsican nationalists, they succeeded in getting the release of hostages held in the Hotel Fesch at Ajaccio and arresting the terrorists without firing a single shot.

"We have proved our worth in 84 different actions, an average of 14 a year," declared Captain Prouteau. "We have liberated 212 hostages, and made 63 arrests. Back in 1973–4 there were between 18 and 20 hostage-takings a year and now the number has fallen to three or four."

Of course, most of the incidents he mentioned were caused by armed criminals rather than terrorists, but the dangers are the same. The commander of GIGN himself was wounded in 1980 by bullets fired by a gunman who barricaded himself in a house at Pauillac in the Gironde *départment.*

Mystery still surrounds another reported intervention by the group. In January 1980 the French magazine *Le Point* claimed that five men of the GIGN had flown to Saudi Arabia the previous November to take charge of Saudi security troops in the recapture of the Great Mosque at Mecca. This, the most holy place of Islam, had been seized by armed religious fanatics making a political protest against the regime of King Khalid and it took the Saudi National Guard days of attacks with heavy casualties before the rebels were cleared out. Gendarmerie headquarters in Paris refused to comment on the report and the French government was remarkably coy about the matter even though the Saudi Arabians coldly denied that French forces were "responsible" for the defeat of insurgents. They pointed out that only Moslems were allowed to visit Mecca. American sources in Jeddah later told us that the French, although they were helping to train the National Guard, played no part in the operations and added, "If a country gets praise for helping with a worthy action why would they go out of their way to deny it?"

The attitude of GIGN is a police attitude deriving from the civilian law and order role of the Gendarmerie Nationale rather than from its military tradition. That is no doubt one of the reasons why the French government chose this branch of the service for the anti-terrorist role. There is an old legal maxim in France that "Sagesse commence avec la peur du gendarme" (Good behavior begins with fear of the gendarme).

If fear imposed by GIGN is not sufficient to deter modern terrorists and a greater degree of force and counter aggression is needed, France does not lack for bigger and heavier forces. It keeps a professional force of 27,000 men earmarked for rapid intervention overseas. Included in this formidable array is the 11th Parachute Division, 12,000 strong, garrisoned in southwest France and on Corsica. A Marine commando division of 10,000 men is also based at Vannes in Brittany.

Both these units saw active service in 1978 when they flew to Zaire to the rescue of French citizens in danger from guerilla forces coming up from Angola, and in to protect French interests in Chad. Squads from this force which has it own Transall and

C 130 Hercules troops transports could rapidly intervene on the terrorist front if they were needed.

Police forces and military units are all very well to provide the sinews of anti-terrorist warfare but they are powerless to act without the kind of direction that can only be provided by good intelligence. And in the field of military and civilian intelligence organization the French once again have a profusion of services.

When they were first mobilized for action against the new enemy, Raymond Marcellin, an excitable Gaullist enthusiast, had been Minister of the Interior since the Paris student revolution of 1968. He began making use of the Renseignements Généraux, the RG, whose task had always been to keep an eye upon political movements suspected of extremism, rather in the manner of the FBI and the British Special Branch.

From informers and from their dirty tricks department skilled in telephone tapping, opening letters and clandestine searches, they soon amassed copious dossiers under the general heading MR (revolutionary movements). In 1975 they provided useful information which led to the attempted arrest of Carlos, the international terrorist, in a seedy apartment in Rue Toullier on the Left Bank. Unfortunately the operation went badly wrong and he shot and killed two inspectors and wounded another senior officer. All three men belonged to another security organization known by its initials, DST, which stand for Direction of Surveillance of the Territory, the internal espionage body. From that time onwards the DST, enraged by the killings, became predominant in providing intelligence about terrorists despite the fact that those sections of the RG dealing with extremism had been heavily reinforced. The DST also works closely with another branch of the intelligence service which deals with foreign espionage and counter-espionage, the SDECE. The two branches set up a joint operational group to specialize in anti-subversion and anti-terrorism.

In 1978 the government re-organized the DST and divided it into three divisions. There is now a Counter-Espionage group and a curiously named "Counter-Interference" group known as CI, and both make use of the third division which provides the technical back-up for their activities.

The CI, which has its office in the Rue Rembrandt in Paris, has now assumed responsibility for providing information about terrorist activities. One of its sections specializes in Europe and the Middle East and another in South American and Cuban terror networks. It takes no action against the terrorists but passes on its information to the recently created special terrorist section of the Criminal Investigation Department of the Paris police *(police judiciaire)*.

The Counter-Interference group takes little interest in home grown terrorists. For example, it only became involved with a group of Corsican guerillas when it was revealed that they had been trained in one of Colonel Qaddafi's Libyan camps. Similarly a ten man team was sent to Bayonne in south west France, not to look into local terrorism, but to investigate links between Basque nationalists operating across the Spanish border and the Irish Republican Army.

Because France has been spared the experience of dealing with any home grown archetypal terrorist organization comparable to the Red Army Faction in Germany or the Red Brigades in Italy, she has been able to rely largely upon ordinary criminal law and normal police methods. The one exception is the GIGN which was intended partly as a symbolic gesture of preparedness, and partly to deal capably with alien acts of terrorism on French soil. For the same reason it has not been necessary to enact emergency legislation giving greater executive powers. In any case the French state is by nature somewhat authoritarian, and General de Gaulle, when he was president, greatly strengthened emergency powers to deal with the Algerian crisis and its domestic consequences.

France is a nation with a tradition of terrorism, part of its revolutionary inheritance; but also with an equally strong tradition of centralized authority in government and, as we have seen, powerful police resources. When President François Mitterand replaced Giscard d'Estaing, and secured a socialist majority in the National Assembly, it began to look as though the political tilt in France was towards the revolutionary and liberal tradition. The new President gave amnesty to 31 convicted terrorists of various kinds when announcing his intention of abolishing the State Security Court which, since it was established by General de Gaulle in 1963, has had jurisdiction over such offenses.

The first impact of the new violence in France came when foreign terrorist groups began using French soil either as a base or as a battleground. French governments had always maintained a tradition of welcoming political émigrés but their generosity was unsuitably rewarded by Paris becoming a world capital of terrorism.

In 1968, according to Raymond Marcellin, the French police had a list of 44 terrorist organizations in the world of which 20 had connections in France. Carlos operated there. Arabs, Israelis, Latin Americans, Armenians and Iranians have all carried on their bloodthirsty trade on French soil. Italian Red Brigades have used France, so have Basques, and the West German Red Army Faction held their hostage Hans-Martin Schleyer somewhere in France. His body was finally discovered at Mulhouse.

Distressing though this was in many ways, it did not greatly harm the fabric of French life. The foreign epidemic was handled by the police bureaucracy, which in general took care not to become too embroiled in other peoples' business; and by the Foreign Ministry which skilfully arranged the expulsion of captured terrorists rather than risk more incidents by having them held in France.

What did affect France more directly were the growing activities of nationalist irredentist movements, in particular acts of terror organized by the Bretons and the Corsicans. These militant movements may be compared with the IRA in Northern Ireland and with the ETA in the Basque country of Spain. Indeed in south-western France there is an overspill of the Basque campaign for independence from the central Spanish government. French Basques to some extent help their friends on the other side of the Pyrenees, and a danger exists that they might themselves make militant demands for regional independence from France. For this reason the French government keeps a careful watch on developments. The danger perhaps lessened with the election of President Mitterand who is sympathetic to the idea of regional revolution.

The Bretons, seeking autonomy for the ancient province of Brittany, made their presence felt through militant actions by the Breton Liberation Front (FLB) sometimes supplemented by the Breton Revolutionary Army (ARB). Unlike most such movements they had no friendly frontier across which help and refuge could be found, and French police were able to prevent any but small and symbolic raids. They hit such targets as gendarmerie local headquarters, electricity installations and tax offices. In 1978 they chose a more spectacular target, and over-ambitiously placed a bomb in a renovated room at the Palace of Versailles, which destroyed mainly large paintings depicting famous victories of Napoleon. They had gone too far, and the full force of police power was brought to bear in investigations which led to the arrest of Breton leaders. The eight charged admitted making 26 attacks and the FLB/ARB was listed as having made 206 attacks over the previous three years. Since then they have been notably less involved in terror acts.

Corsican nationalist groups have been busy on the French mainland as well as on Corsica, especially the National Front for the Liberation of Corsica, which was formed in 1976. In 1980 they were reported to be responsible for 463 explosions. When, as one of his last Presidential acts Giscard d'Estaing visited the island before the elections, a bomb was exploded at Ajaccio airport shortly before his arrival.

In retaliation against the NFLC, loyalist extremists, many of them veterans of the OAS Secret Army of French Settlers and soldiers in Algeria who later settled in Corsica, have retaliated by setting up a counter-terror group. It is know as FRANCIA and its targets are the Corsican independence movement and its supporters. It fights violence with violence in the same way that the Ulster Defense Association fights the IRA, and causes an equal amount of trouble to the security forces.

French security men who had learned their tactics in the hard school of fighting Secret Army terrorists in the plastic explosives campaigns of the fifties, and in action against Algerian Arab terrorists, did not find it too difficult to keep these unsupported regionalist groups under control. But they have still not entirely mastered the tactics of how to deal with the new generation of indigenous terrorists now operating in France.

It has been called "soft" terrorism on the analogy of "soft porn." There are, for example, violent small ecological groups which have demonstrated at and then made attacks upon, motorway toll stations, holiday centers and beach facilities.

Even tougher police measures were adopted, and with public sympathy, in their attempts to cope with the so-called "autonomists," people who, incidentally, had nothing whatsoever to do with regional autonomy but who were violent anarchists. The favorite tactics of these, mostly young people, were to tag along at the end of a procession or march hell-bent on making touble.

Among the pseudo-terrorist groups of the left-wing fringe are two whose methods, though not the intensity of them, bear comparison with the Red Armies of Italy and West Germany. They are the Armed Nuclei for Proletarian Autonomy (NAPAP) and the International Revolutionary Action Group (GARI). Both appear to have contacts with the international movements and made a number of bomb and shooting sorties against public figures in the mid seventies. NAPAP bombed the front door of the Justice Minister, and its members were involved in the murder of the Bolivian Ambassador. GARI members were probably responsible for trying to bomb the Minister of the Interior in Toulouse. Their device exploded prematurely killing two bomb planters.

Such groups are small in number of supporters, some of whom shift effortlessly from one grandly-named revolutionary cluster to another. The successor to NAPAP and GARI is Direct Action, and it too has made violent threats and movements. The organization, which in 1980 attacked and damaged computers of the International Computers Ltd. at Toulouse after several assaults upon similar installations, was probably an offshoot of this movement.

In late 1981 and early 1982, two high-ranking officials of the U.S. embassy were the targets of what appears to be, as of this writing, a lone assassin. In the first attack on Nov. 12, 1981, Christian Chapman was fired at as he left his home for work but escaped injury by crouching behind his armor-plated embassy car. However, on Jan. 18, 1982, Lt. Col. Robert Ray was fatally wounded by a shot fired by an assassin. Both French and American authorities have speculated that both attacks were the work of Libyan hit men sent out by Col. Qaddafi in answer to the Reagan Administration's hostility to his regime.

What really alarmed France during the autumn of 1980 was an ugly eruption of right wing "Black Terrorism," as it is called. Neo-Nazis detonated a bomb outside the synagogue in a fashionable district of central Paris which killed four people. This attack was followed by a bomb that exploded outside the Bourse, the Paris stock exchange, and a series of attacks on French Jews. These attacks, following the bomb outrages at Bologna railway station and the Munich beer festival, both the work of right-wing extremists, gave rise to fear that resurgent Nazis of Europe were again becoming a serious threat.

In France there were strong suggestions that the police had been infiltrated by right-wing extremists. It also seemed that police officers had been fighting the fanatics of the left for so long they had themselves become fanatics at the other end of the political spectrum.

Although the government later denied that the police in France were riddled with Fascists, there can be little doubt that in its ranks are many who sympathize with the ideas of the new right. Jewish opinion in France was outraged by the attacks upon its community, and there was strong middle of the road support for a purge of the police. Certainly this is a field where counter action is needed to prevent politicization of the police. Strong measures are needed to fight against left-wing terrorism, but if the price is power growth of the extreme right, then the price is too high and would represent a victory for terrorist methods.

8.

Italy: The Carabinieri Fight Back

The terrorist threats facing the two most important countries at the Mediterranean end of Europe was different in quality from that which confronted their northern neighbors. Both Italy and Spain were under attack from compatriot Marxist-Leninist groups of gunmen from 1969 onwards. But, although there is no doubt about their links with the other groups such as the West German Baader-Meinhof gang, they were essentially nationalist in their operations. Tactically they confined themselves to traditional methods of assassination, bombing and kidnapping. They also became expert at intimidating their opponents by shooting them in the legs with crippling effect.

They did not, however, favor the methods exploited by Palestinians and Latin-Americans of hijacking and hostage-taking on an international scale. For this reason the authorities in Spain and Italy felt less pressure to create a special forces army in the manner of Britain and Germany. When it came to counter measures they relied instead on units of traditional *gendarmerie,* in Italy the Carabinieri, who were more opulently equipped with small arms and better trained in their use than ordinary police.

If this was an advantage in many respects, Italy's unpleasant recent political past tended to inhibit the effective use of such force. Italy did not want to slip back into the old ways by creating police forces too strong to be contained by the relatively fragile democratic governments which had finally come to power. One of the principal aims of terrorist groups is to bring about the collapse of such liberal democracies by forcing them to take repressive measures which become so tyrannical that the people rise against the government and so create an atmosphere of revolution. Because it was aware of this danger, the Italian government was perhaps over-cautious in forging the weapons to counter the assault of the terrorists.

Terrorism in Italy is by no means exclusively an affair of left-wing fanatics. In Rome and in Northern Italy high fascist groups such as the Ordine Nuovo are at work with the same violent objectives in mind. The MSI, Movimento Sociale Italiano, provided a cloak of political respectability for the extreme right. Italy therefore had to face terrorists on two fronts.

The first notable terrorist attack in Italy was the explosion of a bomb in the Piazza della Fontana, Milan, on December 12, 1969, which killed 14 and injured 80. That was the work of right-wing militants, but the reaction of the police was to arrest a well-known anarchist, Pietro Valpreda. It was no less than nine years before the case was finally closed with the acquittal of Valpreda. During this period two neo-fascists convicted for the attack fled while under house arrest.

This demonstrated not only the lethargy of Italian judicial machinery, but also the inefficiency of the police. Even worse for the cause of law and order were ugly facts which emerged during the trial about the involvement of the security forces themselves in the manipulation of right-wing terrorism. It was a time of indiscriminate right-wing terrorism and serious rioting in the same cause in Reggio Calabria, and this came to be known as the "strategy of tension," with the aim of producing the atmosphere of panic and chaos which they hoped would enable the neo-fascists to seize power by a *Coup d'état*. Meanwhile the MSI in parliament and the neo-fascists outside set themselves up as the patriots, using public sympathy for police officers killed on duty to stir up more riots and at the same time to create tension within the police forces.

Left-wing groups, such as the early Red Brigades under their founding father Rento Curcio, took to the streets in opposition and then moved into clandestine operations in the cause of "proletarian justice," themselves seeking to draw the Italian workers along behind them. In 1972 Giangiacomo Feltrinelli, a millionaire publisher who had turned to the left-wing cause and founded the Partisan Action Groups in order to combat the fascists, killed himself when explosives detonated as he placed them by an electric pylon near Milan. It was later revealed that this had been a training exercise, for he was unskilled with high explosives. But at the time it was firmly believed that this was all part of the "strategy of tension," provocative right-wing terrorism manipulated by the security forces, so as to discredit the left.

There is little doubt that the secret intelligence services and many police officers were indeed active sympathizers with the neo-fascist cause and in numerous cases they were right-wing activists. Evidence has come to light that the secret intelligence services sometimes knew in advance of neo-fascist operations and did nothing to prevent them. An example was the plan by right-wing militants to seize and occupy the Ministry of the Interior in Rome in 1970. There was a similar plot in 1974.

During the 30-year period of rule by one party, the Christian Democrats, through a series of coalitions, successive Prime Ministers and Ministers concerned with security had encouraged the security services (then known as SID and SDS) to infiltrate both left–and right-wing groups. The then head of SID, General Vito Miceli, who later became a right-wing Deputy, supervised the relationship between his officers and the neo-fascists. It now appears that the penetration of militant groups on both wings corrupted security officers and also promoted inefficiency, for in neither case did the undercover work lead to the prevention of terrorism.

The Italian public were rightly cynical from the start about their ever-changing governments and deeply suspicious about the motives of their security services. Throughout the post-war period all intelligence operations were theoretically supervised by the President of the Republic who had the duty to be informed on all state security matters by the Prime Minister and his Defense Minister. But the services were not accountable to parliament. They depend heavily on the sources of their NATO allies, and in particular the U.S., and their main function was to keep watch of Soviet and Communist activities.

Plotting was already rife in the service in 1964 when General De Lorenzo, head of military intelligence, was accused of using his position to launch a *coup*. Yet parliament showed no great enthusiasm for demanding investigations and stronger control, fearing, it is suspected, that many unpleasant skeletons might emerge from the security cupboard. Nonetheless, there were demands for reform and re-organization after court evidence had emerged for the connections between the services and terrorists in 1974 and 1975.

In the latter year the *Corriere dell' Aviatore* revealed that a *coup* from the right was being plotted as a "therapeutic measure," to resolve "a dangerous political situation."

After these revelations a number of high-ranking officers were charged with incitement to subversion. The general suspicion was that the intelligence services and the armed forces were dominated by neo-fascist sympathizers, and therefore their information about left-wing groups was untrustworthy. There were even dark suppositions, totally unproven, that behind all the plotting was one extraordinary mastermind obscurely referred to only as the *grande vecchio,* the grand old man.

Be that as it may, demands for a more thorough reform of intelligence services before the June 1976 election resulted in the dissolution of SID and SDS. They were replaced by the Democratic Security Information Service (SISDE) and the Military Security Information Service (SISMI) to deal respectively with internal security and espionage and counter espionage. Clearer terms of reference were established and links with parliament were ordered through a coordinating committee called CESIS. The main difficulty was to find a suitable head for SISMI, a post which remained vacant for some time. Many senior officers were dismissed, others resigned; and for some time chaos reigned in the service.

In addition, the intelligence services scandal brought popular demand for easier access for inspection of personal files kept by the authorities, as it had in the post-Watergate United States. Not only terrorists, but also criminals took advantage of this liberal move. Their lawyers demanded to see the dossiers, and examining magistrates were forced to grant many such requests. The advantage for the wrongdoers was that even though the intelligence files did not record the names of informants against them, it was not difficult from close examination of the record to guess their identities. A number of police informers were either murdered or "knee-capped" by criminals and terrorists, thus terrifying into silence people who might have been inclined to pass on information. Police sources of information dried up, and as a result there was a dramatic rise both in terror incidents and in criminal kidnappings in 1976–8.

Therefore, at precisely that moment in the mid seventies when terrorism both from right and left began to offer its most serious challenge, the Italian intelligence services were at their weakest and most divided. During the decade there were no less than 9,361 terrorist attacks, 116 people were killed and 355 were wounded, and the rate of arrest and imprisonment of those responsible was remarkably low. There can be no doubt that a major factor in this situation was the total disorganization of the intelligence service.

In 1978 the freedom of information law was amended so that intelligence agencies might only be ordered to produce personal files on the orders of the Cabinet Anti-Terrorist Committee, the chairman of which was the Prime Minister, with the Minister of the Interior as his chief executive. Even so, much remained to be done to make the intelligence-gathering organizations efficient, for even in 1979 the two branches of the service were only up to 70 percent and 50 percent of their authorized strength.

The splitting of SID into two parts led to a clash of influence, for the military wing was far from pleased to see its anti-subversion mission on home territory passing exclusively into the hands of SISDE. This bureaucratic tiff led to a further complication when the Italian police set up their own intelligence unit at the Ministry of the Interior, and named it UCIGOS (Ufficio centrale per le investigazioni generale e per le operazioni speciali). It concentrates on the anti-terrorist campaign and operates its own special units in the field.

Long after northern European countries had begun improving

their defenses as a protection against the new onslaught of terrorists, Italy remained in great danger through the weakness and inefficiency of its security forces. The threat came not only from the terrorists but also from organized crime. Since the middle seventies up to 80 people a year have been kidnapped in Italy. Even though 90 percent of these kidnappings were criminal rather than political, the fact remained that something needed to be done to strengthen the forces of law and order all round.

The event that convinced the Italian authorities of the urgent need for action against the growing threat of the Red Brigades was the kidnap and murder in 1978 of Aldo Moro, the Christian Democrat former Prime Minister, who was expected to become Italy's next President. On the morning of March 16, a well-drilled squad of the Red Brigade ambushed his car, killed his five bodyguards and abducted the old man. They held him for 54 days, during that time they conducted a mockery of a trial and demanded the release of Red Brigade terrorists in an exchange deal. This the government rejected. On May 9th they shot Moro dead with a Skorpion machine pistol and dumped his body in the boot of a Renault parked in a Roman street half way between the party HQ of the Communists and the Christian Democrats.

It was one of the well-known high-water marks of terrorist brutality, of "armed public relations" comparable to the killing of Hans-Martin Schleyer, or indeed to the Munich massacre. The Moro affair gave impetus to a more aggressive policy of dealing with terrorism in Italy.

On the day he became Prime Minister, Giulio Andreotti, a protege of Moro's, summoned his Inter-Ministerial Committee on Security (CIS). It consisted of diplomats, the military, police and intelligence men. He told them of his worries about the low morale of the Italian public and the danger of panic. The Prime Minister at once proposed special laws permitting preventive arrest, making telephone tapping easier and allowing the bugging of prison cells in Turin occupied by members of the Red Brigade.

He also took the first steps toward bringing together the traditionally rival forces of Italian police. There were three main groups and each was operated by a different ministry. There was the Public Security Guard (GPS)—50,000 strong, composed originally of urban police forces—which was under the orders of the Ministry of the Interior. There was the paramilitary Carabinieri—85,000 strong—operated by the Ministry of Defense of rural police work and frontier protection. As Italy became industrialized and cities grew in size the work of the police and of the Carabinieri overlapped in many places and rivalry grew between the two groups. Then there were the 42,000 men of the Finance Guards (GE) whose main task was to deal with currency and smuggling offenses on behalf of the Ministry of Finance. The GE have become increasingly important in the war on terrorists because of their involvement in investigating the payment of ransom money, the tracing of its origins and in preventing smugglers from bringing weapons across frontiers.

Already in 1974 the government had made one attempt to coordinate Caribinieri and police by establishing the General Inspectorate for Action against Terrorism, which had achieved something at national level, though regionally and locally the forces were as divided as ever.

The first urgent task was to reorganize anti-terrorist forces and to ensure that the three groups exchanged information among themselves—not an easy business. But although there is still rivalry, they now work together on internal security tasks under the orders of the Ministry of the Interior. The working rule is that whoever arrives first on the scene of the terrorist attack handles the case. All action is now directed by an examining magistrate, a state legal official, whose task it is to coordinate and control the course of the investigations.

As the Moro affair continued the Interior Minister, Francesco Cossiga, formed a kind of think-tank to help him to track down the kidnappers. He asked for assistance from the British SAS and from West Germany, for he knew the value of their computerized technology, and had been greatly impressed by the Mogadishu exploit of the GSG9. Both these Common Market partners of Italy replied with prompt offers of assistance.

The United States, which traditionally has strong links with Italy, was also asked to give a hand but the CIA felt unable to help. At one time such a call would have been answered at once. But after wrestling with the problem for two weeks, Stansfield Turner, then the director of the Agency, came to the conclusion that Congressional restrictions imposed upon him after the Watergate scandals made it impossible for the CIA to help. Signor Cossiga then asked for the advisory services of an American crisis manager, Dr. Steve R. Pieczenic, a deputy assistant Secretary of State at the State Department. In conditions of high secrecy he was permitted to go to Rome and advise. Dr. Piec-zenic's claim to be a specialist at the age of 34, apart from the fact that he was a Harvard-trained psychiatrist and a political scientist from MIT, was largely based on his successes in handling the Hanafi Muslim siege in Washington, and also the hijacking of an airliner by Croatian émigrés in New York. His task was to advise on strategies and tactics in the Moro affair.

He realized at once that the abduction of Moro was an entirely new development in terrorism. It was the first time a senior statesmen had been kidnapped for political purposes without any specific demands being made. (The suggested exchange of Red Brigade prisoners for Moro came very late in the affair.) After talking to the Minister of the Interior he came to the conclusion that the purpose of the Red Brigades was the classic one of creating conditions for a civil war by provoking repressive measures.

"It is also the strongest attempt we in the Western world have seen by terrorists to destabilize a democracy." For that reason he considered it necessary to demonstrate that "no man is indispensable to the viability of the nation state."

There can be no doubt that by the time this emergency developed in Italy, the Red Brigades, or rather the second wave of the Red Brigades who were altogether tougher and more professional than the "historic" first generation, were a powerful force.

They had used millions of pounds worth of lira stolen in bank raids to establish what they called "columns" in Genoa, Turin, Milan and Rome. They were estimated to have some 400 hard-core men and women working and shooting for the cause full time. And they were backed by a similar number of enthusiasts who could be called upon for assistance. The kidnapping of Aldo Moro had been carried out by a specially-trained force drawn from among the professionals. Clearly the Brigades represented a serious challenge to government and the time had come for the government to take counter action.

The first consequence of the crisis was that the Christian Democrats and the powerful Italian Communist Party formed an unlikely alliance to condemn the methods of the extremists of which they equally disapproved. It was this *de facto* agreement that ultimately made it possible to strengthen the hand of the security forces.

But in the months following the death of Moro, the nation was wracked by crisis and indecision.

The public was shocked that killers could stalk the streets of the great Italian cities, that it was unsafe to go out at night to eat in a restaurant, that men were shot down on their way to work. Terrorism had become a dreadful sub-culture in Italian life. Was it caused by unemployment, the educational crisis, or was it the result of frustration brought on by the inefficient bureaucracy and the rapid industrialization of Italy? Dozens of newspaper articles and books on terrorism explored every possibility, and in their enthusiasm for the new *deus ex machina* of sociology they found dozens of explanations, none of which seemed entirely to fit the case.

None of the political solutions on offer seemed to help very much either. The traditional right demanded strong measures. The noisy Social Movement Party called upon the government to take exceptional powers under Article of the 217 of the Public Security Act. The more emotional demanded that a state of emergency be declared.

It was at this time that Signor Viginio Rognoni, the Minister of the Interior, who had succeeded the unfortunate Francesco Cossiga when he was forced to resign over the Moro murder, reported that a new terrorist group called *Prima Lina* was competing in the terrorist business with the old established Red Brigades. What seemed even more alarming was his report that the university oriented terrorists, the spoiled brats of revolution, seemed to be succeeding at last in drawing to their cause militants from young Italian factory workers. This distressed the traditional Communists as greatly as it alarmed the right wing.

While the search still continued for the killers of Aldo Moro, the government took note of a "situation of emergency" and imposed a series of strict measures. Included among the decrees was one making it possible to impose a maximum penalty of life imprisonment for kidnappers who killed their victims. Wisely the government did not bring back the death penalty even though there was popular clamor that they should. Instead increased powers were given to the police in the matter of detention, interrogation and wire-tapping.

At the same time the authorities called in a special military squad that had been in training in Sardinia in anti-terrorist techniques. Little has been heard of this military unit established as such squads were in every European country after the Munich affair. For the Italians decided to leave anti-terrorism in the hands of the police and Carabinieri, and so far they have not had to face overseas terrorist operations.

To hit back at the terrorists in Italy the government chose, not a squad of amazingly fit and well-trained young men as favored by the British and the Germans, but a portly 57-year-old general of the Carabinieri named Carlo Alberto Dalla Chiesa. In his photographs he appears to be the very soul of braggadocio—all medals and glorious peaked cap—the kind of man that central casting might have chosen for a part originally planned for Vittorio De Sica. We say appears to be, for Dalla Chiesa is a secretive officer not given to holding forth in public or allowing himself to be interviewed.

At heart he seems to be an old fashioned policeman. All his male relations have served in the Carabinieri. He seems to enjoy the discipline of it all, and he relishes the chase. It is not for nothing that they call him the "Fox." Before he became known to a wider public as a hero of the terrorist wars, the general already had an impressive record. After fighting in the Italian resistance in World War II he was posted to Sicily in 1945 and took vigorous action there against the Mafia. His record shows that he was responsible for the arrest of 77 Mafiosa, including the notorious Frank Coppola.

The general had experience of fighting the Red Brigades even before the Moro affair. Using traditional police methods he had managed to infiltrate the terrorist organization and had persuaded captured members to inform on their ex-comrades.

Indeed Dalla Chiesa is the officer credited with the eventual capture of Renato Curcio, the original leader of the Red Brigades. He had previously been in charge of prisons, and after a number of terrorist escapes from these ramshackle and crowded establishments he was responsible for setting up high-security prisons. He now began to use his knowledge of prison life, and successfully placed some of his undercover officers inside, to spy upon their cell-mates. He used his underworld contacts, bought information and kept his men following suspects until finally they made a mistake. In fact he employed the old, tried and sometimes unsavory methods of the professional law enforcer.

A decree on August 10, 1978 appointed him coordinator of anti-terrorist operations though he had no title other than general of Carabinieri, to control with extremely wide-reaching powers a special anti-terrorist group which combined men from the police, the Caribinieri, the Finance Guards and from the secret service. He was to be responsible only to the Ministry of the Interior and the Prime Minister, but had a large and secret budget and achieved more or less complete independence as his methods were seen to succeed. The Italian press at once invented a title for him and began calling him the "super terror hunter."

He went about his job methodically, starting by reading the dossiers and by studying the terrorists' own literature, as well as what had been written about terrorism Then he went into action. He had 50 men initially and eventually built up a carefully chosen team of 150. He impressed them when it came to a big raid by leading it himself, automatic pistol in hand.

The general's methods soon produced results. Within three months he had achieved more than all the police intelligence men had managed before his appointment. Fourteen members of the Red Brigades were arrested, numerous arms caches were discovered and the Italians began to breath more freely. Of course that was not the end of terrorism but General Dalla Chiesa had made a promising start.

It was not surprising that after a while there were criticisms of his methods, for the general is a hard man. He became virtually independent of political control and his great powers have been compared to those of a military governor in Franco's Spain.

Whatever critics think about his methods, there can be no doubt that Dalla Chiesa got on with the job and produced results. That was the view of the politicians when all the major parties supported his re-appointment in August 1979.

Certainly Italian governments appeared to approve of the methods adopted by the anti-terrorist squad. In December 1979 an otherwise feeble government enacted a number of decrees which appeared to be in line with his thinking. The killing of policemen, judges, lawyers and union leaders was to be punished by life sentences, to be enforced to the letter. Terrorists who wounded people in their raids would automatically get double the normal sentence. Even suspected terrorists were automatically refused bail, and abetting terrorism became a crime too.

The decrees also widened police powers, allowing them to hold suspects longer for questioning and to search without a warrant. In addition, any person starting a new bank account with more than $20,000 would have to provide proof of identity, which makes it easier for the police to investigate how they had obtained the money in the first place. The security forces were also authorized to interrogate suspects legally in the absence of a defense lawyer.

In mid 1980 General Dalla Chiesa was dispatched to Milan as commander of the 25,000 Carabinieri in Northern Italy, the principal battlefield of the terrorists. He was given wide-ranging powers and took with him many of his original anti-terror squad. To replace him in his role as national coordinator the government set up a National Commission for Order and Public Security.

Although the government had pondered these measures for some time, they were announced in response to another wave of terrorist attacks. Terrorists had burst into a business school in Turin, selected five students and five teachers and shot them in the legs as a doctrinal warning "not to become servants of the multinationals." Some factory workers were also murdered and three Carabinieri were shot dead in the streets. These attacks convinced the authorities that the two main terrorist bands, the Red Brigades and the Front Movement had joined forces and were working together.

But by the end of 1980 it appeared that the strength of the left-wing terror groups had been greatly reduced by General Chiesa's operations, and by the re-organization of security forces. In the earlier months of that year some 240 left-wing terrorists and 90 right-wing terrorists were sent to prison. In the course of security operations police seized nearly 6,000 weapons and 350,000 rounds of ammunition. They also rounded up 3,000 kilos of explosives, mortars and grenade throwers. The number of terror attacks fell in 1980 to 1,264 from a record 2,395 in 1978.

Official statistics showed that there were still 39 members of the Red Brigades on wanted lists, while 322 were held in prison. One hundred and fifty-five of the Armed Proletarian Nuclei were under arrest with only five still wanted. Front Line had 180 of its members in jail while 46 were still being sought.

But it would be wrong to deduce from such successes that the battle against terrorism in Italy is over and won. For even as the left-wing urban guerillas suffered setbacks the right-wing Armed Revolutionary Nuclei, NAR (not to be confused with NAP, the left-wing Armed *Proletarian* Nuclei) placed a time bomb in the railway station at Bologna in August 1980 which killed 84 people and wounded another 200. The aims of Fascist terror groups are the same as those on the extreme left—to bomb Italy into a state of tension and destabilization which will eventually lead to totalitarian rule.

So far as the anti-terrorist campaign against the Red Brigades and the other main left-wing group Front Line is concerned, the Italian authorities believe that the worst is over. Speaking at the beginning of 1981, General Umberto Cappuzzo, overall commander of the Carabinieri, and the most senior officer concerned in the struggle, reported that 700 suspects were arrested the previous year. Front Line, he declared, had almost been liquidated together with a number of smaller groups. "They have failed politically and now capture terrorists who confess are making more uncertainty for them."

The same feeling is apparent in Italian public opinion. The Carabinieri in particular have again become popular. Great sympathy with them was apparent after the murder by Red Brigades of General Enrico Galvaligi, the chief aide of Dalla Chiesa, as he returned with his wife from New Year's midnight mass. The terrorists carried a gift-wrapped basket of wine as though they were delivering it, and they shot the general at close range as he reached into his pocket for money to tip them.

As the head of the Carabiniere said, "Terrorism can still strike hard. They always have the initiative and they need only a group of four or five." Or even one, we might add. For in early summer of 1981 a Turkish loner made his way to St. Peter's Square in Rome and shot and wounded the Pope.

The Red Brigades proved they still had striking power in December 1981 when they kidnapped U.S. Brig. General James L. Dozier from his Verona apartment. But the Italian authorities struck back even harder 42 days later, freeing Dozier unharmed and capturing five armed terrorists in a Padua apartment.

At this writing, only a few days after Dozier was freed, not all of the facts are in. However, it is apparent that his liberation represents a major defeat for Italian terrorists. First of all, the signs clearly indicate that the police were led to the terrorists' hideout by information from captured or defecting members of the Red Brigades. Secondly, during the nationwide manhunt for Dozier's captors, involving more than 5,000 personnel, more than 20 members of the Red Brigades or The Front Line were captured, including Giovanni Senzani, one of the leading figures in the Red Brigades. Thirdly, the information developed in the investigation of the Dozier kidnapping was expected to quickly lead to the capture of other terrorists. And finally, the success of the operation was certain to boost the morale of the police and to dishearten the terrorists and their sympathizers.

9.

Spain: The King Goes to War

Spain is the European country most threatened by terrorism. It is also the nation least well equipped, and least capable of defending itself against a complicated threat which comes simultaneously from two diametrically opposite directions.

On the one hand are the few hundred regional terrorists of ETA, the Basque separatist movement, whose aim is to establish a socialist Basque peoples' republic in the northern provinces. Their tactic is to murder officers and off-duty soldiers of the Spanish army; they have already killed a number of generals and others of field rank, and wounded the chief military aide of King Juan Carlos. Were they to succeed in provoking the armed forces by this tactic into launching a successful *coup d'état* they would destroy the fragile plant of Spanish democracy.

The brutal Basque campaign interacts upon the other notable menace to the continuance of the liberal state in Spain. For there are many senior officers in the armed forces, and in the head-quarters of the security forces, determined to eliminate Basque terrorism, indeed all terrorism, by imposing military government upon the nation. Their aim is to overthrow the democratic monarchy in order to restore the glories, and the law and order of the defunct Franco régime.

Caught between this hammer and this anvil are the courageous young King Juan Carlos, the middle-of-the-road parliamentary parties and the business community. Their ambition is to make Spain a prosperous member of the European Common Market, and of NATO; and to restore the nation to a respectable position within the European community. The liberal society is still a novelty. Franco died in 1975, and three years later the new constitution brought the first taste of democracy for 37 years. That the change was popular is shown by the fact that fewer than 2 percent of the voters in free elections voted for the far right which for so long had governed the country, claiming that it represented a majority.

For years the question had been: what will happen to Spain after Franco? The great fear was that the army, the mainspring of Franco's dictatorial power, would move their armor on Madrid and seize power to perpetuate the old régime; then the powerful Spanish Communist Party would strike back with the big battalions of workers, and a fresh civil war like the one which tore Spain apart in the thirties would break out. But things had changed in Europe and Fascism seemed to most Europeans as well as to most Spaniards merely a curious survival from an earlier age. Fearful though the older generation of Spaniards were at the passing of a régime which, whatever else it had done, succeeded in imposing law and order for 40 years, they were ready to see power transferred to a new democracy. The process of change was confirmed by King Juan Carlos, designated and trained as the new leader by Franco himself, who offered the influence and prestige of his Crown to the new régime. Through loyalty to the Crown even the most diehard of the old generals accepted the changeover, though some of them with ill grace and foreboding.

The terrorists then began their distructive operations. Warning signs of the new perils facing Spain had already appeared in the sunset of the Franco years. The ETA Basques had embarked upon armed action in 1967, and in 1973 they performed their first big horrifying act of terror by murdering Admiral Carrero Blanco, the Prime Minister. Such was their expertise, and the quantity of explosive used, that his car was blown over a four story building. It was a declaration of terrorist war.

ETA developed their campaign most actively in the Basque country itself. But they also began a deliberate attack against high-ranking military officers, killing two generals in Madrid in the first year of the new constitution. Their aim even then was to provoke the army into unconstitutional action so as to enlarge the conflict. It was notable that they also chose as targets for murder members of the middle-of-the-road Democratic Center Party.

General elections placed a middle-of-the-road government in power under a capable Prime Minister, Adolfo Suarez. The Communist Party became legal, gaining only 10 percent of the vote. Content for the moment with its new found freedom to take seats in the assembly, it accepted the democratic framework—to the intensive dislike of the Franco generals still in command of the army. It began to look as though Spain could settle down as a stable member of the European club.

But other forces were at work. A number of extreme rightist militant groups, such as New Force and the Warriors of Christ the King, began to take to the streets, and then moved toward violence. The Apostolic Anti-Communist Alliance modelled itself on the Argentinian Triple A (Alianza Anti-Communista Argentina) which had gone into hard terror, torturing and murdering leftists.

At the other end of the spectrum was GRAPO, Grupa de Resistencia, Antifascista Primo Octobre, named in memory of the day when four Madrid policemen were assassinated in retaliation for the execution of five convicted urban guerillas in 1975. They launched a campaign of kidnapping, murdering police officers, bank robberies to finance their activities, and political murders. It is believed that they were responsible for an attempt on the life of the King during a visit to Majorca. A senior police officer described them as, "the armed wing of a radical breakaway group of the Spanish Communist Party," though others considered them to be Maoists. Despite the arrest of 21 of their members after police undercover men had penetrated their cells in 1978 they were still able to mount operations the following year. But the police by this time knew a great deal about them, having discovered their safe houses and taken away documents and equipment. A further setback came when their 29-year-old leader, Juan Carlos Delgado de Codex, was shot dead while resisting arrest. After his death GRAPO took another knock when their explosives expert and bomb-maker was arrested in Valencia.

At that stage the morale of the security forces was still high. The parliamentary monarchy had inherited from General Franco one of the most powerful and numerous police organizations in Europe. They were trained and encouraged in intelligence work to detect enemies of the Fascist régime, and clearly organizations like GRAPO and ETA were such enemies. The undercover men operated efficiently without caring too much who they hurt in the process of investigation. Several times they have claimed GRAPO had been broken, and once asserted 100 of its 130 activists were in prison. Yet the terror group still murders.

The National police force consists of 40,000 men, backed up by the *gendarmerie* force of the 60,000 strong *Guardia Civil.* The Civil Guard, originally established to rid Spain of bandits on the roads, are conspicuous for their tricorn patent-leather helmets. In addition, the 240,000 strong Spanish army was trained in internal security duties and had its own well-informed intelligence units. The army is handicapped by the fact that it also has no less than 1,400 generals, including 404 of them on the active list. It is probably the oldest corps of officers in the world and the army is still led by generals who fought in the Civil War in the thirties. An attempt is currently being made with the Army Reform Bill to force officers to retire at the age of 66, but there is still resistance because this would result in a purge of right-wing soldiers.

The most powerful terrorist group confronted by the army and security forces is ETA, initials standing for the Basque words *Euzkadi Ta Askatusuna*—the Basque Homeland and Liberty Group. It is an intensely nationalist formation with its roots in the long struggle of the Basques to achieve independence, and in that respect it is comparable with the IRA. It is deeply conscious of Basque history and pitiless in its methods of operation. The present organization dates from 1959 when it developed as a radical splinter group from the Basque Nationalist Party.

To counter its activities in 1968 General Franco declared a state of emergency and tried to break the organization; he failed and ETA has pursued an unremitting and increasingly violent campaign of bombing, kidnapping and assassination ever since. Insofar as the organization's aims were originally nationalist they enjoyed a good deal of popular support in the northern provinces of Spain.

In an attempt to defuse the crisis and bring an end to terrorism by political means in the cause of national harmony, King Juan Carlos made a number of concessions early in his reign to the revolutionary ambitions of the Basques. Their national flag was given official recognition, and so was the Basque language which had been banned by Franco. The King went further, and in 1978 legalized the political wing of ETA. These measures did indeed satisfy many moderate nationalists, and they were the first steps towards reconciliation between the Basques and Spain.

The Basque region is now an autonomous area with its own regional government, accepted by popular vote despite efforts from ETA to wreck a referendum on the subject. Presiding over the government is Carlos Garaicoetxea, leader of the middle-of-the-road Basque Nationalist Party. There was even an agreement from the central government that they would gradually withdraw Spanish security forces from the region. Yet even this is not enough to satisfy the wild men of ETA. It is now their declared, and seemingly impossible, aim to set up a new country comprising four provinces of Spain including Navarre, and three districts of France across the Pyrenees. The hardcore terrorist leaders of what is now known as ETAM (standing for military, the other wing being political) call themselves Marxist-Leninist and insist that the greater Basque state must also be socialist. In the words of a Basque historian who, with 30 others, signed a letter opposing terrorism, "ETA's idea of a military solution is crazy."

Continuing Basque terrorism provides a sad reinforcement for the argument that in dealing with guerilla groups no government can hope to gain peace by making reasonable concessions. These are not reasonable people and the only way to deal with them is to make it impossible for their violent plans to succeed.

ETA is a problem not only for the Spanish government but for the regional Basque government as well. For unless the Basque government can take measures strong enough to cope with its militants there is a grave danger of civil war breaking out within the autonomous region itself. It all hinges upon how quickly the Basques can set up an effective police force, for not until then will it be possible for Spanish Civil Guards to leave the region.

Only native Basque police officers can hope to get the cooperation and information needed to crush terrorism.

At present the Madrid government tends to post their young
police officers untainted by service and training under the Franco
régime into the Basque region. But in the nature of things they
lack the professional experience vital for their difficult task.
They are targets for the terrorists, and it is not surprising that they
leave as soon as they have a chance of getting transferred to a less
bloodthirsty part of Spain.

After gunmen raided a bar at Zarauz on the Biscay coast in
November 1980 and killed four off-duty traffic officers of the
Civil Guard, the Basque regional government issued a statement
warning that the spiral of violence would lead the area to
catastrophe. It also reminded the central government of the
urgency of setting up Basque security forces. The Madrid Interior
Ministry believes it will take at least three years before such
forces can be deployed, and even then they will contain only a
bare majority of Basques. Meanwhile the Basque authorities
began seeking outside advice on how to cope with security in
their own country. In the summer of 1980 they called in private
security advice from a London firm employing former SAS
troopers and ex-Commandos from the Royal Marines. Negotiations were later reported under way for an official training
mission from the SAS to take over the training course. It is not
only the Basques, but also the Spanish Civil Guards, brought up
in the old dictatorial school of repression, who lack training in
sophisticated methods of coping with terrorists.

Basque terrorism also has international dimensions. There are
French Basques living north of the Pyrenees, and there is no
doubt that they give help to people they consider to be compatriots in Spain. ETA men on the run frequently cross the border to
find refuge in safe houses in France.

In the summer of 1980 Juan Jose Roson, the Spanish Interior
Minister, spoke harshly to the French after a wave of terrorist
bombing had hit Spanish Mediterranean holiday resorts, frightening off the tourists and damaging the economy.

At the end of 1980 a diplomatic incident occurred when men of
a Spanish counter-terror unit crossed into the French town of
Hendaye, entered a bar and killed two men and injured ten
others. Pursued by the French police, they returned to Spain with

the help of frontier officials. The café was well known as a meeting place for ETA sympathizers.

The French Foreign Minister protested strongly and warned Spain not to use French territory in attempts to resolve "an internal Spanish problem." France has no wish to become involved in Basque terrorism though French security men are well aware that an extensive cross-border terrorist network existed within their territory. While Franco was still in power they turned a blind eye to such activities, partly because the Franco government had tolerated the presence of French officers of the Secret Army when it was plotting against General de Gaulle in the fifties. In 1979, and ostensibly because Spain had now become a democracy, the French government became less tolerant of Basque plotters and removed their status as political refugees, sending a number of them into forced residence elsewhere.

After the Royal government in Madrid had put into effect its more liberal policy towards the Basques it began to look as though they might succeed in removing popular support in the Basque country for ETA. The gesture made by the King in legalizing the political side of the movement did indeed satisfy the majority of moderate nationalists. But as is often the case with terrorists, the hard core simply regarded it as proof that their brutal methods were succeeding and demanded more concessions. ETA leaders had become so accustomed to terrorism as a way of life, that they refused to abandon terrorism in order to achieve a reasonable compromise. They stepped up their campaign and turned their guns upon compatriots who showed signs of going along with the new policies of Madrid.

The aggressive military wing of ETA struck back at the Spanish government by stepping up its assassination campaign against officers and men of the army and of the Civil Guard, with the deliberate aim of provoking the army into action against the new constitution. And their provocations fell on fertile soil, for the armed forces were already restless and fretting against the evils for which they blamed the new democracy.

Already senior officers were voicing their anxieties about the state of the nation. The commander of one military region spoke gloomily of post-Franco Spain, a place of "terrorism, insecurity, inflation, economic crisis, unemployment, pornography and the lack of authority." Elderly generals looked back with nostalgia to the 40 years of stable order under Franco. There were emotional demonstrations at the funerals of soldiers killed by the terrorists, and a captain-general criticized lack of effective action to crush terrorism. "Spain is dying under our eyes," he said. A group of right-wing soldiers was arrested for plotting against the government.

King Juan Carlos, who pointedly drew attention to his function as head of the armed forces by wearing full military regalia when he signed the new constitution, reminded his soldiers: "An army that lacks discipline is no longer an army... The spectacle of indiscipline and disrespect caused by momentary excitement is frankly degrading." Under the new constitution it is laid down that the army exists not only to protect the sovereignty of the nation but also the "constitutional edifice." That the officer corps interpreted this obligation differently from the parliament became clear later.

A group of senior generals and colonels met secretly in Madrid in the winter of 1980 to voice their alarm that the government of Prime Minister Adolfo Suarez was leading the nation to disaster. Emissaries were sent to ask the King to remove him, which he had no power to do, and manifestos began to appear demanding "a corrective solution." This was the beginning of the military plot to overthrow the civil government.

There were in fact two plots. The first, which came to nothing, was for a bloodless *coup* whereby the King and the military were to take over from parliament with the promise to restore democracy once terrorism had been eradicated. It centered around General Alfonso Armada Comyn, who had been closely associated with the King as his teacher and aide. The plan was stillborn because the King refused to go along with it.

Instead other generals organized a more violent plan to seize the government and parliament, a plan which in fact turned them into terrorists, though they did not see it in that light. The timing was arranged to take advantage of the unexpected resignation of Prime Minister Suarez, and the most active organizer of it was Lieutenant Colonel Antonio Tejero de Molino, a Civil Guard officer who had already been found guilty of a previous attempt to seize the Prime Minister.

For the plotting officers the final straw was the visit paid to the Basque provinces by the King, which they interpreted as an official confirmation of Basque autonomy. At Guernica, the ancient Basque capital, Juan Carlos was insulted by Basque radicals.

On February 23, 1981 Colonel Tejero de Molino rounded up 200 Civil Guards, telling them that they were needed to deal with a terrorist crisis in the Cortes, the Spanish Parliament. He took them to the building in a fleet of buses which had secretly been bought by his wife a little while before. Just as the deputies began voting for a new prime minister, Tejero led 200 khaki-clad Civil Guardsmen and plain-clothes police officers into the parliament building. With sub-machine guns blazing the Guards, ignorant of their true mission, stormed the chamber, and took hostage the entire cabinet and 300 deputies.

Colonel Tejero, a portly officer wearing his khaki uniform and the traditional three cornered hat, mounted the rostrum and, finger on the trigger, brandished his automatic threateningly at the Speaker. His Guards ordered the parliamentarians to lie down on the floor. In pictures taken during the attack the whole scene appeared slightly ridiculous, and the colonel looked absurdly operatic. Yet it was a moment of serious danger, for here was an officer whose task was to uphold law and order taking hostge the entire government of Spain, something which not even ETA had ever dared to try.

It soon became clear that the Colonel was by no means alone in the plot. He left the chamber to report over the telephone to General Milans del Busch, the 65-year-old commander of the Valencia military region, and he used the emotive civil war code phrase, "No news, my general," meaning mission accomplished.

Within an hour troops under the orders of General Milans del Busch had taken over the radio building near his headquarters in Valencia which promptly broadcast a statement declaring a state of emergency in that military region. The general, a bitter enemy of democracy, and a veteran of Franco's Blue Division which fought alongside Nazi troops on the Eastern Front in World War II, suspended all constitutional rights and assumed complete power in the region. To make the point clear he sent out his armor to patrol the streets. He then telephoned a number of other officers commanding the other ten military districts of Spain, claiming that he was acting in the name of the King.

From his Zarzela Palace King Juan Carlos was fighting back

and determined to master his rebellious generals. He began telephoning regional commanders to demand their loyalty. He told one general, it was reported later, that the *coup* would succeed "only over my dead body," He ordered General Milans del Busch to end the state of emergency he had declared, and pull back his tanks, which he reluctantly did at dawn. But it was still touch and go, for 13 jeep loads of military police from the crack Brunete armored division joined the military hostage-takers in the parliament building during the night.

It was not until noon the following day that Colonel Tejero was finally convinced the plot had failed and that he must surrender. By this time the King was making plans for an assault on the armed soldiers in parliament which would have been spearheaded by a specially trained, para-military, anti-terrorist unit, GEO, the Special Operations Group.

But at midday the colonel surrendered. The attempted *coup* was over but it left behind a divided army and an anxious nation. King Juan Carlos had to proceed cautiously in bringing to justice those responsible, for harsh measures might have produced another military revolt. Leaders of the majority parties who had themselves been held hostage for 18 hours by terrorists in uniform told the King that at all costs he must avoid humiliating the army, and the King knew that during his crucial night of telephone conversations with army commanders only three of the regional commanders had expressed their immediate loyalty to him as commander-in-chief of the armed forces.

In fact the armed forces in Spain consider themselves a state within a state. This was dramatically demonstrated when lawyers acting for a major who had been charged with plotting to form armed bands, under new anti-terrorist legislation, disputed the right of a civilian court to indict an army officer. Civil courts had only just been given the right to charge officers, even for criminal offenses, when the post-Franco government began reforming army criminal code.

Eventually 30 officers, including three generals, and 17 Civil Guards who took part in the raid on parliament were charged with military rebellion. Their trial was long delayed.

The only people in Spain to derive satisfaction from the events of February were the wild men of ETA military wing and GRAPO terrorists by then working in conjunction with them. They were the true culprits of the army attack on parliament, for their violent acts had goaded the army to rebellion. That is why the King, treading the high wire of policy, decided to take new measures against the terrorists.

In March, after the assassination of more officers, the King told armed forces heads: "It is necessary to act with decisiveness, passing from a posture of patient defense to an energetic offensive." The night before the government of the new Prime Minister, Leopoldo Calva Sotelo, had announced the setting up of a single unified anti-terrorist command, drawing in armed forces representatives together with those of the state security forces, the national police and the Civil Guard. It was to be a ten-man command structure presided over by the Prime Minister himself.

An even more important cabinet decision was to use units of the armed forces for anti-terrorist duties in the northern provinces in combatting Basque terrorists, and to strengthen defenses on the frontier with France. Two aims were in the Prime Minister's mind: to take dramatic measures against ETA without offending moderate Basque opinion; and to give the army a military task to its liking and thereby distract its officers from further political plotting. The danger was, that by sending troops ill-trained and badly equipped for anti-terrorist work they would simply provide the ETA with more targets on their home ground.

To back these military moves the government also initiated legislation to give it new powers of declaring a state of emergency and a state of siege. It became an offense even to join an armed band. Such measures were no doubt helpful to the executive but a grave dilemma still faced the democratic government: how to keep under control over the security forces which were still staffed by Franco officers and which were needed to fight against terrorists. For example, the head of the Security Police was still a devoted follower of Franco. Yet neither the King nor the government dared to carry out a real purge either in the armed forces or in the police and security forces, fearful that it might provoke a new armed rebellion.

That men of the old régime were still in charge and still using the brutal methods of an older generation became apparent in two important cases which roused public opinion. After GRAPO had shot dead a general and three policemen, and ETA wounded the chief military aide of the King, killed a general, a colonel and two soldiers, the security forces were again pushed into counter measures. Three young men arrested as terrorist suspects in the overheated atmosphere of the time died in mysterious circumstances while under arrest. Security men claimed that they tried to escape and had died in a road accident, but bullet wounds were found in the bodies. An investigation was ordered and the prosecution in Almeria demanded the indictment for homicide of a colonel and two Civil Guardsmen.

A second incident concerned the death of an ETA militant named José Arregui who died after being held incommunicado for ten days of interrogation by Madrid police. His body bore marks of torture, including burns on the soles of his feet. In the subsequent scandal the head of the Spanish police and five other senior officers resigned in protest against hostile public reaction to the police.

In an earlier affair allegations were made that police under Manuel Ballesteros, head of police intelligence who was also an officer implicated in the Arregui business, had collaborated with right-wing terrorists. He was alleged to have helped them to recruit right-wing hit men to start a "dirty war" of counter-terrorist armed attacks upon the gunmen of ETA in the Basque country.

All these cases called in question the credibility of the anti-terrorist forces marshalled by the democratic government. They illustrate the special difficulties facing the government of the new Spain under constant pressure to do something about the Basque terrorists, and the terrorists of left-wing groups. For when their murderous campaigns first began the newly-elected government was still in process of changing the laws in order to grant civil rights to a population long deprived of them. Hardly was the ink dry in signatures to new laws before the government had to face the task of granting more powers to the police, giving them a right to hold suspects longer. And these increased powers were wielded by officers brought up in the stern and repressive school of General Franco's state. It is in this respect that Spain differs so strongly from all the other countries whose anti-terrorist precautions are reviewed in this book.

Despite all these difficulties, the summer of 1981 brought some encouraging signs. In May security forces arrested 30 suspects in raids in the Basque country and in Madrid. The new anti-terror command in Madrid, anxious to show that its forces were making an impact, announced that a plot to free ETA terrorists from prison had been uncovered, and 50 more people had been arrested for their connections with ETA.

The one clear and straightforward victory of the government forces in Spain, and the one which gives hope for the future, was the model operation in Barcelona where neo-fascists seized a bank and took over 200 hostages, conducted by the newly-formed Special Operations Group known as GEO. This was its first full-scale intervention.

In May 1981 a band of heavily-armed gunmen burst into the Banco Central, in Plaza de Cataluna, in the center of Barcelona, just as the bank opened for business. They took as hostage at least 200 members of the staff and early customers before making their first demands to police negotiators who had surrounded the bank. What they wanted was the immediate release of Lt. Colonel Antonio Tejero, the ground commander of the attempted *coup* three months earlier. This seemed to prove at once that they were right wingers of a neo-fascist movement.

They also wanted the immediate release of three generals being charged with rebellion after their involvement in the seizing of parliament. Other demands included provision of an aircraft to fly them to Argentina, and a second plane to take the terrorists into exile. If the authorities refused to give in, the terrorist spokesman describing himself only as "numero uno," told police negotiators he would kill the hostages one at a time. A curious feature about what appeared to be a classic terrorist hostage-taking operation was that both Colonel Tejero and the New Force neo-fascist group denied they had any connection with it.

In Madrid, Prime Minister Sotelo summoned his crisis control committee, and the heads of the new anti-terrorist organization. They ordered the stand-by unit of the Special Operations Group to fly to Barcelona. Within hours the 60-strong task force was driven up to the bank in army vehicles, and the commander made a reconnaissance. GEO men in yellow oilskins made their way into the sewers just outside the bank, and began preparing to dig and blast their way into the bank from underground. Their snipers took up positions round the bank to cover doors and windows.

Little attempt seems to have been made to talk the 24 armed men from the building. The government was determined to show on this occasion, the first great hostage-taking drama in recent terrorist history in Spain, that it had the will and the trained men to force surrender. The siege began early on Saturday and as night fell on Sunday the GEO squads were on start lines for their assault operation.

Sub-machine guns blazing, they assaulted the five-story building through doors and windows. The high level of their firearms training may be judged from the fact that in all this firing only one terrorist was killed, and just one of the hostages was wounded. Even more remarkable was the fact that about the time the attack had begun, a number of hostages who had managed to escape the attention of their terrorist guards themselves began breaking out of the besieged building. If the operation had been conducted by less skillful, the number of casualties would have been much greater.

As soon as the first wave had gotten into the bank it was followed by a bomb squad to deal with explosive devices which the terrorists claimed they had positioned within the bank.

The Special Operations Group had been training for months, after a difficult period of its initial recruitment. The Spanish government was determined to build up a force equal in skill to the other crack anti-terrorist forces in Europe. But because of the special political difficulties in Spain in reconciling campaigns against terrorism from two directions, they had to be even more careful in selecting their men. Most of the troopers in the unit came from security police and the Civil Guard. The commander selected young men and young officers not tainted with the fascist past of these forces. The unit called upon foreign advisers to help with their apolitical instruction in the art of anti-terrorist operations. A high standard of discipline was demanded, and it was stressed that the force should be ready for action against any kind of terrorist. Training patterns were the familiar ones pioneered by other European units in the same field, carried out in close secrecy. Even the name of the force commander has been kept secret.

The GEO troops wear khaki uniforms and a distinctive brown beret. They trained both with Heckler and Koch sub-machine guns, and with Uzzi weapons. They also have special sniping rifles, and the whole range of tear gas and stun-grenades. In the bank siege the only weapons necessary were the sub-machine guns, though as we have seen they also used explosives to blast their way into the bank below street level so as to coordinate a surprise assault with the main break in attack.

The only disappointing feature in the break up of the bank siege was that a surprisingly large number of terrorists managed to escape. Of the estimated 24 hooded men who originally went in only ten were arrested. Because of the large number of hostages involved it is likely that some were able to slip away by mingling with the hostages. Even so, had the GEO troopers had more experience in this kind of operation, they would have rounded up the hostages too, so as to sort out any lurking terrorists, as the SAS did in the Iranian Embassy siege in London.

It was, however, a good, professional operation by the new force. Only after the gunsmoke had dispelled did the mystery of who conducted the siege come to light. Even the government seemed far from certain who they were. Three of the arrested men had violent neo-fascist records, and were suspected of having links with Italian and other ultra groups. Large sums of money had been paid out to the terrorists across the border at Perpignan in France, and it is suspected that at least some of the gunmen were hired mercenaries.

The organizers of the raid deliberately drew attention to the earlier failed attempt to overthrow the Spanish government. There is some evidence that they hoped the Barcelona affair would end in bloodshed, which would have further destablized Spain at a critical time and might again have goaded the army to attempt to establish a military government of "national renewal." The fact is prompt intervention by GEO won popular approval, and also gave the King and his government much-needed time to restore their authority.

While security police continued to search flats that had been occupied by the bank gunmen, they came across evidence which led them to the discovery that a tunnel had been secretly dug under the route to the taken by the King on a ceremonial parade the following Sunday. Only 9 feet of the tunnel had been completed but it came to a point only 30 yards from where the King was supposed to be. No explosives were found, but it was considered probable that extremists had planned a large explosion to mark the Kings's appearance in Barcelona for Army Week celebrations. It is certainly in the style of extreme right-wing terrorists to use the tactic of massive explosions, causing the maximum number of casualties, to further their attempts at destablizing democracies. The same tactic had earlier been used by Italian fascists.

Despite these alarms King Juan Carlos duly appeared in

Barcelona for the ceremony and he was cheered by the crowds for his courage in standing up to terrorist attacks from both the right and the left. Indeed, his visit was a triumph for the monarchy and for the new style of Spanish government. Symbolically, while the King in uniform took the salute he was protected by troopers of the Special Operations Group who also had sharpshooters on the roof tops with telescopic lenses on their rifles, and other guards near the Royal saluting base.

Spain has just begun to achieve some results in preparing to counterattack the terrorists. But the real question which must be asked in considering Spanish defense against terrorism is not what has been done in building armed units, but whether the democratic monarchy of King Juan Carlos can first succeed in controlling the army and the security forces, ridding them of terrorists within, and preventing a return to the bad old ways.

10.

Private Enterprise vs. the Terrorists

It is difficult to know for certain which came first. Was it the terrorist threat to international business and its executives, or was it the attempts by the private security industry to convince international business and its executives that they needed the expensive protection of electronic gadgets, private army body-guards and kidnap insurance?

Certainly the private enterprise security business existed long before the present wave of terrorist murders and kidnapping began. Indeed, it can be argued that protection from criminals was first provided by private enterprise, and that official police forces furnished at government expense developed from them.

And, of course, individuals have a perfect right to protect themselves, or to hire people to protect them and their property.

Back in 1855 Allan Pinkerton formed the North Western Police to protect six railroads in the American Midwest. For 50 years he had the field to himself, and it was not until 1909 that William J. Burns established the International Detective Agency. It is now a great multinational corporation with 30,000 employees and an income in 1973 of nearly $2 billion. Wackenhut Corporation, another of the big five American security companies did not go into business until 1954. The other major concerns in the field are Walter Kidde & Co, (Globe Security System) and Wells Fargo.

In Britain and in Europe development of such companies was slower, though there is now an important security industry in most Western countries. They developed in these countries for the same reason they had flourished on the other side of the Atlantic: notably because citizens felt the that official police forces could not provide them with needed security. The fact is that police forces can no longer be relied upon for effective protection against criminals.

This is especially true in the U.S., where an official report announced in 1980 that no less than 30 percent of American households had been touched by crime in some form, and 6 percent of them by violent crime.

In such a situation it is not surprising that the private side of security should have developed. By 1976 a Task Force on Private Security set up by the National Advisary Committee on Criminal Justice Standards and Goals reported that some six billion dollars a year were spent on the industry and the estimated growth rate was up to 12 percent a year. Later estimates put the figure now at around $10 billion annually.

In 1981 an American business research firm predicted a growth rate of 12.5 percent for that year in the commercial and industrial security market. They expected the market would soon be worth $12.5 billion. They also forecast a world market of $5.3 billion for the period 1980–85 in intruder detection sales alone with North America taking half of the cake and Europe some 41 percent.

By then a million people were employed by the industry, a force which far outnumbered the 650,000 law enforcement officers. In the United Kingdom an even more extraordinary picture emerged in the late seventies. Dr. Clutterbuck estimated that private security employed 250,000 men and women, whereas there were only 156,000 soldiers in the British army and the total police forces could only muster 140,000.

The industry had come into being to help individuals and businesses to ward off attacks by criminals, but it was well prepared to expand its activities. While the governments in Western countries were still developing their tactics and marshalling their special forces for campaigns against terrorists, the private armies responded to the threat because they saw a possibility of greatly expanding their market. From resources already developed in the fight against crime of all kinds, the industry was able to offer a variety of services. It could provide guards to protect the homes and offices of potential targets; it could offer bodyguards to ward off terrorists. Even more important, security companies were mass producers of a whole arsenal of equipment—hidden cameras, sensors, electronic surveillance systems, bullet-proof cars, radios—which could be sold to companies and individuals to protect them against terrorist assaults.

There is a commercial bonanza in all this equipment. International exhibitions are held like automotive or boat shows in all major cities to display the latest inventions and models. International security conferences are held in major U.S. cities, many sponsored by ASIS, the American Society for Industrial Security, a powerful organization grouping more than 7,000 executives in the industry. Although terrorists have so far made little impact on life within the U.S., attempts are being made to persuade executives of the need for massive precautions against such activities, just in case.

Eugene L. Fuss, the security systems planning manager for Honeywell's Commercial Divison, writing in *Security Management,* the ASIS magazine, warned, "the full impact of terrorist activity has yet to hit the U.S. but it may well in the next few years." That is why he was recommending equipment designed to turn an executive office into an electronic fortress with a data gathering panel, duress switch, closed-circuit TV monitor, cameras and audible signals. It incorporates microwave motion detectors and videotape recordings. Fuss also suggested the construction of a secret passage for the executive to make his escape and a man-trap system to catch the terrorist. But the unfortunate executive would never himself escape surveillance, always being on camera and having in addtion a miniature radio transmitter so that the console operator would always know where he was.

However rational such suggestions may be, and however horrible the fate of an executive in the hands of a terrorist, such "Brave New World" scenarios do send a tremor down the spine. We quote them to demonstrate how seriously the terrorist threat is being taken be private security.

Even such a cool tactician in the terror wars as Dr. Clutter-buck, who is also a director of Control Risks Ltd., a British insurance and security firm, advocates the need to provide high-risk kidnap targets with "in-depth" protection based on a series of concentric rings. These concentric rings may include: first a general attitude towards security both by those at risk and other staff; then a perimeter; then a more closely protected area; and a final refuge or "keep." Among the items of equipment he detailed are lights, vibratory detectors, acoustic detectors, photo-electric equipment, closed-circuit TV, radio link TV, infrared or microwave beams of buried line sensors.

Even if, by such extreme measures, the potential victim of kidnap or assassination can be protected at home or in his office, he remains vulnerable outside, and in particular in his car. From this fact has developed one of the busiest branches of the security industry—the armoring of cars. In Italy and West Germany after the Moro and Schleyer kidnappings, many garages turned to welding armor plate into cars, especially Mercedes, which have the sturdy construction needed to carry the weight.

Fontauto, the leading Italian car armorers, take things a logical step further by providing a counterattack system, fitting its cars with nozzles which spray attackers with various solutions of noxious chemicals.

In Britian the government has a fleet of "security modified" Rover 3500s which are issued to Cabinet Ministers and leading members of the Opposition. In the private sector, Crayford Engineering of Westerham concentrate on armoring Mercedes-Benz 350s and 450 SELs with a layering of ceramic and plastic which adds 1,000 lb to the weight of the car and costs the owner $150,000. For that price he also gets windows of 30 mm armored glass, floor-protection against grenades rolled under the car, bullet-resistant tires, explosion-proof fuel tanks and a number of electronic gadgets.

Another leading British company, Hotspur Armored Cars, is based in Wales in a discreet little factory where Mercedes, Ford Granadas and even Rolls-Royces are modified to protect their owners.

Hotspur uses a specially toughened light plate which it imports from America. They test each plate by cutting a foot square piece out of opposite corners and then test firing a British Army SLR rifle against them at Bisley. Any plate that does not withstand this test is rejected.

Hotspur craftsmen set out to build a "ballistic monocoque pod" individually tailored to each car. First the car, usually pristine from the showroom, is stripped completely. Everything, even the dashboard and trim, is taken out and steel plating cut to size and slotted together into an overlapping jigsaw is fitted into the inside. There are no chinks, the door armor overlaps, the windows do not open—that lesson was learned in Beirut when an American ambassador was killed because his driver had opened his electrically controlled window. Special plastic templates of the car's windshield are made and shipped to the Goodyear Aerospace Corp. in the U.S. who make windshields in armored glass laminated with a Polycarbonate lining which prevents the sharding of glass if it is stuck by a bullet. Each windshield costs $10,000.

Gas tanks are stripped out and filled with expanded aluminium foil which holds the gasoline in a multitude of tiny cells where it can burn but not explode. Fire sensors and extinguishers are fitted to the trunk and engine. Electronically controlled bolts are built into the doors so that they cannot be opened. Even if the car is blown up by a land mine the pod construction should save the passenger. Compartmentalized tires mean that the driver will have traction as he attempts to escape and he has a fast reverse gear box to help him back out of an ambush. Then if the attackers penetrate these defenses, a master switch is installed in the ignition which prevents the car being driven away. This additional hardware means that heavy duty springs and brakes must be fitted and they too add to the weight; each car loses ten to 15 percent of its performance when it is armored.

How much does it cost to armor a car? "Before I can answer that," say Gerald Davies of Hotspur, "you must decide what you are trying a stop. We armor our cars to withstand a 7.62 mm round from a SLR at 40 metres. Our armor will withstand a burst of automatic fire and so will the glass." The armor will not stop a special armor-piercing bullet and it is therefore incorrect to call the cars bullet-proof, a nicety which is sometimes overlooked by the less scrupulous manufacturers. A Rolls totally retrimmed will cost $185,000. But if its requirement is to withstand handgun fire only $18,000 will be cut off the bill. The Mercedes costs between $120,000 to armor on top of the cost price and the Ford Granada about the same. Protection is an expensive business.

"Every time a terrorist attacks, the business gets a little bigger," says Thomas Nelson, President of Odin International Ltd., sales agent for Advanced Materials Technology Inc. in Virginia. He claims that automobiles are the targets for 80 percent of all terrorist attacks. AMT and the dozen or so U.S. firms that specialize in armoring cars are secretive about their customers, but AMT sells at least 25 a year including ten to the State Department. They offer two models one proof against pistols and sub-machine gunfire and standard hand grenades, and a more expensive one which is bomb proof. Prices vary between $75,000 and $105,000.

Hess & Eisenhardt International Ltd. have been in the business of armoring Presidential cars since the Roosevelt era. They also offer models that go on the offensive with grenade launchers and hostile fire location systems at prices of up to $250,000. Favored cars for the protection treatment in the U.S. are Mercedes, Cadillacs, Oldsmobile 88s, Chrysler New Yorkers, Lincolns or Jeeps and vans.

At the other end of the scale is Rickey Newmayer, President of Newbilt Enterprises, who announced in 1981 he had a clear plastic cube made of one and a quarter inch General Electric Lexguard Laminate, which could be fitted into almost any car to make it bullet proof. The advantage, he claimed apart from the modest price of $32,000 including fitting, was that the protective case could not even be noticed in a moving vehicle. It is called Ballistic Cube 2000.

Armor plating is not enough to provide complete protection. The driver must have the skills needed to know what to do when confronted by terrorists at a roadblock. Courses are now being offered internationally in "defensive driving."

Switzerland has a number of such schools which cater to Italians who want to learn how to do the "bootlegger's turn." The British School of Motoring in London offers a one-day

course for about $275. The course, says BSM, was put together
"utilizing the experience gained in the Special Air Service
Regiment, Class I Police Training Programs and security operations."

A more sustained course is offered by Cititel who claim they
are among the best in the world in teaching "defensive" driving.
Air-Vice-Marshall Arthur Griffiths (now retired) includes a
three-day course among the services offered by his consultancy.
His instructors are ex-servicemen who have been trained in the
art of VIP/Protective driving by the army.

"We know that there is no such thing as 100% safety."
Griffiths says, "But what we can do is reduce the risk. We teach
the drivers to watch out for the signs of kidnappers reconnoitering
a target. We teach the drivers and their bosses to avoid a pattern
of normality. The idea is that they should recognize signs of
trouble before they hit it."

Drivers taking the Cititel course go out to private roads to
practice the various evasion techniques. Cititel uses Ford Granadas, and burn out a full set of tires during each day's tuition. The
idea is to show and then to teach the drivers what to do when
confronted by a roadblock. The simplest and most effective is the
fast "reverse out"—simply go backwards out of danger. The
second is the "handbrake turn"—brake, down shift, then snatch
on the emergency brake and lock the steering wheel hard over.
This will spin a car on a dime. The third is the "J turn" which
entails reversing out and then pivoting the car through 180
degrees. The drivers are made to practice until they can perform
such turns automatically when confronted by a roadblock.

Similar courses are offered worldwide by the International
Security Group, Inc., based in San Antonio, Texas. They teach
evasive driving, and the course includes classroom instruction
with videotape presentations as well as actual driving experience
in simulated situations. The company offers what it describes as
the best armored vehicle available, built by itself and always in
stock. It claims that its lightweight ballistic armor provides the
same protection as heavier tungsten-steel plate protected cars.

As the number of terrorist incidents throughout the world
increased during the seventies and the security industry stepped
up its marketing to convince businessmen of the need to take
protective measures, there was a further development. In the
U.S. a number of organizations went into business to provide the

executive world with up-to-date information on the true facts about terrorism, with emphasis on the kidnapping of business-men.

The report of one private research organization, The Confer-ence Board, stated clearly: "There is no doubt that terrorism has begun to affect the corporate lifestyle overseas, including the way executives live and travel. Ultimately this trend may well influ-ence many business-investment decisions abroad." At that time terrorist incidents were running at up to 300 a month throughout the world, and Conference Board statistics showed that between 1970 and 1978, 567 Americans were kidnapped abroad, of whom more than half were businessmen.

Another new venture in 1979 was the setting up of Risks International to sell information on terrorist activities processed by its computerized data base. The man behind it was Charles A. Russell, a former chief of the Air Force aquisition and analysis division in the Office of Special Investigation. On retirement he established Risks International and says that all his information now comes from open sources such as the press. The service, operated from Alexandria, Virginia, is bought for $1,000 a year by many big enterprises, such as the Chase Manhattan Bank.

Brian Jenkins, of the Rand Corporation, said, "I have a great respect for Mr. Russell's analytic capability and for his data base. It's one of the best inside or outside the Government." Jenkins has had some sharp things to say about the terrorism branch of the security industry which by 1975 was estimated to be doing up to $3 billion worth of business in the U.S. alone. Most of that went on equipment of various kinds and Jenkins declared, "I'm kind of sceptical of the big corporations buying all the hardware. It think they have been spooked into buying a lot of stuff they don't need."

One very useful contribution made by Risks International was publication of executive risk assessments. One paper analyzed the 59 kidnap for ransom operations carried out between March 1972 and January 1979. In every case the kidnappers had demanded a million dollars or more in ransom. Most had taken place in Latin America though the victims were mostly Ameri-can, British and European.

The wave of kidnappings raised the question in corporate circles not only of what precautions might be taken to prevent them, but whether ransoms should be paid or not. It further confronted international companies with the problem about whether they should insure against kidnapping. Business International Corporation put the case for and against. The argument for paying up was that there was an overriding obligation on the company to protect the lives of its employees, and only on that condition would executives accept assignments in high-risk areas. The other side of the argument was the principle that by refusing to pay a ransom companies would help to reduce the danger of more kidnappings. And adversely, money paid to terrorists would help to finance terrorism and put more lives at risk.

On the whole big companies settled for the principle that they should pay and therefore they must insure. In this they were of course encouraged by the insurance companies. The American International Group, Inc., a holding company whose insurance subsidiaries covered a whole range of companies with worldwide jurisdictions, put the matter bodly in a whole page advertisement in the *Wall Street Journal:* "Your chances of being kidnapped are greater than your chances of being killed in a plane crash . . . Kidnapping is not a subject anyone wants to talk about . . . An insurance policy is one form of protection every business executive should consider."

INA Corporation of Philadelphia, the Insurance Company of North America, had already done the same kind of advertising. They pointed out that ransom demands might run into millions and offered frightening information, advice on how to avoid such unpleasantness and finally offered kidnap and ransom insurance. As the sums demanded by terrorists rose—$14.2 million was asked for Victor Samuelson, an Exxon executive in Buenos Aires in 1973—and $5–10 million became the norm, most firms paid up, had also taken out insurance. There was a dramatic leap in the late seventies and now at least three-quarters of the top 200 international firms are carrying coverage of some kind.

American insurance firms were in fact trying to catch up because for a long time the London insurance market had held a clear lead in kidnap insurance. It began when Lloyds of London entered the field in 1933 to underwrite such insurance after the kidnap of the Lindbergh baby.

Anthony A. Cassidy, a Lloyd's underwriter and a director of an underwriting agency, and an established expert on the subject, declared in 1976, "It is true to say that at this point in time, the lion's share of the kidnap/ransom market is supported by

Lloyds." At the time he reported that since 1972, 42 claims had been paid and added, "The present worldwide gross annual income from kidnap/ransom insurance is probably well below $70 million . . . Only because we effectively led the market in these high hazard areas were we able, by adjusting rates, reducing maximum sums insured, and offering limited periods of cover on new risks, to maintain some sort of market in the problem areas where companies most needed it, and most insurers would have deemed it prudent to cut their losses."

Once the company has decided that it will pay the ransom in order to save the employee's life, it is in the interest both of the company and the insurer to make sure the ransom is as small as possible. To negotiate with terrorists or criminals in such circumstances a highly specialized kind of consultant-negotiator has come into being. There are few such men available.

Andrew Nightingale, a former SAS major with much experience in fighting terrorism was one of them. He worked for Lawn West—the name has no significance—a consultancy which performs the functions of loss management in kidnapping insurance and is part of the London based Saladin, KMS group of companies. He later died tragically when his car overturned in Oman.

Nightingale led us through the ritual which is now established for dealing with kidnappers.

> When the chairman of a company is lifted the terrorist who has done the deed usually makes contact with some representative of the company or with his family. My first task is to try to discover who is responsible for the kidnap from the person contacted, then to try to get a voice sound and to establish whether the kidnap claim is genuine. We need to get as much information as possible from the initial contact calls.

It is most important from the insurer's point of view that contact should be made with representative of the company who know about the insurance policy. Ideally only the chief executive officer and one other person ought to know all the details, because if it becomes generally known that a man is insured he becomes an attractive target for kidnappers.

> Before flying off to the scene of the crime, I need a quick

conference with the underwriters, so that everyone is informed. My first check on the spot is to make sure that the local police have been informed, even in parts of the world where the local force cannot entirely be trusted.

Then I must bring myself up to date with the family, or the victim's colleagues on the spot. In the early stages it is better to use a local national to talk to the kidnappers when they make contact, for he will speak the language and be quicker to detect local nuances. Even so the outside negotiator who has long experience of such situations, who has done his intelligence work, can give valuable advice on handling the situation.

Nightingale added, "The negotiator is often a man who in many capacities has faced terrorists before." He has certainly done that because he spent 18 months on an undercover SAS assignment in Northern Ireland before he was "blown."

Another negotiator with experience is Arish Turle, also a former SAS major who is a director of Control Risks, a subsidiary of London insurance brokers Hogg Robinson. Turle has conducted a number of delicate negotiations, including those which led to the release of two executives, Ian Massie and Michael Chattenton, of Lloyds Bank in exchange for $10 million paid to a rebel group in El Salvador. Turle and one of his colleagues were jailed for a time by the Colombian authorites after they had paid $450,000 in a previous ransom deal.

By now the moves in the game are as formalized as a ritual folklore dance, with each side knowing fairly well what the other's reactions will be. For the insurance negotiator there must also be long consultations with the underwriters as well as with the terrorists. He needs to perform the high-wire act of bringing the original exaggerated demand for money down to a level somewhere around, and preferably below, the sum for which the victim is insured without revealing to the kidnappers what that sum is. And he must also try to persuade them to abandon political demands.

"While doing this," explained Nightingale, "you also have to build up a rapport with the kidnappers, find out about them, and then try to dominate them by setting the pattern of the negotiations." In order to safeguard the life of the victim it is necessary to emphasize that if the terrorists do kill him they will lose their bargaining power, and the authorities will be free to attack.

How many people are insured against such kidnap risks? Because of the secrecy maintained by consultants and underwriters it is impossible to produce a precise figure. But one informed insurance man was prepared to tell us that he believed the number must be counted in "tens of thousands." This is not surprising, for the growth of terrorism has demonstrated that company executives and middle-class businessmen are every bit as vulnerable to kidnap, especially when working abroad, as are millionaires. By seizing them terrorists can not only hope to get money, but also to make doctrinal left-wing points against the "wickedness" of multinational companies.

The average cost of such insurance is one percent each year on an estimated ransom demand. If the two Lloyds Bank executives already mentioned were insured, the policy would have cost the bank $100,000 a year, probably more than the cost of the two men's salaries.

It is important to remember that when the insurers are called in they do not themselves pay the ransom. Their job is to reimburse the insured after a full investigation of the claim. This is done partly to deflect criticism that the insurance companies are encouraging kidnappers by paying them off. Their role is that they never pay the kidnappers, they only pay the victim's family or company—whoever has insured him—after deciding to make the payment. If they refuse to pay the ransom then the insurers will not pay out. Nevertheless there is criticism of their role. But one is bound to ask which is the more immoral course of action: to pay off the kidnappers and rescue the men or allow them to be killed on a point of principle?

There is a wide range of public figures for whom governments do not provide the same kind of protection they are able to afford to statesmen. In this field the international private security companies fill a gap in the struggle against terrorists and make good money by providing bodyguards. These days, hardly any self-respecting Arab shiek or his wife would dream of going shopping in New York, London or Paris without a discreet bodyguard at the elbow.

Whenever Sheik Yamani moves outside Saudi Arabia he is protected by a 24-hour a day team. They are British ex-servicemen supplied by Colonel Jim Johnson of the London firm, KMS who are constantly reminded that it is only a few years ago, and before he had such bodyguards, that Sheik Yamani was seized in Vienna by Carlos, the notorious international terrorist.

At the top end of the business first-class service is provided for hefty fees. In London Commander Rollo Watts, former operations commander of the Metropolitan Police Special Branch, trains his beefy recruits and lectures them on the background of international terror. His officers, all in plain clothes, are taught to look after the clients with a minimum of fuss and minimum use of force, for it is irksome for a rich and powerful man to subject himself to being guarded around the clock.

The ultimate task of a bodyguard is to protect his client from an assassin. Commander Watts argues that ideally the guard should never allow his man to get into a situation where guns are used. "Your man can be dead while you are still going for your gun. The task is not to shoot terrorists, but to protect your charge." He is full of commendation for the way Secret Servicemen in Washington acted on this principle when the attempt was made on the life of President Reagan. He says they behaved correctly in bundling him into his car and getting him away from the scene in case a second assassin threatened.

Careful drills are worked out for client protection. There is an element of choreography in all this though the guard must always use his own initiative in the end. Both in America and Britain reputable security companies always stress how important it is for bodyguards to work within the law. In neither country does a private security officer have any right of arrest other than that enjoyed by ordinary citizens. In Britain security officers are not allowed even to carry guns, or indeed so-called offensive weapons, such as nightsticks.

Watt's group often sends teams on jobs abroad to places where it is essential for them to be armed. A two-man team carries a mixture of weapons. One will have a 9 mm Browning pistol with a 13-round magazine loaded and a 20-round magazine in his pocket. The other man will carry a Ruger .357 Magnum with a two and three quarter inch barrel. The point of this combination is to allow the man with the block-busting Magnum to fire six bullets quickly in an emergency. His colleague can then hold off the attackers with his larger supply of ammunition while the first reloads.

Whether in the use of firearms or other techniques good

training is essential. That is why there exists so much resentment in the good firms, both American and British, about the bad reputation acquired by smaller and more unscrupulus outfits.

E. Patrick Mcguire in a report on International Terrorism and Business Security remarked that the competence of individuals offering protection services varied widely and quoted one analyst saying: "Some of the people providing executive protection are really competent. But there are an awful lot of others around who were taking photographs in hotel rooms just a few years ago and really don't know the first thing about providing effective executive protection."

A Rand Corporation report on Private Police in America, expressed concern about the lack of training of some of the officers employed and their low standards of education. It described firearms training in private forces as "woefully inadequate" among those who were allowed to carry guns. The unwarranted use of firearms and illegal arrests by some guards are a constant source of worry to regular police forces.

There are questions too which cause anxiety for respectable and well-organized security companies in both countries. They also worry the general public who have to submit to airport searches. Women out shopping find themselves ordered about by a uniformed security guard in a shopping mall. Such events raise the question of the accountability of men looking and acting like policemen.

Graver fears have also been expressed that security organizations might be used ultimately to provide strong-arm support either for or against a political cause. With companies on both sides of the Atlantic involved in the terrorist wars they might be dragged more closely into political activities.

If the involvement in the politics of terrorism becomes closer still it will reinforce the case made by those both in the industry and the general public for stricter governmental controls over private security armies.

11.

Democracy on the Warpath

By 1981 the countries of Western Europe and the U.S. and Canada had completed the first stages in building their defense against international and national terrorism that had ran amok in the previous decade. This does not mean that terrorism is dead. The terrorists, like the poor, are always with us, but at least their worst excesses have been contained.

Protective measures successfully kept the hijackers at bay. The decisive step by each of the governments whose activities are surveyed in this book was a decision not to give in to armed blackmail. Each country in turn created special forces, and equipped thcm to fight those militant squads who shoot their way into embassies, banks and other public buildings to seize hostages, to murder and to bomb. By so doing they discouraged fresh attacks. New tactics were developed to combat terrorist operations; military and police technology was improved to provide

177

the weapons and devices to help with their task. The need for better intelligence was recognized so as to prevent violence before it happened. Computer technology was pressed into service by the police in order to pre-empt terrorists by discovering in advance who they were. The phenomenon has been studied to death, some would claim, and attempts have been made to explain the nature of the threat to the public at large.

In short, each Western nation has put up a modification of the old zoo sign, "This animal is dangerous. When attacked it defends itself." In order to make life more difficult for the people of violence laws have reluctantly been modified, the security forces have been given greater license to arrest, hold and question suspects in all European countries. A degree of international cooperation and mutual aid has been achieved.

The result is that terrorists no longer have things all their own way. The West Germans have the Red Army Faction on the run, the Italians have sapped the strength of the Red Brigades and allied movements; the amazing Japanese Red Army which operated in Europe and the Middle East has publicly announced that it was wrong and has gone out of the terrorist business altogether. There have been defectors from the terrorist ranks such an Hans Joachim Klein, the Red Army Faction international.

In Spain, for historical-political reasons, the fight is still at a crucial stage. In Nothern Ireland the British are still at grips with the IRA, and the intractable problem of Ireland.

Early in 1981 it appeared that the IRA and Irish National Liberation Army (INLA) were concentrating on a propaganda campaign centering on hunger strikes to the death. By October no less than ten convicted Irish terrorists had deliberately starved themselves to death in sequence at the Maze prison near Belfast. The British government refused to give in to demands that they should be treated as political prisoners. But the hunger strike was broken, not by the determination of Whitehall but by mounting opposition from the families of the prisoners and the resistance to the idea of death fasts from the Roman Catholic Church in Ireland. As this macabre campaign ended the IRA returned to the attack by planting a succession of bombs in London. It also provoked a Protestant backlash in Northern Ireland by murdering a Loyalist member of Parliament.

The never-ending war between Jew and Arab continues in all its forms, but the Palestine Liberation Organization has become quasi-governmental and turns to lobbying and diplomacy as well as to terrorism.

The tide of terror has receded, though there are ominous signs of new waves already gathering. Terrorists made their appearance in Greece in the summer of 1981. Leftist groups placed fire bombs in Athenean department stores, and blasted British council offices in Salonika.

In Portugal, bombs were detonated and politicians were assassinated. Indeed, as the defenses built up it seemed that assassination was again becoming a favorite tactic because it is so difficult to prevent. President Reagan and the Pope were wounded, and Queen Elizabeth was the target of a boy with a replica revolver firing blanks—a replica terrorist.

Iranian leaders who had used terrorist warfare against the Americans themselves became the victims of their own opposition when terrorists killed President Ali Rajai and Prime Minister Bahoner in August 1981. Even the Russians, who had given so much help and encouragement to outside terrorists, fell victim to Afghan assaults—indeed they began to train their own Red Army special forces in the art of combatting guerillas in Afghanistan.

In the nature of things terrorists always have the initiative, for they are the ones who choose where, how and when to strike. Surprise is always on their side, and in the West there is no lack of targets.

Modern industrial society provides many areas for attack which are difficult to defend. Power lines, oil pipelines, reservoirs, dams, electricity generators, and especially nuclear targets, are all vulnerable. When one considers the disorder and confusion created in New York by the accidental disruption of the electricity supply there, it is not difficult to imagine what might happen in case of a deliberate and planned electric power cut combined with other terrorist activity.

There is even a threat in more rural areas where the risks at present seem remote. "The state of Oklahoma may represent the new battlefield where terrorist tactics could be conducted," suggests Professor Stephen Sloan. In a survey of preparedness on state and local level in the U.S. he drew attention to the possibility that terrorists might choose to exploit the less secure facilities in rural areas. "Because of economic considerations many corporations have not only left the central city and the suburbs, but have also chosen to establish their new headquarters around smaller towns and in less populated areas. Consequently, terrorists can now attempt 'to bring the war home' against multinationals within the countryside.''

A further source of anxiety is the number of armories stacked with modern weapons around the countryside in the U.S. and in Europe, seemingly without effective protection. A Contemporary Affairs Briefing, written by William Boyers or Aberdeen University in Scotland on the international arms trade and terrorism, quoted a U.S. army report that in the seventies terrorists had stolen enough weapons to equip ten battalions.

One hundred and twenty automatic rifles disappeared in a single raid on a Norwegian Home Guard armory, and some of them were later identified in various parts of the world including El Salvador and Bangladesh. Not all such weapons are stolen by terrorists. The private trade in arms at international level is also to blame for thefts of weapons later sold to terrorists. Terrorists find it only too easy to acquire powerful weapons. The Soviet bloc is willing to sell them, and sometimes to give them, not only small arms, but also for example, RPG7 rocket launchers. Third party governments such as Libya and the People's Republic of South Yemen which receive military aid from the Soviet Union are willing to pass on weapons to terrorist groups. Such sources of supply are extremely difficult to block. But the time has come for European and North American authorities to defend their stores of weapons more diligently, so that it will be more difficult for terrorists and their friends to steal and sell them. More careful control is also needed over the licensing of the sale of arms for export.

It has become commonplace for all writers on terrorism to draw attention to the threat of ''nuclear terrorism,'' and to sketch out scenarios of terrorists seizing atomic weapons. It is a danger that should not be neglected, but nor should it be over-estimated. For nuclear weapons are firmly in the hands of the armed forces and the secret services of the major powers who take great care to protect them. In addition, their use is controlled by a highly complicated and secret code of procedures. Despite this there is need for vigilance. More than any other country the U.S., as the superpower that has the greatest stocks of nuclear material, is vulnerable to this form of attack. A police state like the Soviet Union, which also has a great nuclear arsenal, is much less at risk from this form of subversive warfare. The Americans have done a great deal to improve their defenses by placing military guards and on rocket sites and on stockpiles of nuclear weapons. Some 25,000 troops keep watch over an estimated 30,000 such weapons in various parts of the country. Nuclear raw material is now conveyed in special security trailers and railroad cars, all of them carefully guarded. They are further protected with a variety of devices including sprayers of disabling gas and sticky foam. Strong defenses are now in position but the study of terrorist activities show how ingenious violent groups are at penetrating defenses. The principal danger is that a technological terrorist band might lay its hands upon plutonium and the technical means to build a nuclear weapon which they might use for purposes of supreme blackmail. After a number of nuclear scares in several American cities the government created a special organization known as NEST, the Nuclear Emergency Search Team, whose task it is to find and identify with the aid of sophisticated equipment, any "improvised nuclear device" or I.N.D., which might be constructed by terrorists or blackmailers. It is also their duty to render harmless any such device. NEST had a budget for 1981 of $50 million, a sign that Washington takes seriously the fear that one day the government may have to contend with a threat from such a device.

In their recent investigative novel *The Fifth Horseman*, Larry Collins and Dominique Lapierre sketched a highly realistic scenario of a terrorist blackmail threat. In a highly credible tale of nuclear blackmail it imagined that Col. Qaddafi had persuaded a Palestinian scientist to steal nuclear fuel from the French, and after getting his own nuclear bomb, made a demonstration test of it in the desert, before arranging for terrorists to place a device with sophisticated mechanisms in New York City. The threat was that unless the President compelled the Israelis to quit their West Bank settlements the terrorists would destroy the city and its population. This well researched work of fiction makes a terrifying point about a new form of nuclear terrorist blackmail. There is nothing fictional about the desire of the Libyan leader to acquire a bomb of his own. And Libya is just one of a number of Third World countries that are not far away from achieving their desire. Iraq is pressing on with plans to build a nuclear bomb, even after the Israelis sabotaged and bombed their nuclear plant near Baghdad. Colonel Qadaffi who has boasted that he intends to get the "Islamic Bomb" is helping to finance Pakistan's nuclear program, and he will want a return for his investment. There is now a real and alarming prospect that wildcat regimes may, in the not too distant future, control nuclear weapons which they would not hesitate to use either in war or in terrorist campaigns to achieve political aims.

No government can afford to ignore such risks of what has been called "mini-proliferation." The best answer to it is greater protection for stores and transport of nuclear material, and a closer watch upon the activities of all who have access to it.

Less alarming manifestations are also emerging in the field of "soft terrorisms." As some ecological and conservationist groups whose aims are in themselves peaceful and humane become more militant, their activities cross the borderline into such activity. International groups of anti-nuclear power activists have mounted violent demonstrations at nuclear power sites in France, Germany and in the U.S.

In 1975 a group calling itself the "Commando of Opposition by Explosives to the Self-Destruction of the Universe" bombed the Paris offices of a manufacturer of nuclear fuel elements and then a uranium mine in south-west France, causing extensive damage. In November 1979 Swiss saboteurs attacked the nuclear power plant at Goesgen and put it out of action for 12 hours. There were eight successful acts of sabotage against nuclear installations in Germany between 1977 and 1979 and, in a sinister twist to the campaign, 35-page "Handbook for Self-Help" appeared in left-wing bookshops. It was a professional instruction manual. It told readers how to make bombs and plant them against security fences, building and power pylons. It told how would-be saboteurs could accustom themselves to heights in order to climb pylons. It warned against direct attacks on the reactor because of the danger of radiation. And it included a detailed drawing of the reactor site at Esenhamm near Bremerhaven.

Nuclear power stations are not the only industrial infrastructure targets to come under attack. Early in 1980 there was a rash of sabotage attacks on computer istallations in France by a left-wing organization called Direct Action and by the hitherto unknown organization called the "Computer Liquidation and Hijacking Committee." They completely destroyed the CII-Honeywell Bull computer at Toulouse. Such attacks high-lighted the vulnerability of computer installations and their importance to the structure of modern society. As *Le Figaro* pointed out, the destruction of a computer could cause far more damage than the murder of a politician.

Even the people who want to save those most peaceful of creatures, the whales, have uncovered a seam of violence. The Canadian conservationist Paul Watson offered a $20,000 reward in June 1980 to anyone who would sink a pirate whaler in the Atlantic. "I'm trying to encourage the crew members to sink their own ships. It could be done by opening the seacocks and flooding the engines." The reward could only be collected, he said, if the ship was sunk without death or injury. But he added that he would accept responsibility if anyone was hurt because whaling was illegal.

A much more dangerous form of violence is the brand which can be designated "offical state terror." One example was the seizure of the U.S. embassy in Teheran by zealots who held the 53 American hostages with the collaboration of the Iranian government. Col. Qaddafi of Libya is an outstanding practitioner of this form. He sent Libyan hit squads out to Europe and America to murder expatriot political opponents. One of his men even gave poisoned peanuts to the children of a Libyan living in England. When we asked Qaddafi about Libyan murders in Britain, he replied that this had nothing to do with the British people or government: "This is purely a Libyan matter . . . the new Libya is getting rid of the old Libya."

After he had taken the same attitude to other murders committed in the U.S. President Reagan denounced Libyan hit men in America and ordered the expulsion of the entire staff of the Libyan Embassy in Washinton. This served as a warning while the government began weighing in the balance, the need to punish states which give official aid to terrorists, against possible economic damage caused by Arab oil threats. The U.S. government already has the power to name terrorist states and to take sanctions against them, as has been done in the case of Iran. Under the provisions of the Export Administration Act countries supporting terror, such as Libya, Iraq and Syria have been prevented from buying American warlike stores.

Encouraging signs came from Washington after the election of President Reagan that a much firmer attitude in such matters might be expected. Yet when the President condemned terrorists and guerillas, Yasser Arafat, chairman of the PLO, did not hesitate to speak out, and threaten action against U.S. military bases in the Arab world in retaliation. "We are a great revolution that can never be intimidated," he said. "We have connections with all revolutionary movements around the world, in Salvador, in Nicaragua—and I reiterate Salvador—and elsewhere in the world."

The Soviet Union also has such connections and it is indisputable that the Russians have given money, help and instruction to terrorist movements. It is important that steps be taken now to discourage the Soviet Union from giving its official blessing to so many violent enterprises. In this matter, a lead must be taken by the American administration. Of course, it is too much to hope that President Leonid Brezhnev or his successors could be persuaded to relinquish the Soviet Union's role as the leader of world revolution. But, by stressing the linkage between the USSR's support for terrorist organizations and U.S.–Soviet relations, and indeed Atlantic Alliance relations, some headway might be made in persuading the Kremlin to be less zealous in its godfatherly role towards terrorists.

The subject has already been raised at the European Security Review Conference which involves both the U.S. and the USSR. The best hope of getting some established ground rules governing support for terrorists would be to avoid the thorny question of definitions. What is needed is a code of international conduct to govern such things, rather as the Geneva Convention furnished some rules for the civilized conduct of big wars. If the Soviet Union refuses to accept such a code it must be made to understand that it will have to face the political, economic and military consequences. These are matters of high diplomacy that can be conducted by the Atlantic Alliance only if the American President is prepared to give a strong lead.

In the field of anti-terrorist tactics so many changes have taken place that the time has come to survey the forces established both by the military and by the police, and to pose the question whether they themselves may not be a danger to the democratic countries which created them. Anxiety centers in particular upon the crack units formed for the counter assault on terror such as the Israeli unit, GSG9 and the SAS.

Because of the circumstances in which it was conducted in the center of London and under the cameras of television crews, the Iranian Embassy siege operation by the SAS is the counter-

terrorist action most available for detailed analysis. By the time
the one survivor was brought to trial the relief and elation had
passed, and questions were being asked.

Was the carnage really necessary? Among those who expressed their doubts in letters to newspapers at the time was John
La Carré, author of the best-selling Smiley novels of espionage
who described the action in these terms,

> It is the courage of the thug put to social use. At Princes Gate,
> counter terror vanquished terror. We should indeed be thankful
> that the extreme recourse succeeded. But we should be scared stiff
> by the sight of shock troops storming London's streets, and a little
> ashamed of having them billed as our national—racial—
> champions.

This is a highly emotive expression of doubt felt by many
Britons.

The answer must be that it is essential to have such a force as
the SAS as a protection against terrorists storming London's
embassies and ministries. The troopers at the embassy were right
to take no chances with men who had already killed one hostage,
and were obviously ready to kill more. Their response was a
disciplined one.

But another lesson is to be learned, which applies also to the
Delta unit now formed in the U.S. as well as the other special
units in Europe, and that is they must only be allowed to act
within the tight framework of the law and under very strict
government control. In the British example, the SAS were called
in at first under the authority of the police and utimately the
government. They were in charge of the operation only for a
limited time under the law which allows the military to be called
in support of the civil power. Once their mission was accomplished they handed over to the Metropolitan Police, and returned
to barracks. In America such an operation by troops might not
have been permissable, because of the provisions of the Posse
Comitatus Act, and that the task would have fallen to an FBI
tactics squad, which does not have the aggressive military training to handle things so expeditiously.

It is important to stress that in the aftermath of the London
siege the surviving terrorist was brought to trial before a court

which not only found him guilty, but also examined the facts of the case. Had the court considered that the SAS troopers exceeded their powers, they could perfectly well have been charged with manslaughter or murder. For there are plenty of precedents in British law for so charging soldiers, who indeed cannot defend themselves by claiming they were simply obeying orders. This same rule of law applies even in the violent conditions of Northern Ireland. British soldiers do not have a license to kill except in war. Those on duty in Ulster carry cards setting down clearly under what controlled circumstances they may open fire.

But the confrontation between terrorist violence and military force used by a democratic government is not the only issue posed by the special intervention groups. Like all soldiers their life consists of long periods of inaction, punctuated by short bursts of extreme tension and very violent action. It is not easy to maintain morale, and constant training of various kinds, necessary though it is, does not necessarily fill the gap. The temptations of politicking apply in particular to the units in Spain and Italy, where there is a long history of army involvement in political plotting, rather than in Britain and the U.S., where the armed forces have mercifully been immune from such activities. The best defense against such dangers is in careful selection of the commander, and of his officers and men, and by keeping a watchful eye over such units in quiet times.

Another point worthy of consideration is that the creation of special units to handle terrorist raids in a way plays into the hands of the terrorists. For if crack units are necessary for operations against them, that confers a special status upon the terrorists. If they can only be mastered by army units, surely that means that terrorist bands are in fact military units themselves. If that is accepted, then it goes some way towards justifying their demands to be treated as prisoners of war when captured, and allows them to claim the right not to be interrogated after giving their name, rank and number. Captured terrorists already claim special status for themselves in prison. IRA men have even fasted to the death to assert such rights, which are denied by the British government. One of the strongest arguments in law against terrorists in the countries of the West is that they are to be regarded as criminals and not as political prisoners. Many countries, for example, will only consider allowing extradition for those wanted as criminals, and if they can prove they are political prisoners then the long traditions of asylum for political refugees come into play. There is a distinct danger that by using the armed services in response to terror attacks, rather than uniformed police who normally deal with criminal affairs, Western governments do give a degree of legitimacy to the terrorists.

Despite these perils, arguments have been put forward in favor of an international anti-terrorist force, notably by Lord Chalfont, a former British Minister concerned with defense. At an international conference on terrorism organized by the Israelis he said: "It is at least worthwhile examining the possibilities of extending cooperating in an institutionalized form using the national anti-terrorist squads of countries, like West Germany, Britain and Israel as the nuclei of a permanent force."

Apart from the fact that international forces such as those of United Nations enjoy a poor reputation, such a step would be full of political and diplomatic traps. The inclusion of Israel, a country in a state of constant emergency which is ready to turn to counter-terrorism of the most aggressive kind under the leadership of Menachem Begin, who began political life as a terrorist himself, would create far more difficulties than could be solved by an international force.

That seemed to be the opinion too of a fellow delegate at the conference. George Bush, before he became vice president, declared that he did not believe the creation of a truly international force was likely, though he added: "I believe that anti-terrorist paramilitary units, closely co-ordinated by democratic states, are a viable answer to the threat."

Bush stressed, rather, the need for cooperation in the field of intelligence and counter intelligence among the Western powers, with the proviso that "intelligence is accountable to the people." He declared, "We should strive vigorously to shape and utilize this important capability in the fight against international terrorism. You may be assured that I will do all I can to bring this about."

Bush, of course, is a former CIA director, and is conscious of the fact that the use of special forces by that agency in Latin America and in Vietnam, and its other shortcomings, prompted the radical and liberal human rights campaign which, as we have seen in Chapter 3, hamstrung American intelligence in the early years of the terrorist threat. The restrictions placed upon intelligence work affected not only the United States but also its allies.

An example of this was provided when the Italian government at the height of the Aldo Moro crisis asked America for special surveillance equipment. It was not forthcoming because the Ryan Amendment forbade covert CIA operations without Presidential approval, and limited its activities against terrorists to "international terrorism." At that time the Red Brigades were deemed to be "domestic terrorists" and therefore outside the scope of CIA assistance.

Equally, when the West Germans had asked for technical help on how to break into the Lufthansa Boeing aircraft hijacked to Mogadishu, their request was turned down because an amendment to the Foreign Assistance Act in 1975 had made it illegal to use foreign aid dollars to assist with foreign policy operations.

It seems more than likely that the new administration will do better in the matter of helping members of the Atlantic Alliance against the terrorist scourge. Americans are commendably active in protecting their civil rights. So far their principal preoccupation has been to prevent excesses in the activities of the CIA and FBI.

After the election of President Reagan, as it became apparent that he intended to put teeth back into the CIA, organizations in the "anti-intelligence lobby", such as the American Civil Liberties Union which played such a role in the original attacks upon the CIA and the FBI, began mobilizing for renewed activity. Willaim Casey, the new director of the CIA, who is also a close friend of the President, declared, "The difficulties of the past decade are behind us," and announced that the agency was again going secret. As more capable agents were recruited into the service he abolished the agency's public affairs office.

Casey, who served as secret intelligence chief in London during the Second World War, intended to restore CIA morale and provide "desperately needed" intelligence capability. Another of his aims was to restore the confidence of friendly intelligence abroad.

To restore intelligence capability is one thing, but if ever the U.S. felt it necessary to increase police powers and make changes in the law on the scale which had proved necessary in Britain and Western Europe, for defense against terrorists, there would be a great outcry from American liberals. Indeed it has been stated that such steps would not be possible within the terms of the American Constitution.

Yet Abraham Lincoln did not hesitate to suspend *habeas corpus* when he believed the occasion demanded it. And he argued that no government, however democratic and liberal, can be expected to stand by and see itself destroyed by people who neither recognize the law nor any restrictions on their violence. That in a nutshell is the argument of Britain and the other European nations facing up to the same people. They have all, and with reluctance, removed a number of legal safeguards built into the constitutional practice to deal with an emergency.

Apart from West Germany, it is Britain which has taken the most far-reaching measures in this field in order to combat the IRA in Northern Ireland and in the rest of Britain. The main provisions of the two most important pieces of legislation, the Northern Ireland (Emergency Provisions) Act 1973, and the Prevention of Terrorism (Temporary Provisions) Act 1974, have been described earlier in this book.

There is no doubt that they go further than any other peacetime acts to change traditional ways of doing things, but in exceptional circumstances exceptional measures are necessary. Unpleasant though it is to have to take them, they do not vastly affect the population at large. Of course there is strong opposition to them, especially from the National Council of Civil Liberties (the British equivalent of the ACLU), which constantly opposes emergency legislation on the grounds that it diminishes the rights of all citizens. And indeed, it is true that the Home Secretary can exclude a UK citizen from entering Northern Ireland and a citizen may be detained legally with no right to *habeas corpus*.

But the citizens in question are ones suspected of terrorist activities, and usually with good reason. Obviously the police and the security forces make mistakes and draconian rules sometimes lead to unjust consequences. But despite many protests, there is a consensus among the political parties that stern measures are necessary and must be kept in force until things get better. Although some members of the British Labor Party have attacked the emergency legislation it enjoys general support in parliament.

The independent Republic of Ireland also protects itself against the terrorism of the IRA. Like the British it fights on two fronts, against the IRA and against "Loyalist" Ulster terrorists active on both sides of the border. The Republic has even stronger anti-terrorist laws than the British. The Republic still has the death penalty and in 1981 in Dublin a Belfast IRA man was sentenced to be hanged for shooting a policeman while driving a van carrying explosives for shipment to Britain for a bombing campaign the Christmas before. The Irish President commuted his sentence to 40 years imprisonment. IRA men are not allowed to be interviewed on TV in the Republic, although they still appear on the BBC in Britain to argue their case.

There is a clear conflict between the preservation of civil liberties and the need to protect lives and property from terrorist attack. For it is not possible to take the powers needed to deal with terrorism without to some extent reducing the freedom of innocent citizens. Yet it has to be done.

The most irritating feature of this is that such measures bring satisfaction to the terrorists because they sow the seeds of doubt about democratic government, and it is the long-term aim of terrorists, in so far as they have one, to overthrow such government in order to impose their own views under threat of bomb and bullet.

Special measures are necessary, so are special forces to hit back at some terrorist enterprises. Yet neither can succeed in destroying this late-twentieth-century phenomenon. As the counterattack on terrorism got under way, there were victories to match the earlier defeats. In the long run, provided that the liberal states of the West maintain their traditions and remain on the alert again all excesses, whether terrorist or counter terrorist, there is hope that the threat will recede. We must all remain cool and watchful, and remember the words of Oliver Cromwell: "Place your trust in God, but keep your powder dry."

Bibliography

Annual of Power and Conflict 1979–1981 (London: Institute for the Study of Conflict).

Becker, Jillian, *Hitler's Children.* 1977. (Philadelphia, PA: Lippincott).

Ben Gurion, David, *Israel: Years of Challenge.* 1963. (New York, N.Y.: Holt, Rinehart & Winston).

Ben Gurion, David, *Israel: A Personal History.* 1971. (New York, N.Y.: Funk & Wagnalls).

Bell, J. Bowyer, *Terror Out of Zion.* 1977. (New York, N.Y.: St. Martin).

Bolz, Frank and Hershey, Edward, *Hostage Cop.* 1980. (New York, N.Y.: Rawson Wade).

Crelinsten, Ronald D. and Szabo, Denis, *Hostage-Taking.* 1979. (Lexington, MA: Lexington Books).

Clutterbuck, Richard, *Living with Terrorism.* 1979. (Westport, CT: Arlington House).

Clutterbuck, Richard, *Kidnap & Ransom* (London: Macmillan).

Clutterbuck, Richard, *The Media and Political Violence* (London: Macmillan).

Coogan, Tim Pat, *The I.R.A.* (London: Fontana).

Dewar, Michael, *Internal Security Weapons and Equipment of the World* (Middlesex: Ian Allan Ltd.).

Dayan, Moshe, *Story of My Life.* 1978. (New York, N.Y.: William Morrow).

Dobson, Christopher, *Black September.* 1974. (New York, N.Y.: Macmillan).

Dobson, Christopher and Payne, Ronald, *The Carlos Complex.* 1977. (New York, N.Y.: Putnam).

Dobson, Christopher and Payne, Ronald, *The Terrorists.* 1979. (New York, N.Y.: Facts On File).

Farran, Roy, *Winged Dagger* (London: Elmsfield Press).

Frankel, William, *Israel Observed* (London: Thames & Hudson).

Geraghty, Tony, *Who Dares Win* (London: Arms and Armour Press).

Greenwood, Colin, *Police Tactics in Armed Operations.* 1979. (Boulder, CO: Paladin Press).

Hastings, Max, *Yoni, Hero of Entebbe.* 1979. (New York, N.Y.: Dial Press).

Hirst, David, *The Gun and the Olive Branch* (London: Faber and Faber).

Katz, Robert, *Days of Wrath.* 1980. (New York, N.Y.: Doubleday).

Koch, Peter and Hermann, Kai, *Assault at Mogadishu* (London: Corgi).

Laqueur, Walter, *Terrorism.* 1979. (Boston, MA: Little, Brown & Co.).

Lodge, Juliet (ed.), *Terrorism, A Challenge to the State* (Oxford: Martin Robertson).

Luttwak, Edward and Horwitz, Dan, *The Israeli Army.* 1975. (New York, N.Y.: Harper & Row).

Meir, Golda, *My Life.* 1975. (New York, N.Y.: Putnam).

Moorehead, Caroline, *Fortune's Hostages* (London: Hamish Hamilton).

Netanyahu, Benjamin (ed.), *International Terrorism, Challenge and Response* (Jerusalem: Jonathan Institute).

O'Brien, Conor Cruise, *Herod, Reflections on Political Violence* (London: Hutchinson).

Ofer, Yehuda, *Operation Thunder* (Harmondsworth: Penguin

Books).

Peres, Shimon, *David's Sling*. 1970. (New York, N.Y.: Random House).

Rabin, Yitzhak, *The Rabin Memoirs*. 1979. (Boston, MA: Little, Brown & Co.).

Royal United Services Institute for Defense Studies, *Ten Years of Terrorism: Collected Views*. 1979. (New York, N.Y.: Crane, Russak & Co.).

Rumbelow, Donald, *The Houndsditch Murders* (London: Macmillan).

Stanhope, Henry, *The Soldiers* (London: Hamish Hamilton).

Sterling, Claire, *The Terror Network*. 1981. (New York, N.Y.: Holt, Rinehart & Winston).

Stevenson, William and Dan, Uri, *Ninety Minutes at Entebbe*. 1976. (New York, N.Y.: Bantam).

Warner, Philip, *The Special Air Service* (London: William Kimber).

Watson, Peter, *War on the Mind*. 1978. (New York, N.Y.: Basic Books).

Wilkinson, Paul, *Terrorism and the Liberal State*. 1978. (New York, N.Y.: Halsted Press).

INDEX

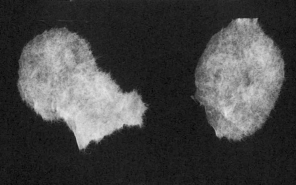